DATE DUE

APR 29 1998			
GAYLORD			PRINTED IN U.S.A.

Developing Motivation in Young Children

Developing Motivation in Young Children

Stanley Coopersmith, Editor

Albion Publishing Company
San Francisco

ALBION PUBLISHING COMPANY
1736 Stockton Street
San Francisco, California 94133

Library of Congress Catalog Card Number 75-16006

ISBN 87843-621-9

Acknowledgment

This collection of articles on affective education was granted as part of a larger effort to provide materials that would describe and promote effective early education programs. With that need in mind the Office of Economic Opportunity and the Office of Child Development established a project (Grant#H-9708) to develop materials, guidelines and principles for early childhood programs in the United States. This volume is part of that project and received support through a subcontract through Research for Better Schools. The materials were designed to be employed in training and teaching programs. They are deliberately written in nontechnical language and are designed for the educator and general reader interested in gaining perspective and information on "affective education." We should like to acknowledge that:

> Partial (or total) financial support for this project was provided by the Office of Child Development (O.C.D.) and the Office of Economic Opportunity (O.E.O.), Grant #H-9807, through Research for Better Schools, Ronald K. Parker, principal investigator. The opinions expressed in this publication do not necessarily reflect the position or policy of O.C.D. or O.E.O. and no official endorsement by these agencies should be inferred.

Stanley Coopersmith
El Cerrito, California

Contents

Developing Motivation in Young Children

1

The Role of Emotions in Education

Stanley Coopersmith
University of California, Davis

A major concern of this book is to examine the role and significance of emotion in the processes of early education and development. This aspect of child behavior has been avoided and rejected by many teachers. It is my belief that this avoidance has had unfortunate consequences for learning and motivation. The importance of emotion in learning has been largely sidestepped by many educators, because of long-term cultural reservations and uncertainties about the role of emotions in our lives and the conviction that emotions are out of place in our schools. Parents and teachers tend to follow their own convictions about when, where, and how much emotion should be expressed. Alternative views may be regarded as challenges to their values and way of life. We are on the verge of developing programs for young children that could make for more effective performance and happier personal lives, and many psychologists and educators have raised the prospect that certain types and (moderate) levels of emotions can be highly constructive sources of energy and involvement. At a point when many schools report problems with discipline, disinterest, and drugs, educators and observers have proposed that student interest, enthusiasm, awareness, and concern for learning may stem largely from emotional components of the learning process (see Bibliography). They suggest that emotions are a valuable, largely unexplored aspect of child education. They also suggest that the proper use of emotional expression may represent a partial solution to some of the problems schools now face. According to their view, objective examination of the evidence relating emotion and learning may lead us to conclude that cultural restrictions have blinded us to an important resource for helping our children to grow.

1

CULTURAL ATTITUDES TOWARD EMOTIONAL EXPRESSION

The place of emotions in contemporary American life is an issue that extends beyond personal and familial matters to the theories and practices of American education. As a people we have been noted for our industry, optimism, and overt friendliness rather than for our expressiveness or depth of feelings. Such early observers as de Tocqueville commented that Americans are generally good spirited, tend to act close to the surface, and are not given to self-examination. These characteristics of extroversion and energetic confrontation with the physical world may be associated with our earlier expanding frontier that provided an escape valve for restless spirits or with an expanding economy that provided an impersonal vehicle for initiative and aggression. Whatever their sources, it is clear that the bulk of America's concerns and energies have been directed outward rather than inward. As a people we appear to be more attentive to manipulating the external, physical environment than to examining and expressing the internal world of our feelings, ideas, and imagination. Although orientation to the external, physical world may have been functional in the past, there are numerous reasons to believe that its importance is being reduced and tempered in contemporary life. The great issues in our country today are those that arouse feelings and require an ability to deal with them. The conflicts and barriers are between people and within people; the new frontiers are the treatment of difficulties associated with poverty, race, crime, drugs, loneliness, and sex, all of which are emotionally arousing. To deal with those issues we shall have to look within and examine our feelings as well as our budgets and materials.

In discussing American attitudes towards affect, I do not intend to suggest that other countries and cultures do not have similar attitudes. The world has grown too small for such sharp distinctions; the insistent development of urbanized, sub-urbanized, industrialized mass media societies has made for greater commonality of values and styles of life than citizens in different countries often recognize or acknowledge. I will use American attitudes as examples rather than as unique and isolated phenomena. These observations are not intended to be critical of earlier or traditional practices. I do believe that attitudes towards affect that may have been useful in the past are interfering and possibly destructive today. It may have been necessary to hold certain emotions in check while we explored, shaped, and developed our country, but the days of physical expansiveness are largely past. Different attitudes and postures may be functional in the 1970s than were in the 1870s. To teach the children of today requires that we look at the values, beliefs, and attitudes that exist today and seek to determine what is desirable and functional in contemporary times as well as in historical perspective. Values shift; what is effective in one period may be dysfunctional in another, and there is always the possibility that new scientific evidence will force us to reconsider the "truth" of earlier convictions.

Let us begin our examination by considering several aspects of prevailing cultural attitudes towards emotion. First and perhaps foremost, emotions are regarded generally as bad, particularly in relation to learning and thinking processes. In this sense, emotions per se are regarded as an indication that logic, reason, and the capacity for objective analysis are no longer operating at maximum potential. Emotions are seen as largely intrusive and disruptive; so, their presence is an indication that the most efficient and reasonable outcome will not be attained. This opposition of emotion to reason has an ancient and honorable tradition going back to the days of Aristotelian analysis. Aristotelian analysis differentiated various categories of mental processes and established logic and reason as the highest and most human of all faculties, and emotion was given a lower and more primitive position.

Emotions were and in many cases still are regarded as an indication of weakness. Traditionally, females have been portrayed as being overwhelmed with feelings and weakened in their resolutions because of feelings of love and devotion. To show emotion has not been regarded generally as strong and masculine behavior. According to many people, showing emotions indicates vulnerability and excessive sensitivity. The male who shows feelings by his warmth, tears, and sensitivities has not been regarded as being strongly masculine but rather as lacking in stamina and resolution. Since children, who by their very nature are less physically mature than adults, are also more emotionally expressive, such expressiveness is often regarded as immature and childlike. Women and children who are regarded as weaker and more sensitive and vulnerable than adult males are also regarded as more unstable and emotional. The mature male, on the contrary, is presumably characterized by his ability to control and repress his emotions.

Another expression of the negative, disruptive, and weak connotations frequently assigned to emotions is the belief that psychological difficulties often result from very strong feelings that are out of control. In this context, neuroses are termed emotional disorders, and therapy is viewed as a process of gaining control over emotions and getting emotions out, i.e., catharsis. At the opposite extreme of psychological functioning, i.e., that of great effectiveness, the general opinion is that very competent people operate at a rational, logical level and either have their emotions under tight control or learn to operate without feelings.

The social connotations of emotion have several features in common. The term "emotion" is associated generally with strong and extreme expression of feelings. Emotions are associated with "emotionality," that is with extreme, disruptive states and with an agitation of feelings in contrast to a moderate or average level of response. It is important to note that a formal (Webster) dictionary definition of emotion is "a departure from the normal calm state of an organism of such nature as to include strong feeling, an impulse toward open action and certain internal physical reactions." Another general connotation is that emotion is more likely to be negative than positive and more likely to be distressing than satisfying. We find in the dictionary definition of emotion the following listing of states: fear, anger, disgust, grief, joy, surprise, and yearning. Joy is the only clearly positive state listed with the others that carry various negative connotations. Popular usage further assumes that negative emotions such as sadness, anger, and fear are generally inappropriate for public expression. Even such positive emotions as happiness, enthusiasm, and acceptance are appropriate only if they are moderately expressed and under control. In emotions as in attitudes, the culture advocates what benefits of moderation and restraint are considered essential. Although it is regarded as appropriate to show pleasure and happiness when a desired event occurs, even then cultural norms favor a dignified and controlled expression of feelings. A person who expresses tears, great joy, or extreme anger in public situations will probably be regarded as unrestrained and out of control. Frequently such actions are thought of as public exposures of private matters and hence inappropriate if not indecent. Feelings are, in effect, personal affairs, and the presence of other people should act as a restraint upon their expression. Whether or not people do regard such expressions of feelings as negatively as is assumed, it appears that the great majority of Americans believe that if they themselves openly express feelings other people will judge *them* to be immoderate.

On the basis of the preceding discussion, we can draw several conclusions about the usage and significance of emotion in the schools. It would appear that expressions of emotion in the schools are thought of as inappropriate and disruptive in a public setting that is designated as a training center for skills of reason, logic, and intellect. Emotional expressions presumably interfere with the efficiency of learning and also encourage weakness. According to this code of efficiency and appropriate conduct, teachers who encourage or permit emotional expression are allowing a "bad" thing to happen; such expressions disrupt task performance, encourage immoderation, and may contribute to psychological difficulties. Schools are task-oriented — to teach skills and information, to instill control and focus, and to establish basic rules of conduct and discipline. It is no accident that children learn they should not express their feelings in schools and soon lose their spontaneity and enthusiasm. Many classrooms are joyless and emotionless by deliberate policy and practice. Accordingly, it appears that a principal cause of the loss of children's curiosity, enthusiasm, and spontaneity is their response to the school's unstated policy of emotional repression. The children have learned their lessons well and suppress their interests and excitement. It may well be that they have lost their enthusiasms outside of school as well and may seek to regain them via drugs, speed and other thrill-seeking actions.

The cultural norms regarding emotion and the school's interpretation of those norms represent a strong, generalized, and inaccurate judgment of the influences of emotion in learning. Attitudes regarding emotion are so loaded with emotion that they are accepted uncritically and are overgeneralized and closed to examination. An unfortunate consequence of the taboos against emotional expression may be the current difficulties in motivation, involvement, and task orientation that are prevalent in our nation's classrooms.

AFFECT IN LEARNING AND PERSONALITY DEVELOPMENT

One of the most striking features about the taboo against affect in education is the certainty and conviction about what would happen if emotions were permitted or encouraged in our schools. Supporters of the subject matter, strong discipline approach believe that encouraging emotional expression would mark the end of the educational system. Advocates of the more extreme versions of humanistic, expressive, and self-discovery procedures believe that schools pursuing their programs and procedures would develop self-directed, involved individuals. From my own perspective, it appears that neither group has looked beyond its ideological prejudices to examine the issues and evidence regarding affect in learning and personality development. The rhetoric of intellect and performance tests opposes the rhetoric of emotional expression and creativity, and neither looks directly at the underlying issues or evidence relating emotion and learning. Although the relationship between affect and learning has not been extensively studied, what we do know suggests that emotion can play a constructive role in education. The issue is not whether emotions should be expressed but how and to what extent they should be expressed to gain motivation, interest, and involvement.

The point of departure for examining the role of emotions in learning is to place the concept of emotions in a broader context of evidence and values. I would like to emphasize that emotions are an integral and inevitable aspect of every man's experience and that they cannot be legislated or denied out of existence. Man does have feelings, and those feelings have moved, colored, and directed his actions since the beginning of his species. Each person, child or adult, lives with feelings and must learn to use them and cope with them if he is to survive, succeed, and be happy. It is naive and dangerous to maintain that feelings should be eliminated from the schools because some earlier authorities labeled them as primitive, lower, and irrational. To eliminate emotions from man is to dehumanize man; to eliminate emotions from the schools is to dehumanize education. Man is what he is; if we are to educate him and help his growth and development, we are forced to confront his emotions as well as his intellect. The issue that confronts each of us is how to become aware of and accept feelings as part of ourselves and how to live and cope with their messages and consequences.

I do not intend to say that feelings are either good, bad, constructive, or destructive. What I am saying is that feelings are inevitable and always present. Emotions are involved in building cathedrals, writing symphonies, establishing businesses, playing baseball, and reading a story. They are also involved in fighting a war, stealing goods, hating minorities, and fearing the loss of a job. When we try to eliminate feelings we are attempting to eliminate a major source of the world's great art, music, writing, and science as well as the source of war and conflict. If we eliminate emotions, we remove the source of interest, enthusiasm, ideals, and concerns. If we eliminate emotions from the home, we remove warmth, concern, love, and joy. If we eliminate emotions from the schools, we remove curiosity, enthusiasm, satisfaction, and incentive. If we eliminate emotions from our personal lives, we have lost that part of ourselves that inhibits us from inflicting pain and brings us to deeds of courage, cooperation, and love. In sum, emotions really cannot be eliminated from our lives; if they could, the result almost certainly would be a less concerned, more mechanical, and passive existence.

There is an emerging body of evidence and theory regarding the definition, significance, and role of emotions in learning and personality development. This evidence has been increasing markedly and represents an extensive field in its own right. Inasmuch as emotions are complex, studied from different vantages, and affect a wide range of human behaviors evidence on emotions comes from such diverse fields as physiology, phenomenology, linguistics, and social psychology. Since this chapter focuses on emotions and learning, I will not attempt a comprehensive statement or examine the methodological issues and refinements. In the paragraphs that follow, I shall summarize some of the major conclusions that emerge from recent studies bearing on the role of emotions in education. I should make it clear that while the conclusions are consistent with the spirit and data presented in the original research reports, I have simplified and generalized the results and conclusions. The translation of technical results from specialized areas to people in other fields requires attention to major findings and a deliberate focus upon the significance of these findings for these other fields. Hopefully, these findings and their implications will stimulate the reader to look further into the original research reports. Even if this is not the case, I believe that this summary will provide a more accurate statement of current thinking and knowledge about emotion than has been available to educators.

1. *Emotions are not a separate or isolated type of behavior.* Affect is intermixed with cognition (knowing) and conation (striving) and cannot be considered as a separate state. The separation between feeling, knowing, and acts of will is based on logic arrived at by ancient Greek philosophers in a period that preceded scientific investigation of man's psychological functioning. Such logical categories as cognition and affect are not necessarily psychologically correct or meaningful, and in this case they are clearly in error. In fact, one of Sigmund Freud's major findings was that emotions are able to influence perception, thinking, and memory. Freud found that people tend to be selective in their thinking and memories. They are more apt to remember pleasurable experiences than those touched with pain or failure. He therefore concluded that memory is influenced by emotions and motives as well as by interference from intervening events. Today we see that emotions are not separate and discriminable entities; so, a statement that emotions influence memory becomes redundant. Emotions are an integral, indistinguishable part of psychological events and processes, and are therefore a part of memory.

Other examples of the influence of emotions upon psychological processes come from experimental studies relating needs and values to perception. In one study (McClelland and Atkinson 1948), sailors who were deprived of food for one to sixteen hours were asked to describe the images they saw projected on a screen and estimate the size of various objects. Although no pictures were actually being shown, the sailors reported seeing more food objects than other objects. The sailors who were most deprived of food reported the largest number of food objects. The sailors also estimated that food objects were larger than nonfood objects, although neither kind of object was in fact being projected on the screen. Thus the food deprivation was associated with increased perception of food and with exaggerated size estimates of food objects. A study with nursery school children (Bruner and Goodman 1947) found that children from poorer homes perceived coins to be larger in size than did children from well-to-do homes. Follow-up studies indicated that tokens children received for work and that would be redeemed for candy were perceived as larger after ten days of rewarded learning than at the beginning of the study. Children who were rewarded saw the tokens as being bigger than did children who did not receive the practical benefits from ownership. Needs, wishes, and desires apparently can lead to selective perception — perception of what the individual sees and the organization of those perceptions.

Given the interrelationship of needs, desires, and other emotions with other psychological processes, it appears incorrect and artificial to differentiate the cognitive and emotional aspects of learning. The different aspects of learning interact with one another in such a way that they cannot be separated. One educator (Brown 1968) has proposed the term "confluent" education to encompass the affective and cognitive components of the learning process.

2. *The popular language of emotions is impoverished and misleading.* The language popularly used to describe emotions is very limited. It inadequately describes the different levels and types of emotion people actually experience. Uncritical usage implies that emotions are a relatively simple, unitary entity, and it fails to recognize the diversity and range of intensities, types, and expressions of feeling. For example, the teacher who asks a child not to get "emotional" also refers to calmness, moderation, and positive feelings. Empirically it is now clear that there are several dimensions of emotions (Schlosberg 1954; Block 1957; Davitz 1970). These dimensions include activation levels that range from pleasant to unpleasant and from attentive to rejecting. Most investigators agree that the term "emotions" applies to moderate and low intensities of feeling as well as it does to extreme, stirred-up responses (e.g., Arnold 1970). Researchers also seem to agree that the intensity and quality of

emotion are quite different and independent dimensions of emotion. The popular view that associates intense reactions with negative states would appear to be a result of cultural emphasis and not of operational necessity.

Another source of confusion about emotions is that traditional usage makes sharper distinctions between the concept of emotions and such other concepts as interests, enthusiasms, attention, and curiosity. These distinctions apparently represent intellectual exercises that are not consistent with what we know about the involvement of emotions in arousing and maintaining attention, interest, and enthusiasm. By ignoring other distinctions (e.g., intensity, type, and expression of emotion) we are led to believe that all emotions are the same (negative). In light of the evidence (Schacter and Singer 1962) that we interpret and label our experiences by those terms that are deemed appropriate to the situation by one's social group, it would appear that linguistic usage that encourages us to label negative experiences as emotional is imposing cultural connotations that are not an inherent part of experience itself.

3. *Emotions can and do play a positive role in teaching and learning.* The taboo against emotional expression has led to an overgeneralized, negative interpretation of the role of affect in learning. The result of this interpretation is the belief that introduction of affect into the school will be disruptive and will lead to reduced learning and loss of control. The influences of the taboo are so broad and powerful that many teachers have failed to recognize that the praise and rewards that they employ exert their positive influence by producing positive emotions. The notion of "reinforcement" is based on the finding that actions that are immediately and directly rewarded are more likely to recur, while those that are not rewarded will be extinguished. Even though the behavioristic psychologist may deny that rewards result in favorable, internal states of emotion, his frequent use of candy as reinforcement suggests that he has noted the child's pleasure when he receives and consumes sweets. It is true that extreme and uncontrolled emotions tend to interfere with learning and lead to turmoil in the classroom, but this does not mean that more moderate, open expressions of affect will have the same results. The evidence on the effects of anxiety and punishment provides examples of the benefits of moderate and positive emotions. Research on the relation between anxiety and academic performance indicates that moderate levels of anxiety increase the child's drive to perform, whereas low levels leave him lackadaisical. High levels of anxiety often disrupt performance (Sarason 1960). Very low levels of anxiety may be

associated with effective performance, but they may also be associated with lack of energy and lack of involvement; very high levels of anxiety may result in greater motivation, but they may also be associated with inability to tolerate pressure, with irrelevant learning, and with lessened ability to make visual and auditory discriminations (Mandler and Sarason 1952; Spence 1964).

The research findings of the effects of punishment on learning underscore how integral emotions are in directing and controlling behavior. Although punishment tends to temporarily suppress an undesirable response, that response is not eliminated or weakened and is likely to reappear when punishment ceases (Estes 1944; Azrin, Holz, and Hake 1963). Indeed, children can be controlled by a punitive teacher, but such control is likely to be temporary and have several negative consequences at the same time it is removing the specific, undesired behaviors. Among the possible undesirable consequences of punishment are anger and fear of the teacher and school as well as response to the specific behavior; the possibility that the undesired behavior that is subject to punishment will become permanent rather than disappear; and an increase in unpredictable or abnormal patterns of reaction to school and learning (Potter 1954).

There is abundant evidence that evoking positive emotions via rewards is much more effective than evoking negative emotions via punishment in changing student actions and attitudes. Rewards indicate what is desired and offer an alternative way of acting that can produce favorable feelings and consequences to replace those that have had negative effects. These findings on anxiety, rewards, and punishment do not necessarily mean that schools should limit themselves to moderate or positive emotions. Children do express strong emotions, lack of emotions, and negative emotions, and many academic (and life) problems can result directly from an inability to deal with such feelings. The point here is that there is a considerable body of evidence indicating that emotions such as anxiety, fear, and anger directly influence learning. Talking about punishment and omitting the terms of fear, anger, or rejection does not make the experience of punishment less emotional or more objective. The objective for the educator is to learn how, when, and which emotions can be used to facilitate learning, involvement, and motivation in the classroom. This task requires analysis and clarification of and experimentation on major, relevant factors rather than avoidance of such central issues as the role of emotions in learning. By equating emotion with negative feelings educators have ignored the affective consequences of rewards; by overlooking the influence of needs and values they have failed to use a potential source of interest and motivation; and by assuming that emotions should be dampened or eliminated they have ignored an important source of enthusiasm and involvement.

4. Emotions cannot be voluntarily controlled nor be considered irrational, biased, or nonobjective. People cannot decide to love someone and by an act of will develop feelings of affection, warmth, and arousal. Children cannot decide to become enthusiastic about reading or to like a teacher because a parent or principal tells them to do so. Lectures and talks about trying harder and feeling more positive are doomed to be largely ineffective since emotions cannot be turned on or off, no matter how sincere the interest and commitment. New books, different teachers, an alternate way of teaching, or internal changes that lead to different perception or interpretation may induce enthusiasm and replace prior lethargy. Despite what many parents believe should be the case, children cannot make themselves enthusiastic and motivated when they do not feel that way. They may spend much time at work, extend great effort, and repeat their work until mistakes decrease, but they cannot make themselves feel eager, happy, hopeful, and excited. Children feel emotionally involved and motivated because something in the teacher, subject matter, or classroom situation makes them feel that way, often without their knowledge or even against their will. We do not decide whom we will like, when to blush, and what will frighten us, but we respond directly, immediately, and involuntarily to the people we meet and situations we experience.

One source of confusion about the significance and consequences of emotion is the view that emotions are irrational, prejudiced, and subjective. According to this view, emotions are associated with very personal needs, desires, and convictions and lead to very narrow, illogical, and distorted perceptions and beliefs. An example of this view would be a teacher's belief that certain children cannot perform effectively, even though she has no direct experience with these children and has not assessed their abilities. This example is often cited to indicate that emotions result in sensitivities, blind spots, and emphases that are not in accord with objective evidence or an actual situation. There are several errors in the view equating emotions and irrationality. One error deals with the complex issue of defining and determining what is objective and rational. Since emotions are involuntary phenomena that represent a direct action and reaction in a situation, it is misleading to refer to them in terms of their consequences. Emotions occur; they are neither good nor bad, true or false, effective nor ineffective. We cannot talk about emotions objectively until we define the criterion by which we shall measure such objectivity. Emotions are objective as indices of personal and direct responses to people and events; emotions are objective in that they are involuntary and hence difficult to suppress and distort. The same argument applies to attempts to label emotions as irrational or prejudicial. Emotions can be rational or irrational or both at the same time. Judging emotions in terms of their consequences leads us to evidence indicating that emotions are involved in persistence, creativity, and sustained achievement as well as lethargy, boredom, and failure. As we noted earlier, emotions are not only negative and extreme but also positive and of varied intensities. Since emotions are intertwined with cognition, the statement that "emotions are prejudiced" represents a selective and scientifically meaningless bias of its own. Interpretations or styles of response may be prejudiced, but those prejudices are as likely to be present in the person's thinking as in his emotional reactions.

5. *A child's arousal and attention is associated with his emotional state.* Affect can result in increased attention and improved learning as well as in distraction and determination. Studies (Schlosberg 1954; Duffy 1962) have revealed that the general level of feelings, that is arousal, is related to a person's attention in a given situation. Moderately high levels of arousal are associated with greater attention and the ability to focus upon materials. Low levels of arousal tend to lead to easy distraction and fleeting attention. The teacher who wants to have the students attend to and focus upon their studies should be aware that moderate levels of affective arousal are more likely to accomplish this than a purely cognitive statement, demand for discipline, or absence of emotion. Attention appears to involve at least as much emotion as it does thinking and willing. Concentration and determination are not only intellectual activities but also involve a child's state of emotional arousal (Duffy 1962).

Studies in American and Russian laboratories have clarified the conditions that lead to increased motivational arousal. They reveal that certain types and amounts of changes in the environment trigger responses that orient a person to attend and focus on his world. Such orienting reactions are associated with vigorous and persistent actions on the level of overt behavior, with states of alertness and anticipation on the level of conscious experience, and with stimulating rates of heart, muscle, and brain activity. Orienting responses are seen as pervasive, reflex actions that have helped man to survive by integrating inquisitiveness with preparation for action. Arousal is apt to increase when there is a marked difference between the immediate experience and prior experiences of a similar nature (Hunt 1961).

Arousal is also more apt to increase under conditions of moderate intensity (Sokolov 1958). Under conditions of uncertainty, children seek information that will enable them to clarify the situation and determine what type of reaction is in order (Berlyne 1966). In short, there seems to be an inborn capacity to attend and seek information, and these orienting reactions are associated with arousal, attention, and concentration. The arousal involves emotions as well as intellect and is apt to occur under conditions of moderately intense stimulation.

6. *Emotions are expressed nonverbally as well as verbally.* Emotions are expressed not only in feelings and conscious experience but also in physiological functions and overt physiological actions. Popular usage tends to associate emotions with inner states of feeling and with physiological functions such as heart rate, breathing, and digestion and elimination. More comprehensive and objective examination indicates that emotions have several aspects of a common occurrence and that none of these aspects is independent of the others. These aspects of emotions include a person's experience of particular feelings; overt behaviors indicating feelings by motions, posture, and gestures; activities of the central (voluntary) and autonomic (involuntary) branches of the nervous system; activities of the organs and functions controlled by the autonomic nervous sytem such as breathing, elimination, and heart rate; and glandular activities such as those involving the adrenal, pituitary, and sex glands. Studies have revealed that there are different patterns of physiological reactions to fear and anger (Ax 1953; Funkenstein, King, and Drolette 1957). In subjects exposed to conditions designed to arouse anger heart rate decreased, muscle tension increased, and diastolic blood pressure climbed. In subjects exposed to conditions designed to elicit fear respiration and skin conductance increased, and muscle tension reached a peak. Subjects who openly expressed their anger showed different patterns of physiological reactions from subjects who controlled their expression of such feelings or became anxious. Overt expression of anger and anxiety reactions were associated with the secretion of noradrenalin, but restrained and inward-directed anger was associated with secretion of adrenalin. There is ample evidence that emotions are expressed in nonverbal, bodily changes as well as in personal experiences and feelings.

People can judge another person's emotional state from facial expressions in a fairly reliable manner (Woodworth 1938). They can also use cues of physical distance to interpret friendship or aloofness (Hall 1959). For example, in the northeastern United States a man stands eighteen to twenty inches away from a strange man and twenty-two to twenty-four inches away from a strange woman. A person who stands as close as eight to twelve inches away is either being very friendly or aggressive. People communicate their interest, concern, distress, and distance by an elaborate but interpretable body language (Birdwhistell 1963). Nonverbal cues like postures, hand and leg positions, eye and head movement, and body tonus often represent nonverbal expressions of emotion (Perls, Hefferline, and Goodman 1951; Lowen 1971). An adult or child thus communicates his emotions by a wide range of bodily cues and physiological functions as well as by verbal statements.

The recognition that emotions are communicated nonverbally as well as verbally has significant implications for the processes of learning and teaching. Recognition of nonverbal communication means that the words of teachers and their declarations of interest and concern are only one manifestation of the feelings they hold toward their students. Students observe and interpret the emotional expressions of their teachers and develop their own views as to who is sincerely interested in their welfare and growth. Another implication is that there is nonverbal emotional "contagion" of feelings among students and between students and teachers. Feelings of anxiety, fear, and enthusiasm are communicated within the social environment of the classroom by facial expressions, tones of voice, and body language. Students also learn how to avoid, approach, or accept their emotions as a basis for learning and action. Nonverbal acceptance of a child's emotions by a teacher can often help a child to gain greater awareness and acceptance of himself. Nonverbal communication of emotions adds a depth and added basis for motivating and supporting the student in his classroom activities.

7. *Emotions can be adaptive as well as disruptive.* We now have considerable evidence that emotions can be constructive and facilitating as well as disturbing and debilitating. Several investigators have concluded that the major impact of emotions is to produce disturbance and disorganization (e.g., Young 1961). Judging from the total range of evidence, though, it would appear that this focus on the negative effects of emotion may represent a selective, cultural bias rather than objective assessment. Although it is clear that certain levels and extended states of emotion can have negative consequences, it is also clear that other levels and types of emotion can have beneficial influences upon behavior. There is no basis for the conclusion that disruption and disorganization are integral characteristics of all emotion (Leeper 1948; Leeper 1965).

To answer the question of whether emotions are disruptive or adaptive requires an appreciation of the task, situation, and time span involved. The concept of adaptation carries with it the idea of a fit between an organism and its environment. The concept cannot be used absolutely for all tasks, situations, and persons. We find that emotions generally have positive effects upon tasks of moderate complexity and demand, and they are likely to have negative effects in complex, stressful situations (Patrick 1934). There is also evidence that fear is quite adaptive and increases the effectiveness of behavior. Studies of airmen during World War II indicated that fear made the flyers more alert and sharply increased motivation (Wickert 1945). Studies of students who expressed anger at the poor treatment they received indicated they performed at least as well as nonemotional subjects (Funkenstein, King, and Drolette 1957). In general, moderate emotions of not too long duration and intense emotion of short duration increase involvement and energy and aid performance. Intense, enduring emotions can have disorganizing, disruptive effects that are particularly notable in complex, problem-solving tasks (Goodenough 1931); Lantz 1945; Spielberger 1966). Persistent emotional stresses that are associated with physiological activities are capable of producing such psychosomatic disturbances as ulcers, headaches, and asthma (Dunbar 1955). A level of emotions that is too low may be maladaptive in that it reduces the level of energy available to the individual and may cause his life and work to appear dull or meaningless. Leeper (1965) has proposed that emotions can direct as well as disrupt behavior and that emotions provide cues and memories regarding previous learning and the present physiological state. He maintains that emotions are part of a broader representational process that conveys and synthesizes learning, perception, motivation, and emotions. Since that representational process provides cues and is essentially an information-giving process, there seems to be little point to or basis for labeling emotions as exclusively disruptive.

If we take the view that emotions provide information, energy, and involvement, we are led to a broader and more accepting attitude toward the role of emotions in the educational process. Teachers may be faced with classroom conditions where there is need for more emotions or different emotions rather than lower levels of emotions to achieve academic goals. They may also have to learn how to adapt the level of emotional arousal to the complexity and nature of the tasks they present their students. Students, on their part, differ markedly on how they respond to pressures and whether they perform well or poorly in response to demands for improved or accelerated performance. If we take the interaction between student dispositions, task demands, and situational factors into account, it is simplistic to talk of emotions as disruptive factors in the educational process.

8. *Positive emotions may have an accelerating effect on intellectual and personality development.* An acceleration effect resulting from positive emotions does not necessarily occur in all aspects of intellectual development, but it does appear that the absence of any emotions and presence of negative emotions do impede intellectual growth (Hunt 1961; Goldfarb 1945). The Fels Institute study of parent-child relationships (Baldwin, Kalhorn, and Breese 1945) indicated that children of acceptant-democratic parents showed accelerated intellectual development as compared to children with other types of parents. This acceleration was revealed by higher I. Q. levels, more originality, more emotional security and control, and friendly, nonaggressive social actions. Warm and accepting feelings apparently create a desire in a child to be near and similar to the person who accepts and appreciates him. Children reared in orphanages or under family conditions where warmth is lacking in the early years of life turn out to be socially unresponsive, limited in conscience formation, and relatively alienated from their peers (Goldfarb 1945; Bowlby 1956). In a situation where at least a minimum of warmth is present the child is likely to imitate the parent or teacher model and learn the specific behaviors of the model and his ideals and values. Imitation and internalization of adult values, goals, and actions is unlikely to occur, unless the adult model indicates his concern, interest, and acceptance of the child (Sears, Maccoby, and Levin 1957). Even punishment that is used to suppress a child's undesirable behavior is more effective when it comes from loving parents than from those who are rejecting or indifferent (Bandura and Walters 1963). The child does not respond merely to a given treatment of reward or punishment, but he interprets the meaning and importance of a given act in the context of his broader relationship with the person who rewards or punishes him. A child is more likely to accept guidance, be motivated, gain intellectual skills, and model himself after a warm, accepting adult than after one who is neutral or negative. The advocates of impersonalized treatment, limited affect, or a "hard" educational line should be advised that their position has been largely discredited by the available scientific evidence.

Studies of therapist and teacher effectiveness also indicate the importance of warmth, trust, and acceptance in furthering student growth and learning. Studies that compared psychotherapists who had been most and least effective in treating patients revealed that effective therapists sought active and personal relationships with their clients. They also tended to develop relationships in which the patients felt respected, accepted, and trustworthy (Betz and Whitehorn 1956). Studies comparing different treatment procedures (Heine 1953) indicate that emotional warmth and expressiveness are a major factor in developing positive helping relationships. Among the procedures found most effective were those that developed a sense of trust and understanding and those that provided an opportunity to express and clarify emotions that were only partially recognized and appreciated. Warmth, interest, sensitivity, and appreciation of the person's attitudes without too much emotional involvement appear to be other common features of effective helping relationships (Fiedler 1953). Research on effective teachers indicates that many of these same factors of warmth, interest, respect, and concern also contribute to student development in the academic environment. Parents, teachers, and therapists who facilitate intellectual and personal growth with positive emotional expression appear to have some common features.

9. *Fear of failure and feelings of powerlessness are major sources of poor academic performance and dropping out of school.* The Coleman report (1966) made a very comprehensive examination of American education and concluded that student attitudes regarding their own powers are the most important influence in determining whether students succeed or fail in school. The child who believes that his efforts will make a difference in his achievement of success puts out more effort, persists, and tolerates the difficulties and boredom that long-term schooling generally requires (Wiener 1971). The findings of this report suggest that students are more likely to perform when they believe that their educational environment is aware of and responsive to their needs and interests. It further suggests that students' feelings of powerlessness are reduced when they can influence the direction of their activities and studies. Even young children know when teachers and parents are aware of and responsive to them and willing to consider their views. Coleman found that a student's feelings that he does make a difference were more closely associated with academic performance than class size, yearly expenditure per pupil, or level of teacher's educational preparation. If we judge these findings, students' feelings of acceptance and importance are of central significance; they are not peripheral or incidental to learning as some critics have claimed them to be.

It is important to note that teacher expectations of student performance have a dramatic effect upon how students actually perform (Rosenthal and Jacobsen 1968). A teacher who expects more from a given child and who believes he can succeed communicates these beliefs to the child and apparently raises the child's expectations regarding his own capacities and performance. Such favorable self-expectations have been associated with more focused and persistent work habits (Coopersmith 1967). The teacher who believes that a child can and will succeed conveys her confidence to him and thus establishes a self-fulfilling prophecy of success. The teacher may express her interest, convictions, and attention in such a way that the child believes he "can make it" and is worthy of the teacher's time and effort. At the other extreme, teacher and parent expectations that a given child will fail are likely to rob him of hope, interest, and attention and establish a self-fulfilling prophecy of failure. The teacher who wishes to facilitate performance and growth in students should be aware that actions instilling expectations of success and feelings of significance are among the most powerful tools to use. Emotional commitment to a child effectively increases the likelihood that the child will learn to be capable and effective in his academic and social activities (Baumrind 1967).

10. *Motivation for competence in children may be associated with innate emotional satisfactions.* Psychological research (White 1959) has indicated that people may perform actions because of their inherently satisfying consequences. According to this line of evidence, children are rewarded by internal feelings of increased competency as well as by external motivation. Greater activity, increased ability to explore and manipulate objects, and the search for increased, new, or more complex stimulation appear to be built into our biological heritage. For example, monkeys will take equipment apart and manipulate latches for no other reward than the satisfaction of the activity itself (Harlow, Harlow, and Meyer 1950). Other animals deprived of movement will engage in physical activity for the satisfaction of the activity itself (Hill 1956). Chimpanzees who are presented with unfamiliar objects manipulate them and alter them to investigate their use and significance (Kelleher 1958). A wide range of studies has indicated that curiosity and exploration are motives themselves, and in many cases, they may be more powerful than such physical necessities as food or water (Berlyne 1960). Internal, inherent motives associated with a search for information, activity, stimulation, and manipulation apparently are part of the motivational system. Studies of human infants suggest that they are avid seekers of information who scan their environment, make fine distinctions, and prefer certain types of complex stimuli (Bower 1966; Fantz 1958). Children appear to be biologically programmed to seek, explore, and respond to gain increased information and competence in dealing with

their environment. The motivations for performance include innate emotional satisfactions as well as external sources of reward.

The new evidence regarding innate sources of motivation has considerable, but largely unexplored, implications for school practices. Although there is general agreement that the long-term goal of education is to produce a self-rewarding individual, there are differences of opinion on how such an individual is to be produced. Educators following a behavioristic model assume that external rewards are internalized to become self-rewards. Those educators following an affective, humanistic model assume that the child must define and clarify his own feelings and needs before he can reward himself. The evidence indicating that innate satisfactions are associated with competency suggests that there are internal rewards that precede parent and teacher rewards and that can be utilized to increase student involvement and performance.

A model of education that depends solely or predominantly on external rewards to the student for incentives and direction requires constant, sustained, and individualized attention to each student. Although such persistent attention and reinforcement procedures are a worthy goal, a teacher cannot provide it at all times for each student in a class. As we have stated, such external rewards would not result in the development of a self-directed individual. A model that requires reinforcement from the teacher must also deal with the question of motivation in the absence of external rewards. If we look at the place of rewards in the school, we find that there is no single type of external reward, whether it be candy, praise, or grades, that is equally effective for all children. Children differ individually in the type of reward to which they respond, and teachers are not sufficiently acquainted with all children to apply the most effective reinforcement for each individual. Teachers are not always able to be nearby and responsive when a child performs a desired task or reaches levels that are worthy of notation. Finally, we should note that teachers who depend on external rewards are faced with difficulties and lack of direction when desired responses are not rewarded. Extinction generally occurs in the absence of external rewards accompanied by the loss of the gains in learning and motivation that did occur during the period of reinforcement. We have reason to believe that the child who learns to gain affective satisfaction early in his learning career will persist in his learning, even when external rewards are not readily given or immediately available. Many adults know that they must either learn to persist in activities for the satisfactions tasks themselves give or become automatons in their work. If we encourage the child's awareness of positive and negative affect, we increase the likelihood that he will learn to respond to his internal feelings of success and failure. If the child is aware of such feelings, he can correct himself as he pursues tasks, reward himself for the level of attainment he reaches, and internally recognize the need for changes and improvement. External rewards clearly have a place in the school as a part of the motivational, encouragement process rather than as the entire process itself. External reinforcement can be used to guide and direct children to new materials and subjects, expose them to alternative ways of acting, and consolidate achievements. Rewards used in such a manner can lead children to new and alternative behaviors without creating the illusion that external rewards are the only ones that are effective, necessarily beneficial and capable of always sustaining behavior.

The aspects of emotions that we have outlined above provide us with evidence that current knowledge and thinking about emotions has changed markedly and that this change has great significance for educational theory and practices. Cultural blinders and the weight of tradition previously lead to definitions and emphasis on the negative and disruptive aspects of emotion and their interfering or irrelevant function in the educational process. With the recognition that emotions are not a separate category of behavior and also that emotions are complex, rather than simple occurrences, has come appreciation of the constructive, organizational, and positive effects of learning. Emotions cannot be voluntarily controlled, but teachers who know how to verbally and nonverbally communicate warmth, trust, and respect can significantly improve the motivation and performance of their students. The recent evidence of innate satisfactions gained from increased information and competencies suggests that children are motivated by internal sources of gratification as well as external reinforcement. Emotions are an integral aspect of our heritage, and they cannot be eliminated or avoided. Teachers who accept children as they are recognize and respect affect as a legitimate concern of a school and a society that is involved in motivating and guiding the behavior of its youth. If we affirm emotions, we affirm the reality of our biological heritage and are thereby able to utilize the child's feelings as part of the educational process. If we ignore or reject feelings in students, we have covertly said that learning to count is more important than motivation; that formal science experiments are more important than making sense of experience or creativity; and that education that is arousing and fun is almost inappropriate in the school setting. Beyond the practical issues of self-reward and self-motivation that can facilitate learning and beyond the recognition that learning how to confront, cope with, and utilize feelings can lead to more effective behavior is the value we place upon ourselves as total persons. To suppress emotions in the school is to deny part of every child's humanity; to accept and utilize emotions is to utilize that humanity to increase realization of human capacities.

REFERENCES

Arnold, M.B., ed. *Feelings and Emotions.* New York: Academic Press, Inc., 1970.

Ax, A.F. "The Physiological Differentiation between Fear and Anger in Humans." *Psychosomatic Medicine* 15(1953):433-42.

Azrin, W.H.; Holz, W.C.; and Hake, D.F. "Fixed Ratio Punishment." *Journal of Experimental Analytical Behavior* 6(1963):141-48.

Baldwin, A.L.; Kalhorn, J.; and Breese, F.H. "Patterns of Parent Behavior." *Psychological Monograph* 58(1945):No. 3.

Bandura, A., and Walters, R.H. *Social Learning and Personality Development.* New York: Holt, Rinehart & Winston, 1963.

Baumrind, D. "Child Care Practices Anteceding Three Patterns of Preschool Behavior." *Genetic Psychology Monographs* 75(1967):43-88.

Berlyne, D.E. "Curiosity and Exploration." *Science* 153(1966):25-33.

Betz, B.J., and Whitehorn, J.C. "The Relationship of the Therapist to the Outcome of Therapy in Schizophrenics." *Psychiatric Research Reports* 5(1956):89-117.

Birdwhistell, R.L. "The Kinesic Level in the Investigation of Emotions." In *Expression of the Emotions in Man.* New York: International University Press, 1963.

Block, J. "Studies in the Phenomenology of Emotions." *Journal of Abnormal and Social Psychology* 54(1957):358-63.

Bower, T.G. "The Visual World of Infants." *Scientific American* 215(1966):80-92.

Bowlby, J. *Maternal Care and Mental Health.* Geneva: World Health Organization, 1956.

Brown, G.I. *Now: The Human Dimension.* Esalen Monograph #1. Big Sur, Calif.: Esalen Institute and University of California, Santa Barbara, 1968.

Bruner, J.S., and Goodman, C.C. "Value and Need as Organizing Factors in Perception." *Journal of Abnormal and Social Psychology* 42(1947):33-44.

Coleman, J.S. et.al. *Equality of Educational Opportunity.* Washington, D.C.: U.S. Government Printing Office, 1966.

Coopersmith, S. *The Antecedents of Self-Esteem.* San Francisco: W.H. Freeman and Co., 1967.

Davitz, J. "A Dictionary and Grammer of Emotions." In *Feelings and Emotions,* edited by M.B. Arnold. New York: Academic Press, Inc., 1970.

Duffy, E. *Activation and Behavior.* New York: Wiley, 1962.

Dunbar, F. *Emotions and Bodily Changes: A Survey of Literature on Psychosomatic Interrelationships 1910-1953.* New York: Columbia University Press, 1955.

Estes, W.K. "An Experimental Study of Punishment." *Psychological Monograph* 57(1944):No. 263.

Fantz, R.L. "Pattern Vision in Young Infants." *Psychological Record* 8(1958):43-47.

Fiedler, F.E. "Quantitative Studies on the Role of Therapists' Feelings toward Their Patients." In *Psychotherapy: Theory and Research,* edited by O.H. Mowrer. New York: Ronald Press, 1953.

Funkenstein, D.H.; King, S.H.; and Drolette, M.E. *Mastery of Stress.* Cambridge, Mass.: Harvard University Press, 1957.

Goldfarb, W. "Psychological Privation in Infancy and Subsequent Adjustment." *American Journal of Orthopsychiatry* 15(1945):247-55.

Goodenough, F. "Anger in Young Children." *University of Minnesota Institute of Child Welfare, Monograph Ser.,* 1931, No. 9.

Hall, E.T., Jr. *The Silent Language.* Garden City, N.Y.: Doubleday & Co., Inc. 1959.

Harlow, H.F.; Harlow, M.K.; and Meyer, D.R. "Learning Motivated by a Manipulation Drive." *Journal of Experimental Psychology* 40(1950):228-34.

Heine, R.W. "A Comparison of Patient's Reports on Psychotherapeutic Experiences with Psychoanalytic, Nondirective, and Adlerian Therapists." *American Journal of Psychotherapy* 7(1953):16-23.

Hill, W.F. "Activity as an Autonomous Drive." *Journal Comparative Physiological Psychology* 49(1956):15-19.

Hunt, J. McV. *Intelligence and Experience.* New York: Ronald Press, 1961.

Kelleher, R.T. "Stimulus Producing Responses in Chimpanzees." *Journal of Experimental Analytical Behavior* 1(1958):87-102.

Lantz, B. "Some Dynamic Aspects of Success and Failure." *Psychological Monograph* 59(1945):No. 271.

Leeper, R.W. "A Motivational Theory of Emotion to Replace 'Emotion as Disorganized Response'." *Psychological Review* 55(1948):5-21.

———. "Some Needed Developments in the Motivational Theory of Emotions." In *Nebraska Symposium on Motivation,* edited by M.R. Jones. Lincoln, Neb.: University of Nebraska Press, 1965.

Lowen, A. *Language of the Body.* New York: Collier, 1971.

Mandler, G., and Sarason, S.G. "A Study of Anxiety and Learning." *Journal of Abnormal and Social Psychology* 47(1952):166-73.

McClelland, D.C., and Atkinson, J.W. "The Projection of Needs: I. The Effect of Different Intensities of the Hunger Drive on Perception." *Journal of Psychology* 25(1948)205-22.

Patrick, J.R. "Studies in Rational Behavior and Emotional Excitement: II. The Effect of Emotional Excitement on Rational Behavior in Human Subjects." *Journal Comparative Psychology* 18(1935):153-95.

Perls, F.; Hefferline, R.F.; and Goodman, P. *Gestalt Therapy.* New York: Dell, 1951.

Rotter, J.B. *Social Learning and Clinical Psychology.* New York: Prentice Hall, 1954.

Rosenthal, R., and Jacobsen, L. *Pygmalion in the Classroom: Teacher Expectation and Pupils' Intellectual Development.* New York: Holt, Rinehart & Winston, 1968.

Sarason, S.G. "Empirical Findings and Theoretical Problems in the Use of Anxiety Scales," *Psychological Bulletin* 57(1960):403-15.

Schacter, S., and Singer, J.E. "Cognitive Social and Physiological Determinants of Emotional States." *Psychological Review* 69(1962):379-99.

Schlosberg, H. "Three Dimensions of Emotion." *Psychological Reviews* 61(1954):81-88.

Sears, R.R.; Maccoby, E.E.; and Levin, H. *Patterns of Child Rearing.* Evanston, Ill.: Row, Peterson, 1957.

Sokolov, E.N. *Perception and the Conditioned Reflex.* Moscow: University of Moscow Press, 1958.

Spence, K.W. "Anxiety (Drive) Level and Performance in Eyelid Conditioning." *Psychological Bulletin* 61(1964):129-39.

Spielberger, C.D., ed. *Anxiety and Behavior.* New York: Academic Press, Inc., 1966.

White, R.W. "Motivation Reconsidered: The Concept of Competence." *Psychological Review* 66(1959):297-333.

Wickert, F., ed. *Psychological Research on Problems of Redistribution.* Army Air Force Aviation Psychology Program Research Reports, Report No. 14. Washington, D.C.: U.S. Government Printing Office, 1947.

Wiener, B. et al. *Perceiving the Causes of Success and Failure.* New York: General Learning Press, 1971.

Woodworth, R.S. *Experimental Psychology.* New York: Holt, 1938.

Young, P.T. *Motivation and Emotion.* New York: John Wiley, 1961.

2

Free Social Play:
A Guide to Directed Playing

Rivka R. Eifermann
Psychology Department
The Hebrew University of Jerusalem, Israel

INTRODUCTION [1]

Despite the recent surge of interest in educational and simulation games and in recreation, researchers, in general, have not undertaken any systematic examination of the characteristics of "natural" games or the structure and organization of freely formed, unsupervised children's play groups. As a result, books for teachers and parents on the choice of suitable recreational games have been based on limited personal experience, intuition, or untested theoretical considerations, and the invention and choice of educational games has been rather haphazard. Success in the design, planning, and organization of games — children and adult — largely

1. Most of the facts and findings presented in this chapter are based on large-scale observations conducted by the author with the assistance of some 150 students and teachers who served as observers and recorders of play groups in schools and streets. Though they here remain anonymous, their efforts are reflected throughout. Ruth Steinitz, Amira Ravin, Giora Kronzon and David Salomon are responsible for some of the more important findings presented here that, except for their special efforts, would have remained stored in our files as raw data for a long time to come.

The collection and preliminary analyses of the school data were made possible mainly through support of the PL 480 Education Research Program, U.S. Department of Health, Education and Welfare, Office of Education, Bureau of Research, under Contract No. OE-6-21-010. Support for additional analyses was obtained from the Israel Academy of Sciences and Humanities and The Center for Human Development at the Hebrew University of Jerusalem. The street data was analyzed in part through Grant No. 6 F-5, The Ford Foundation.

depends on the possession of firmly-based knowledge concerning the capacities and interests of the potential players. For example, what is the most suitable time span for a single round of a game designed for a particular age group? Are the children for whom the game is intended capable of sustained strategic thinking? Is this capability reflected often in games of their choice? What part does chance play in children's spontaneous games? To what extent are the players capable of and interested in playing games requiring mutual cooperation? What is the largest reasonable size for a play group in the kind of game children are going to play? The answers to these and many other questions prepare the way for rational planning and for the organization and construction of games that will be accepted by the children as "real" games.

My aim in this chapter is to present some answers to questions about games and children that may be of use to instructors of young children. A few examples will illustrate some of the ways in which we can apply this knowledge.

Let us assume that we are interested in encouraging group cooperation among seven- and eight-year-old boys and that such cooperation can be promoted by playing certain games. If we realize that children of this age rarely play purely cooperative games when left to their own devices, we will instead offer the children a game of a type which is "naturally" more popular among them. Once we know that games involving competition between two groups are more acceptable for children of this age we can choose a competitive game; cooperation within each group will then be actively practiced when participants united against an outside force. Since in our particular example we are concerned with cooperative activity among boys, we will choose a game that will involve some of the skills that are most attractive to boys, such as strategic thinking, rather than memory or attention. We should also choose a game that requires a number of play participants and a time span compatible with the natural inclination of the age group under consideration. We can see an example of this choosing process when we organize games for players of both sexes in mixed groups. In order to reduce friction and to select games attractive to both boys and girls, we find we should choose games with features characterizing boys' and girls' play habits or games that incorporate typical boys' and girls' game features but in which there is a sufficient division of roles as to give members of both sexes the possiblity of exhibiting some particular prowess. If we are ambitious enough to "plant" a game that, hopefully, will be played spontaneously and without supervision and even become a "craze," we should try to model it along the lines of existing "crazes" that we will refer to as *recurrent games.*

In this chapter, I have tried to summarize some major findings relevant to selecting children's games. The findings are based partially on findings of Piaget (1962) and Parten (Parten and Newhall 1943), but predominantly on records obtained in large-scale observations of freely formed, unsupervised play groups of Israeli children and on over 2,000 descriptions of their various games. The observations were conducted during free recess in fourteen schools involving some 7,000 pupils and after school hours in the streets and empty lots in a rather quiet city neighborhood of relatively low socioeconomic level. The cumulative total of players recorded in over a year of observations was in excess of one hundred thousand. The children observed at school ranged from ages six to fourteen. The children observed after school (henceforth abbreviated to "street") ranged in age between three and seventeen years.[2] In this chapter, I shall consider only the play habits of children from ages three to eight. It is, though, an arbitrary age division from the point of view of play habits. The children observed in our research were of various cultural and socioeconomic backgrounds, but the findings indicate considerable overlap in play habits despite marked differences in socialization. There is little observational data available on the group-play habits of children in countries other than Israel, but data that is available suggests that the games that have been recorded in Israel do not differ greatly from those listed and described in various other countries (e.g., Lehman and Witty 1927; Chateau 1955).

GAMES WITH RULES AND GAMES WITHOUT RULES

Perhaps the most obvious division of types of games that can be and is usually made is that between rule-governed games and games without rules (often referred to as "just play"). Examples of *games without rules* are sociodramatic games, e.g., playing house, playing with dolls, playing with trucks or trains, playing doctor and patient, playing bus driver and passengers; constructional games, e.g., building in the sand with wooden bricks or plastic blocks; and action games, e.g., chasing, climbing poles, throwing stones at a target, or free skipping with or without a rope. Some of these games are in fact relaxed versions of rule-governed games such as hopscotch, tag, or jump rope. Sometimes a game without rules is turned into an on-the-

---

2. Specifics concerning the sample of schools and the methods of observation have been described in other publications, in greatest detail in Eifermann, 1968.

spot game with rules during play as the following example that appears in our records will illustrate.

One of two boys (fourth graders) who was standing at a distance of about six feet from a bucket picked up a stone, threw it at the bucket, and hit it. He repeated this activity, sometimes actually getting a stone into the bucket or sometimes missing it altogether. The second boy soon joined the first boy in his game. Initially, each boy merely exclaimed in response to his own or his partner's success or failure, and they threw stones in random order. Soon, however, they began to throw in turn; although, there was no explicit decision to this effect. The second player then suggested scoring a point for each throw into the bucket. Since they rarely succeeded in getting a stone into the bucket, the first boy then suggested that they score one point for hitting the bucket and two for getting a stone inside. Using this agreed method of scoring, the boys continued the game until it was terminated by the school bell.

Such games, rarely if ever, acquire the status of formal rule-governed games. More often than not, the on-the-spot rules created during play are adhered to as long as the specific round of the game lasts. In fact, suggesting rules and arguing about them may become an important part of the play process itself. There will, of course, be some games which fall somewhere in between the two major categories we have described. However, most rule-governed games can be distinguished easily. They have rules that are known before the game starts or are taught by veterans in the game, and the rules are adhered to by all players throughout the game. Such rules usually remain constant no matter when the game is played. Games such as marbles, hide-and-seek, jacks, football, dominoes, blindman's bluff, tag, chess, and tiddelywinks are all rule-governed. There are many variants of most rule-governed games. In Israel alone close to forty variants of tag are played, over twenty of hopscotch, and almost as many of jump-rope. Many examples can be found in Opie and Opie's fascinating book *Childrens' Games in Street and Playground* (1969) and some others in Eifermann's *Determinants of Children's Game Styles* (1970). Variants of games differ from one another in the number and complexity of their specific rules, and all participants are assumed to know before the game starts which variant is to be played according to either a known set of "easy" rules or a different set of "tough" rules. Players decide by declaration or by agreement reached before the game starts which rules they are going to adopt. I would like to add that strict adherence to rules is not always maintained in practice; sometimes children are willing to turn a blind eye to other players' slips, or they simply cheat cheerfully, cheekily, or with a heavy feeling of guilt.[3]

Developmental Trends

The demands imposed on the child when playing rule-governed games are more exacting than those imposed in games without rules. Even willingness to keep to the rules is of itself insufficient; the child must also be intellectually capable of remembering and applying the rules himself and must turn this ability outward to see that others abide by them. He must be capable of social interaction with his peers in ways dictated by a definite set of rules rather than by his own whims, wishes, and imagination. This set of rules is voluntarily accepted, rather than dictated by adults, and must be adhered to as long as the game lasts. Games with rules are not played by toddlers because of these special intellectual and social demands. Parten (Parten and Newall 1943) recorded the play of kindergarten children aged 2-5 and found that even children aged 4 1/2 seldom played rule-governed games. Piaget (1951) who made a thorough, theoretical analysis of young children's games argues that "games with rules rarely occur before stage II (age four to seven)" (p. 142).

Let us examine this development in greater detail by looking at some of the material gathered in Israel. The data presented in Table 1 should be illuminating. It gives the number and the percentages of players of rule-governed games out of all games, both rule-governed and without rules, that were observed and recorded in the street and in the neighborhood school. The school data presented in Table 1 includes players of grades one and two (ages six to seven and seven to eight); the after school data also includes younger children of nursery age (mostly three to six).

A glance at the table reveals a number of noteworthy points:

1. Playing of rule-governed games increases with age.
2. In all cases more girls than boys play rule-governed games. This point is consistent with other characteristics of boys' and girls' play behavior discussed in the section on "Boys and Girls at Play."
3. It is quite evident that relatively more first- and second-grade children engage in playing rule-governed games at school than in the street. Since rule-governed games tend to be more demanding, it appears that the school elicits a higher level of play from first- and second-graders than does the street setting.

---

3. Altogether, children's attitudes to rules change in quality as they grow older. This issue has been extensively treated by Jean Piaget, *The Moral Judgement of the Child* (London: Routledge & Kegan Paul, 1932), and more recently by Lawrence Kohlberg, *Moral Character and Development*, ed. M. Hoffman (Chicago: Aldine Press, 1967).

Table 1

Number of players of rule-governed games and their percentages out of all players, by age and sex

AGE AND SEX OF CHILDREN	STREET		NEIGHBORHOOD SCHOOL	
	Number	Percentage	Number	Percentage
Age 3-6 (nursery)				
Boys	258	32.8	——	——
Girls	213	36.3	——	——
Age 6-7 (1st grade)				
Boys	127	42.2	315	60.9
Girls	167	58.4	395	73.0
Age 7-8 (2nd grade)				
Boys	236	50.0	569	61.3
Girls	273	58.6	553	77.3

Playing in Mixed Age Groups

The finding that greater play is elicited in schools is best understood in relation to another interesting finding. Although, only about one-quarter of the children play in mixed age groups at school, over two-thirds of the children play in such mixed groups in the street. This happens in spite of the fact that in all schools on which our conclusions are based the playground is open to children of all grades. Playing in mixed age groups probably is more common in the street due to the fact that children of the same age are more readily available at school than they are in the street. Even at school the tendency is to mix in play mainly with children who are only a year older or younger. Our records indicate that on the average more than 15 percent of children in the street play in groups with at least one brother or sister. Playing with a brother or sister may often reflect the most congenial solution to the task, imposed by parents, of looking after younger siblings.

Nursery school children tend to play with children older than themselves more often than do school children. As a result, the younger children often "dictate" the style of playing. There is more rule-governed playing among first and second graders who play in the street in groups that do not include nursery school children than there is in groups that do include the younger children. With nursery children it is the other way around; they engage in many more rule-governed games when they mix with school children than when they play on their own. At the same time, we find that when first or second graders play with children older than themselves they become involved in rule-governed games that they do not play among themselves. For example, first graders playing among themselves did not take up certain variants of jumprope, marbles, and tops but were recorded as doing so when playing with older children.

From all of these findings, it appears that when children wish to play and there are insufficient peers of their own age available, they will adapt their level of play to that dictated by circumstance. This will mean that they sometimes play at less than their full potential; at other times, it will give them the chance to participate in older children's games, though often in lesser roles such as turning the rope for the older girls. It is therefore not surprising that quarrels are more frequent in mixed play groups in which extra demands for social adaptation and tolerance have to be met. Play disruption as a result of quarrel is rare. We found that about 2 percent of all games were thus disrupted at school and even fewer than that in the street.

Some Conclusions and Applications

In freely formed, unsupervised play children under six already engage in rule-governed games to quite a considerable extent. This happens particularly when children are playing in the school setting; although, in the school young children still engage in play without rules in about two-thirds of all cases. In the first grade the situation is already reversed, and becomes more pronounced when children play within their own age group. Generally, children prefer playing with their age peers. It appears that when playing with younger children an older child must often adapt himself to the younger and thus lowers the level of play of which he is potentially capable. The opposite also happens; a younger child is compelled to do his best to raise his standards to that of older players. Quarrels are more frequent in age-mixed groups. It seems therefore that if we want to give a child an opportunity to play without extra strain, we will succeed better by limiting the play group to children of the same age.

There are times when we may be particularly interested in giving the child a chance to practice adaptation to less than ideal conditions — to learn to make the most of what is offered. In this case, we should confront him with children a year, or at most two years, younger or older than himself. [4]

The benefits of less than ideal conditions applies not only to the organization of play groups but also to the design of playgrounds. A playground may be open to all or subdivided, either physically or by means of the types of equipment present in different parts. Neither permanent subdivisions nor a completely open play space will result in the best utilization of the various opportunities that playing can offer. The playground that can be adapted to both mixed and nonmixed playing is probably the best; unless those in charge can limit the number of children at any one time. Under those circumstances the playground can remain permanently open to all, and the controlled traffic of children in and out will result either in natural mixing of ages or in age separation in play depending upon the total number of children.

PLAYING WITHOUT RULES

Practice and Symbolic Play

Piaget (1951) distinguishes two major types of games without rules: "practice" and "symbolic." By the age of three, both types of games have appeared often in combination — a "symbolic" game that possesses elements of "practice." Some typical "practice" games taken from our records are the following:

> Two girls of the second grade stepped onto a plank lying on uneven ground and began to rock it by jumping up and down. A girl from the third grade and a boy from the second joined them, and together they rocked on the plank waving their arms to maintain their balance.

> Three boys (grade four) made their way through the playground in the following manners: one walked upright, the second bent forward against the first while holding him by the hips, and the third sat on top of the second, holding onto the "leader's" shoulders. From time to time they stopped and exchanged positions.

According to Piaget, the playful element in such games consists of the child acting on the environment as he wishes, performing skills

---

4. I do not mean to say, of course, that children never play with others much older or younger than themselves — and enjoy it enormously. Indeed, see the example on p. 31. This is the exception rather than the rule.

such as running, pushing, pulling, lifting, or balancing. The child already possesses the skills utilized in such games so that his play is an act of *assimilation* — an expression of mastery over the environment and over his own body. The child plays for "the pleasure of being the cause" of what is happening. "All that he is trying to do is use freely his individual powers, to reproduce his own actions for the pleasure of seeing himself do them and showing them off to others" (Piaget 1951, p. 121). Verbal "practice" games are similar; the child tells stories or communicates in play when he is interested not so much in the content of what he is saying as in the sheer exercise of his verbal skills.

In symbolic play the opposite is the case. The emphasis is on content. The child plays "as if " he is someone or something other than himself — an object (a bus or a bell), an animal (a lion or some imaginary creature), or a human being (a mother or the grocer). Some typical examples of collective "symbolic" play taken from our records are the following:

> The children ran one after the other with short steps, their hands at their sides, making blowing and humming noises, being "buses."

> Three boys (grade 4, 5 and 6) ran along the road. Two of them were each trundling along his hoop, one was riding a scooter, and the rest were just running alongside. Those running with the hoops ("cars") were trying to overtake one another, while the child on the scooter (the "policeman") told them off and warned them that he would give them a ticket. Finally, they staged "a collision," and all the children threw themselves on the street, hands outstretched, screaming "we have been killed." After a while they "came to life," and again ran along as before.

From the age of three onward a child's "symbolic" play tends to become increasingly realistic and detailed. A stick will no longer satisfy him as a substitute for a horse; the toy horse must be as close a model of a real horse as possible. The dramatic roles performed are carried out with increasing consistency and attention to detail, and the dramatic scenes multiply in complexity and elaboration.[5] It is probably

---

5. Recently, strong assertions have been made in Sara Smilansky, *The Effect of Socio-dramatic Play in Disadvantaged Pre-school Children* (New York: Wiley, 1968), with specific reference to Israeli children of North African and Middle-Eastern origin, that they "do not develop the ability to engage in symbolic play." From this to the assertion that such symbolic play was a product of culture rather than a universal phenomenon was but a small step (B. Sutton-Smith, "The Two Cultures of Games," in *Aspects of Contemporary Sport*, ed. G.S. Kenyson, Chicago, 1969). Our own research findings do not support these claims at all, at least in so far as they are based on Israeli children.

for reason of increasing realism in symbolic play that imitation by six- to seven-year-olds centers largely on adult roles rather than on objects or animals. Piaget (1951, p. 131) argues that "just as practice play reproduces . . . each new acquisition of the child, so symbolic play reproduces what he has lived through, but by means of symbolic representation. In both cases the reproduction is primarily a self-assertion for the pleasure of exercising his powers and recapitulating of fleeting experience." However, symbolic play is not only an expression of mastery through repetition of pleasant experiences. Piaget gives some examples in which it fulfills the very important functions of correcting reality, compensating for frustrating experiences, and neutralizing fears which arise out of past experiences or anticipated frightening experiences. A child may play "Mom and Johnny," and in the role of Mom scream at his "Johnny" with the very same words used against him by his own "Mom" or he may pretend to read a newspaper "like Daddy does" or, before the doctor's arrival, he may play at being the doctor. In such play, the child symbolically gains control over unpleasant realities, an achievement which then enables him to cope with them more easily. This aspect of play is particularly emphasized by psychoanalytic theorists (e.g., Beller 1954; Erikson 1963) whose main concern is with the emotional development of the child. They stress the additional, very important point that if the child's fears and frustrations are too great, he will not find expression in play but, on the contrary, cause "play disruption." A child who is overwhelmed by his anxieties is not even able to play "as if " he is mastering them.

Piaget gives little attention to "constructional" games that are characterized by a strong element of adaptation to reality, such as in building brick houses and more particularly, in building models of airplanes or rockets. Some constructional games are even played by way of preparation for other games, and the line between work and play is then not easy to draw, as in the following example:

> Two girls (nursery and third grade) had a long rope which they tied loosely to the railing on two sides of a ground-floor porch so that the rope was hanging slightly above the floor at its midpoint. They then placed a pillow at this point on the rope and sat on it with the obvious intention of swinging. The structure very soon collapsed since they had not succeeded in tying the rope properly. They were in good spirits and persisted in tying the rope and then gently placing themselves on the pillow, even though their swing fell apart after practically every attempt.

Challenge in Play

It is evident to anyone who has observed children that the enjoyment they gain from exercising their skills is often an important motive for play. Children's tendencies to repeat the same activity over and over again without showing any sign of exhaustion or boredom is often quite incomprehensible to adults. It is not always possible for an observer to distinguish play that reflects sheer enjoyment in the exercise of skills from play in which the child symbolically gains some mastery over fear or frustration. If two different players engage in the same activity, they may have quite different motives.

Although there is a great deal of evidence to indicate that the pleasure in the exercise of skills and the reduction of anxiety are both very powerful motives for play, it seems that a certain overemphasis of these two factors has led to the neglect of another — the *challenge* that games offer to their players. For example, challenge is revealed in climbing higher, running faster, thinking quicker, or exerting more influence on one's peers. The challenge found in games in which success and failure are possible and in which the achievement of success requires some effort on the part of the player is an important motive in child play. The challenge factor does not occur only in "motor" games. Sociodramatic games often require imagination, the adoption of roles, and considerable coordination between players and therefore may also offer complex and varied challenges. Two examples taken from our records, one of "practice" play requiring fast and coordinated action and the other of "symbolic" play involving role playing, illustrate the importance of such challenges:

A few children who possessed a long rope encircled a whole group with it so that they themselves were also within the circle. One of them held the two ends of the rope in his hands, facing outward while two or three others held the rope up at the back of the group. The "leader" started running, pulling the rope behind him, while the whole group within the rope ran behind, trying to keep up in order to avoid tripping over one another or being hurt by the rope.

The girls (nursery to third graders) pretend to be young ladies. Sunglasses, handbags, and similar accessories are used. They make believe they are going for a stroll and then to shop. All activities are carried out with the utmost attention to elegance and grace, and the girls clearly try to outdo one another in successful performance.

Many games may be played on more than one level. A child will sometimes build a tower of bricks only so high in order to avoid the risk of its collapse by putting one too many on the top. Often, however, he will try to go one, two and three bricks above complete safety. Even though his attempt may end in tears, he will try again almost invariably. There are vast individual differences among children in the type and degree of challenges they attempt and accept in their play. Yet, all children appear to be occasionally "possessed" by their games; they absolutely cannot stop until they succeed in bouncing their ball twenty times running, skipping perfectly to a set limit, or swinging to a certain height. This response to challenges may reflect a child's overall frustration with being a child and his wish to expand his powers of control. Taking up challenges and successfully meeting them provides more than symbolic satisfactions. It increases control over body, mind, and emotions and adds to social skills. Meeting challenges may result also in a gain in prestige in the eyes of peers and even adults. It represents a test of the world and the child's personal powers with relatively limited danger to his safety and well-being.

Although more analysis is needed, it does appear from our material that as children grow older they turn more often to games characterized by challenge. It seems that when they are younger and very rapidly gaining increasing control over their bodies and an expanding environment, the intoxication with the sheer exercise of these new powers is greater than that experienced at a later age. Once they reach school age, children appear more attracted than their younger peers to games in which there is some risk of failure and in which some effort is required in order to achieve success.

Social Interaction in Play

When children play in groups of two or more participants the extent to which they do in fact play *together* may vary considerably. Parten (mentioned earlier) found that the type of interaction tends to change with age. Very young children play by themselves. Children aged 2 1/2 to 3 1/2 are typically engaged in *parallel play*, as in the case of "two boys spinning around in physical proximity, each screaming 'the house is turning around!' " or "two boys, running parallel each with his own hoop" or "children sitting close together in the sand box each making his own mud pies." The young children play alongside each other and are engaged in corresponding activities, but they do not interact actively in their play. *Associative play* is said to be typical of children aged 3 1/2 to 4 1/2. In associative play all children engage in similar activites such as driving toy trucks, taxis, and trains, and there is interaction in the sense that they borrow and lend play material, follow one another with trains and wagons, and make weak attempts at controlling who may participate. They make no attempt to organize or coordinate the activites themselves. An even higher level of interaction is achieved in *cooperative play* which includes, in Parten's classification, a very wide variety of activities such as games without rules or with on-the-spot rules in which the participants cooperate toward a common goal or even compete.

However, children do not always adhere to this time table. There are great individual differences between children of the same age in the extent to which they engage in each type of play; the more intelligent children tend to play at a higher level of interaction. The appearance of one type of play does not completely replace or substitute an earlier type. We have found that even eighth grade school children engage in parallel play though, of course, to a lesser degree than they did at the age of three or four. Nevertheless, the order in which these different kinds of play generally tend to appear — first solitary, then parallel, then associative, then cooperative — does reflect a gradual development in the social skills of the child, his ability to act in coordination with others, to comprehend and accept others' viewpoints, and to communicate his own wishes and intentions.[6]

Playthings and Play Surfaces

On the basis of what we know now about children's capacities for social play between the ages of three and eight and about the needs motivating such play, it is possible to make certain general statements regarding suitable toys, materials, and equipment. I shall not attempt to list all possible materials and objects or even to present a checklist for the evaluation of toys and other playthings. Such lists have appeared in various other publications.[7] My aim is to state certain

---

6. A very illuminating analysis of the development of some skills required for effective social interaction is presented by John H. Flavell, et. al., *The Development of Role Taking and Communication Skills in Children* (New York: John Wiley and Sons, 1968).

7. Relevant catalogs are obtainable from: *Childplay*, 43 E. 19th St., New York 10003; *Childcraft*, 155 East 23rd St., New York 10010; *Community Playthings*, Rifton, New York 12471; *Creative Playthings, Inc.*, P.O. Box 1100, Princeton, New Jersey; *Novo Education Toy & Equipment Co.*, 585 6th Ave., New York 10011; *Musicon Inc.*, 4200 Blvd., Long Island, New York 11101; *Paul and Majorie Abbatt Limited*, High Wycombe, England; and *Pastorini Spielzeug*, Zurich, Switzerland. Relevand books and articles are: S. Hegeler, *Choosing Toys for Children* (London: Tavistock Publications, 1963); H. Kepler, *The Child and His Play* (New York: Funk & Wagnalls, 1962); E.M. Matterson, *Play and Playthings for the Preschool Child* (Baltimore: Penguin Books, 1967); and S.D. Speeth, "The Rational Design of Toys," *Journal of Creative Behavior* 1(1967):398-410.

principles based on the findings discussed in the preceding pages. The reader himself may, I hope, formulate certain other guildelines that answer his specific needs.

"Creative" play materials are very much the present fashion and it is probably most appropriate to begin with them. I have emphasized the importance of challenge in play and referred to Piaget's comments on how "constructional" games support challenge activites. "Creative" play, in addition to its possible value in stimulating development that is emphasized by optimistic educators, may fulfill well some of the child's basic and intrinsic needs. We cannot emphasize too strongly however, that other kinds of play that are non-creative fulfill needs that are no less important. Children often play games to exhibit complete mastery and control, and in these circumstances they are not at all interested in meeting new challenges. Such wishes are rooted in motives that are as legitimate as those driving them to play creatively. At age three and even at school age children play "as if" games in which teddybears, dolls, trucks, and trains are manipulated and controlled. The common joke about fathers who buy trains for their own pleasure under the guise of interest in their children tends to overshadow the simple fact that possession of a mechanical toy may be one of the child's cherished dreams. This is particularly true at advanced stages of symbolic play in which the child is concerned that his toys be as close a model of reality as possible. The power to put into motion clockwork animals, cars, and planes provides impressive opportunities to express mastery. Such games of pure mastery will tend to lose their attraction for the child sooner than games with a challenge, but they do fulfill important needs.

The needs of the child notwithstanding, we cannot ignore economic considerations. The acquistion of toys or other equipment that is expensive but provides only passing satisfaction, no matter how intense, can rarely be justified. A partial solution to this problem lies in multiple-purpose play apparatuses that can be used in different ways, in games that demand different levels of social interaction and effort. Probably one of the reasons that children return again and again to play with sand and water, dolls, blocks, or a ball is that they can be used just as well in solitary, parallel, associative, or cooperative play; these playthings may be adapted to express mastery, overcome personal frustrations, or meet various challenges. For that reason, we will examine toys and other play objects and materials for their general and multiple-purpose utility. David Aaron and Bonnie P. Winawer in their stimulating book *Child's Play* (1965) present many ideas for the design of playground equipment for multiple uses.

It is interesting to note that our observations in Israel have revealed that on the school playground and in the street the materials used most commonly in children's unrestricted play are those that simply happen to be lying around or are otherwise within easy reach. Sticks and stones, a piece of old string, an old cigarette box, a child's cap, an orange, a pencil, leaves, and a piece of old rubber, all have their multiple uses. Objects specifically designed for play are far less commonly used than simple, common materials! Even though there is clearly an increase in the use of purpose-designed play objects as children grow older, those offered by nature (and neglect) still retain their preferred status.

More than half of the children in the groups we observed in the school playground did not use any play objects in their games without rules; about two-thirds of the children who played in the street used such objects. This difference in the use of play objects was probably due to two reasons: (1) the school playground was cleaner and offered fewer worthy "finds" than the street, and (2) children brought play objects to school less frequently than they did into the street.

Let us examine one other aspect of the playground space: the surface on which the games are conducted. Since school yards and buildings in Israel are not standardized, the fourteen schools of our sample represent a great variety of environments and play surfaces. Some surfaces are paved, and others are not. Some have large lawns, and others have none. Some are mainly natural sand or soil. Yet, it is quite remarkable how similar school children's choice of play surfaces is in all schools. More children tend to play on paved and semipaved surfaces (i.e., asphalt, tiles, and gravel) than on any other type of surface. Next in popularity is natural soil or sand, and lawns, even where they predominate, are only third in popularity. Play in the street is strikingly similar in this respect to play at school, even to the extent of "indoor" play (in the classroom, corridors, and on the staircase at school and on staircases and porches at home). Our findings indicate that among children of school age, more girls than boys play on paved and semipaved surfaces, and more boys than girls play on natural sand and soil. More nursery than school children play on natural sand and soil (there was not one sandbox in the area observed!). The opposite is the case with regard to paved surfaces.

Some Implications of Play without Rules

Children aged three to eight play social games without rules in which they exercise physical and verbal skills and "as if" games in which they take on various human or animal roles or play at being objects such as cars. Games often combine characteristics of the practice type and the symbolic type. Although these games become more elaborate as the child grows older (and more oriented towards reality), most children play their games sometimes at an "easy" level and at other times make them relatively "tough." When a child plays at a level that imposes no demands on him, he enjoys "the pleasure of being the cause," the feeling of mastery which his expanding control over his body and his environment gives him; such play also reduces anxieties from which he may suffer due to his limited control over reality outside of the relaxed game situation. Playing at a "tough" level, meeting new challenges, and not being quite sure of success have their special attractions. The child here tests his powers; if successful, he derives satisfaction from the success itself and from the prestige gained thereby.

Just as children's physical skills and capacities for elaboration and reality orientation increase as they grow older, so do their social skills. Even though the various types of social play — parallel, associative, and cooperative — have all been observed at the age of eight and later, there is a shift in prominence from types of games demanding less social interaction to those demanding more.

It follows that children need toys and other objects of play that help them to meet new challenges, and they also need those objects that aid them in expressing mastery and control. Objects that are suitable for play at different levels of interaction are also important. Multiple-purpose objects may meet these various needs most effectively. Many of these multiple-purpose objects (e.g., stones and sticks) that are never intended to be used as playthings are used more widely than those that are carefully designed and produced.

Evidently, many children's play activities that seem to adults to be a complete waste of time are of importance for the development of the child as a confident and secure being. The child apparently looks for challenges at a level that fits him. If we consider the fact that young children do not cooperate often in their play, we find it may be advisable to design their play equipment so as to avoid cramping the children and to prevent them getting in each other's way. A number of small sandboxes, for example, may be more suitable than one large box and may reduce unnecessary friction. As for play surfaces, more children play on paved than other surfaces, but sand and soil are also popular, in particular with boys.

GAMES WITH RULES

Challenge in Games: Their Life Span

I have found it particularly useful to introduce the following classification of games regarding their occurrence and recurrence in the life of the child. This classification applies only to pure (or ideal) versions of these games and not to mixed activities.

- *Steady Games* which are played more or less constantly at all times, with little variation in intensity. Example: simple tag.
- *Recurrent Games* which are played only intermittently but reach great intensity during each "wave." Example: jump rope or marbles.
- *Sporadic Games* which are also played only intermittently, but in short waves and never reach intensity. Example: simple guessing or fortune-telling games.
- *One-Shot Games* have just one uninterrupted period of existence and reach great intensity during that period. Example: the hula hoop.

This mutually exclusive classification is not meant to be exhaustive. Real games will turn out to be mixtures and variations of these ideal types. Some games will be played only intermittently and reach great intensity on some of their waves and only low intensity on others. Other games will have simultaneously steady appearance in one playground but a sporadic appearance in another playground.

What is it that makes for the *recurrence of games*? Why do such games as hopscotch, marbles, kites, jump rope, jacks, and tops seem to emerge and catch on only to disappear and then recur again? The popular explanation that recurrence is due just to seasonality, such games reappear when the right season for them arrives and disappear when this season is over, has not been able to survive real observations conducted in New Zealand,[8] the United Kingdon,[9] and Israel. Of the five schools we analyzed for recurrence of games, only one exhibited a close correspondence between the recurrence cycle and the seasons; even in that school this cycle held for only one game. The main factors that make for the recurrent character of a game must be sought in the nature of the game itself rather than in external conditions.

An analysis of eighteen recurrent games has shown that these

---

8. B. Sutton-Smith, "Marbles Are In," *Western Folklore* 12 (1953): 186-93.
9. Personal communications with Mrs. Iona Opie.

games possessed some revealing features. Recurrent games tend to be characterized by definite final outcomes and winning; when applicable, they are more frequently associated with material gain. The challenge of all-out competition and the promise of gain are, presumably, features that contribute to the great popularity of such games once they have been reintroduced. Typically, recurrent games are played sequentially by individuals whose activities are independent of each other. Consequently, these games also can be played (or practiced) by an individual child. The games often require specific skills that can be quickly developed through practice, unlike other skills, e.g., competitive running, where improvement can be obtained only slowly and painfully. The challenges inherent in recurrent games last only for a while. Many of the very same features that make for their quick rise also cause their equally quick fall. After a period of training and repeated competition between individuals, a hierarchy of players is stabilized that naturally will tend to reduce the challenge of playing with many of the original potential competitors because they are either "lousy" or "too good." In the relevant cases, many of the poorer players will avoid playing with their obvious superiors out of the fear of unavoidable material loss. Thus the game loses its attraction. It will recur only after a period long enough for the established hierarchy to lose its stability and for new hopes for self-improvement to rise again. During the periods of latency, other games may gain ground and reach their peak.

As we have mentioned, the belief that games recur due to seasonal cycles is not true. We can demonstrate our view by the fact that the very same "seasonal" game may be simultaneously at its peak in one school and utterly dormant in a neighboring school.

The typical form of the curve depicting a recurrent game will be a series of waves that have lines of no activity between them and different amplitudes in different schools or even in the same school. An examination of curves obtained in our analyses of recurrent games such as jump rope, hopscotch, jacks, and marbles shows that a new wave (e.g., jacks) will begin to rise and gain strength only when some other recurrent game (e.g., jump rope) is beyond its peak of attention and popularity. A recurrent game has the best chance of being accepted when there is little competition around at the time.

Other relevant, but secondary, conditions for the appearance of a new wave might be the personalities of the agents who intend to reintroduce the game, the network of communication between children (geographic proximity or similarity in socioeconomic level), seasonal weather (warming-up games in winter), and seasonal availability of implements (apricot pits during the apricot season).

Although the impact of the last two factors seems to have been greatly overestimated, these factors do play some role in the cycle of children's play.

There are very few *steady games*. The profile we obtained for such steady games as simple tag turns out to be quite distinct from that of recurrent games. The popularity of tag may vary, but it is nevertheless steadily present in the playground. What, then, in the inherent nature of simple tag expresses the difference between recurrent and steady games? In tag, too, the hierarchy of the players as to the physical skills (in running and evading) required for good performance will be rather quickly established, but the game will still attract players on a steady basis. Tag in comparison to hopscotch has one factor over which the players have almost complete control: the "it" has considerable freedom in determining how hard he wants to play and whether he will succeed by selecting either an easy or a tough "catch" and the other players can vary their distance from the "it" by either staying safely away or getting temptingly close to him. Control over the extent of the challenge the child is ready to take upon himself is one important factor that provides steadiness in a game. Although this factor is important, it is not necessarily a decisive one and can be cancelled by other factors working in the opposite direction.

My *challenge* explanation for the different lifecycle of the various types of games is, then, briefly as follows: a game is *steady* if in a particular round of the game it allows each participant to adjust the extent of the challenge to his abilities while at the same time still leaving the outcome of that round sufficiently open to the efforts and luck of the players. A game is *recurrent* if after a stable hierarchy of players has been established the outcome of any particular round has become relatively predictable and independent of the challenge and exertions the players are ready to take upon themselves. A game is *sporadic* if it provides only little variation in the extent of the challenge it enables the players to choose for themselves and perhaps little true challenge to their capacities. A game is sporadic if it is too easy or too simple. *One-shot games* (of which one example is the hula hoop) are games with considerable initial challenge but in which the player has no hope of increasing the mastery gained in his initial efforts, even if he were to take it up again after a lapse of a year or two. Such games are not apt to be taken up by the next generation that has never played it before and for which it could have formed a live challenge largely because the game has been lost sight of before the new generation is ready for the challenge.

Cognitive Skills and Chance in Games

There are games in which the outcome depends entirely on memory or on the ability to concentrate or on knowledge or on understanding or on chance. In most games, however, success depends on more than one skill or to some extent on "luck." We have found that children differ in the extent to which they engage in games requiring different kinds of skill. For example, more girls than boys and more "disadvantaged" than "privileged" children play games requiring rote memory. It appears that, other conditions being equal, it does not matter to any great extent whether rote memory is a major or minor requirement of the game. The presence or absence of the rote memory requirement determines which children will play a game with that requirement. From our analysis of this and other components of games we have found that the determination of who is to play a particular game depends on the presence or absence of particular components in the game, rather than on their relative importance.

Let us now discuss the following three classes of games. *Games with strategy* (hencefore abbreviated to Strategy) are games in which the outcome is determined wholly or partially by rational choices between alternative courses of action. Examples are drop the handkerchief, in which the player has to decide where and when to drop the hankie; chess, in which the player has to decide on each of his moves; hide-and-seek, in which players have to choose the best hiding places and to decide whether or when to emerge from them; laughing war, in which one player tries to make the others laugh (the player who succumbs exchanges roles with him) and has to choose his principal "victim"; and tic-tac-toe, in which each player must decide on the most advantageous placing of his sign. *Games with rote memory and/or attention* (Memory) are games in which the outcome is determined, wholly or in part, by rote memory and/or by maintaining an attention span. Examples are jump rope, in which becoming confused in the middle of a jumping rhyme leads to failure; variants of hopscotch that involve numerous successive steps where any failure to perform these in the correct order leads to failure; Simon says, a game that requires paying constant attention; and hands, a hand-clapping coordination game in which concentration is required for proper coordination, and at the same time the exact words of the accompanying rhyme must also be remembered and recited. *Games with chance* (Chance) are games in which the outcome is determined, wholly or partially, by chance. Examples are the various games in which a die or pair of dice is used; guessing and fortune-telling games; war cards, in which the winner is the player who happens to possess "higher" cards; and various counting games such as odds or evens and paper, scissors, or stone.

We have included in the same classes games such as hopscotch and jump rope that require different kinds of rote memory and chess as well as tic-tac-toe that both involve strategic thinking but in which quite different levels of sophistication can be applied. At our present level of analysis we can derive some useful generalizations from our data. Generally, as children grow older they engage in Strategy games to a greater extent whereas the reverse is true with regard to Memory games. These findings suggest that Strategy games are in some sense more difficult for children than are Memory games. Moreover, most games of cognitive skill or chance also have physical skill as one of their components. Nevertheless, it is the presence or absence of nonphysical skills that determines the distribution of players in these games by age, sex, socioeconomic, and scholastic levels. Although there are few pure games of Strategy, Memory, or Chance, there is a rise in the proportion of players of pure Strategy, Memory, or Chance games between the ages of six and eight.

When children play multiple-component games, they most often engage in games combining Memory and Strategy rather than those combining Memory and Chance or Strategy and Chance. They most often engage in games that combine Memory, Chance, and Physical skill rather than those combining Strategy, Memory, and Physical skill or Chance, Strategy, and Physical skill. We have found that players throughout Israel are more likely to be involved in games of Strategy than in games of Memory and are the least involved in games of Chance. Boys are more apt to play Strategy games than girls, but the opposite is true for Memory games and to a lesser extent for Chance games.[10]

These generalizations are applicable in rural and in urban areas as well and among children who differ considerably in their socioeconomic conditions. Nevertheless, there are great differences in the proportion of players who prefer Memory, Strategy, and Chance games in different environments. Particularly, more advantaged than disadvantaged children play Strategy games. Children of the lower

---

10. J.M. Roberts and B. Sutton-Smith have reported (e.g., *Ethnology*, 1962, pp. 166-185) that American girls, rather than boys, show preference for Strategy games. Their findings are based, however, on game checklists in which children were required to indicate their game preferences. Besides the problems involved in generalizing about actual behavior from such declared preferences, it should also be noted that in such analyses each game counts equally, regardless of whether it is constantly played or played hardly at all. Because our findings are based on actual observations and have been repeatedly confirmed among children with marked differences in cultural background, I tend to believe that observations among American children will produce results similar to our own.

socioeconomic strata tend to prefer Memory and Chance games (Eifermann 1971a).

Social Skills in Games

Social, rule-governed games demand that players interact. The interaction does not need to go beyond a comparison of scores as, for example, in a game of darts, but it may be constant and intensive, as in the case of volleyball. Despite the level of interaction, it may be cooperative, competitive, or a combination of both, and the cooperation or competition may be conducted on a strictly egalitarian basis or under conditions of inequality.

In our analyses (Eifermann 1970c and 1970d), we distinguish, among others, the following types of games requiring *cooperation:*

Single party, purely cooperative games are games in which all players act as one party and share a common aim. An example is the game feather. In this game, the players throw up a feather and then collaborate in an effort to keep it up in the air solely by blowing. Another example is cat's cradle in which one player takes over from another a string figure stretched around the fingers of both hands and changes it in the process of transfer. The holder tries to stretch the string at the angle most convenient to his partner, and both aim to continue this collaborative effort of transfer from one player to the other for as long as they can manage. Other examples are some of the hand-clapping and coordination games and some of the fortune-telling games. Our findings indicate that children rarely engage in single party, purely cooperative games. The proportion of such players varies in the different schools from practically zero to a maximum of about 10 percent. To the extent that such games exist, they are more prevalent among nursery and early school age children than among older children and more common among girls than among boys.

Games of cooperation with competing playgroups are games in which members of each of two opposing groups share a common aim. Examples are tug-of-war, basketball, stop ball, and cops-and-robbers.

In games of cooperation within competing play groups there is a steady rise with increasing age in participation in such games. Boys participate in them to a greater extent than girls, often twice as much and more. It is important, however, to draw attention to one additional fact; when comparing the extent of participation in these games among children raised in varying environments, striking differences are revealed. In a kibbutz (voluntary cooperative settlement) where children are raised together in children's homes the proportion of boys participating in games of cooperation within competing play groups was 39.4 percent at age six to seven and 59.6 percent at age seven to eight. The corresponding percentages among family-reared, city children of comparable socioeconomic and scholastic achievement levels were only 22.3 percent and 33.9 percent.

In regard to competition, we distinguish between games of competition where the roles and rules are roughly the same for all players (egalitarian) and games where the roles and rules differ for various players (nonegalitarian).

Singleton games are games in which some players have more privileges than others. Examples are follow the leader, Simon says, and some variants of leapfrog with a more-or-less permanent "back."

Singleton games with interchangeable roles are games in which the rules for all players are roughly the same. Examples are the games of jacks in which each player, in his turn, goes through the same steps and stages of the game; marbles in which each player, in turn, tries to hit his opponent's marble; lotto; and checkers.

Games of one versus two or more singletons are games such as variants of tag, twenty questions, and hide-and-seek.

There is a considerable difference in the degree of egalitarianism in the street and the school. In the street about 50 percent of all singleton games played by nursery to second grade children are egalitarian games, whereas, the corresponding proportion at school is only about 20 percent. One reason for this may be that children at school feel more protected than in the street. They can, in principle, always complain to a teacher — though we have recorded hardly any interventions by teachers in these games. Since children can afford to quarrel in the street more, they do not need to insist as much on strictly fair play. Among the age groups considered, there is a definite increase in participation in egalitarian games and a greater likelihood for boys rather than girls to engage in such games. More boys than girls engage in games of one versus two or more singletons, but there is a decline in participation in this type of game with increasing age. Out of all singleton games, the style of one against many prevails at school but not in the street. The second type of nonegalitarian game, the one with some players having more privileges than others, gains in predominance with increasing age and is played consistently more often by girls than boys.

Some Implications of Games with Rules

The life span of games, their intensity, and duration over longer or shorter periods is strongly related to the extent and type of challenge they offer. Features such as a definite final outcome, playing in sequence rather than simultaneously, and the possibility of practicing alone and improving one's skills are characteristic of recurrent games. Steady games, on the other hand, allow each participant to adjust the extent of the challenge to the level of his skills. Sporadic games offer little challenge at all.

The skills incorporated in a game are cognitive, social, and physical. Among other observations we have made we have seen that as children grow older more of them tend to engage in games involving strategy and less in games involving memory and attention. We have also seen more boys than girls play Strategy games, but more girls than boys play Memory games. As for social skills, we have found that even nursery age children are already involved to some extent in games of cooperation within competing play groups that, on the whole, represent the most complex form of social interaction. Purely cooperative games are not played to any great extent. Since children are capable of cooperating in play, as indicated by two-party group games, the question arises as to whether it is possible (if considered desirable) to educate children in such a way as to produce a greater desire for pure cooperation.

We cannot answer this question easily. We have found, to our surprise, that kibbutz children who are raised in the spirit of cooperation engage in purely cooperative games to a lesser extent than children reared in other environments! Whether this is due to an overdose of organized cooperation or other unassessed influences remains an open question. Egalitarian games of competition between singletons increase in popularity with age. Perhaps, this is partly the result of an increasing understanding of what competition is. As such understanding increases, the value of competition under conditions of strict equality is enhanced, because success is more easily evaluated by direct comparison. In nonegalitarian games equality is preserved to some extent since the leader, the underprivileged player, and the one who plays against many tend to exchange roles during play. We have found that, on the whole, players in such games do not get the same chance for equality as they do in games with interchangeable roles, if only because the number of players in such games tends to be larger. The larger number of players diminishes the likelihood that all competitors will get equal opportunities to play various roles.

Besides the developmental implications of these and other findings, they should be of interest not only to those in charge of selecting appropriate and attractive games for children, but also to the inventor and designer of games. In this connection, let me focus particular attention on *simulation games*. In simulation games varied aspects of reality, both individual and social, are simulated. Examples are

Community Disaster (Inbar 1970), the Dream Process (Bresnitz and Lieblich 1970), a High School Game, a Family Game, Seal Hunting, and others mentioned in Coleman (1967), Boocock and Schild (1968), and Abt (1969). Some of the special advantages of these games are that they are learning games in which the child is given the opportunity to *experience* the consequences of his actions in lifelike situations before encountering them in real life. Through such personal involvement a child can grasp more fully and effectively complex social or psychological processes over which he could not gain command through conventional learning methods. In constructing these games, a great deal of effort has been put into creating accurate *simulations* (indeed, if this were not so, such games would be misleading rather than instructive). These simulation activities have been made into *games*, however, largely by trial-and-error methods since the investigators had few general guidelines which they could apply. It is one thing to say, as does a major proponent of simulation games (Coleman 1967), that "if a game has the appropriate mixture of chance and skill, persons of somewhat different abilities can play together, and success will depend in part, but not entirely, upon their relative skill," but quite another to be able to tell what such "appropriate mixtures" are and what other mixtures are appropriate under specified conditions. Our analyses aim at reaching just such conclusions.

BOYS AND GIRLS AT PLAY

Playing in Mixed Groups

Between the ages of three and eight there is a gradual separation of the sexes in group play. Generally speaking, by age seven or eight no more than 5 percent of all spontaneous play groups comprise children of both sexes. This fact should, however, be understood in relation to another, namely, that a very high proportion of *all* play groups consists of just two children, whereas play in sex-mixed groups *at school* occurs almost without exception in groups of five or more participants. Even in the second grade about 15 to 30 percent of the children still have some experience in playing with children of the opposite sex, although, there appear to be wide cultural differences on this matter. The proportion of boys and girls playing together is much larger in the street than at school. This is probably due to the same factor that causes so much more mixing of age groups in the street. In other words, when a sufficient number of children of their own sex are available, boys and girls tend to play apart, but they do not reject members of the opposite sex when "no one better is available." It is interesting to add that mixed groups more often than not consist of a majority of girls and a minority of boys.

Sex Differences in Typical Game Characteristics

"Sex differences in play behavior have been overemphasized by previous investigators," say Lehman and Witty in their book *The Psychology of Play Activity*, published in 1927. Nevertheless, they present tables listing an impressive number of play activities more commonly engaged in by boys and others by girls. The long-term value of such lists is strongly questioned by Sutton-Smith and Rosenberg (1961) who compared the order of game preference among boys and girls in response to questionnaires circulated in 1898, 1921, and 1959. The investigators conclude (1) that there is increasing similarity in the games preferred by boys and girls and (2) that some games have even lost favor with boys and gained favor with girls (e.g., leapfrog and marbles). Our material, though collected in a very small country, indicates that such lists differ greatly from culture to culture (Arab and Jewish), subculture to subculture (kibbutz and town), and even from one part of a town to another. We found very few games that could be described consistently as either boys' or girls' games. The number of exceptions to sex specific games is large enough to raise serious questions as to the significance and usefulness of lists of sex-differentiated games.

It is not worthwhile to attempt to analyze sex differences as reflected in "typical" boys' and girls' games, if we wish our conclusions to apply to more than just a limited environment. Although there are few games that can be described as being universally either boys' or girls' games, this does not necessarily imply that specific *characteristics of games* may not be universally associated with one of the sexes. Let me illustrate with an example. In comparing two of our schools, we found that the proportion of boys who play games that require the employment of physical strength (out of all players of such games) is practically the same in both schools. This is not immediately evident when we confine our comparisons between the schools to specific games alone. A certain form of catch ball, for example, that requires the employment of strength in throwing the ball is played by boys in 100 percent of the cases in the one school; yet, in the other school it is girls who play it in more than two-thirds of the cases. However, in another game in which physical strength is also employed the picture is somewhat reversed. When the overall comparison between the schools is made, taking account of all games, it is possible for a characteristic to be consistently typical of boys (employment of physical strength, in our example), even though no one game alone reveals this consistency.

After we compiled a list of characteristics, we checked their presence or absence in each of some one hundred games played in different schools. The characteristics were then ranked separately for each school according to the proportion of boy players (out of all players) associated with each. The rankings thus obtained in the separate schools were very similar. The list we have developed starts with the characteristics most typical of boys and ends with those least typical of them, the latter being those which are also the most typical of girls. The characteristics that appear in the middle of the list are more or less typical of both sexes.

1. Large play space (as in soccer or tag, in contrast with hop-scotch). [11]
2. Employment of physical strength (e.g., tug-of-war and wrestling).
3. Competition between teams (e.g., basketball).
4. Success achieved through active interference in other players' activities (e.g., football, in contrast with volleyball).
5. Well-defined outcome (e.g., dominoes, prisoner's base, as opposed to jumprope).
6. Room for personal initiative (e.g., hide-and-seek as opposed to jacks).
7. Continuous flow of activity (e.g., tag).
8. Motor activity involving the whole body (e.g., running and skipping games).
9. Players acting simultaneously (e.g., dodgeball).
10. Leader-follower relationships (as in games in which a leader is chosen before the game starts).
11. Risk taking (as in games of chance, in which players decide on the size of the stakes).
12. Concentration necessary for accurate performance (e.g., headball and marbles).
13. Verbal aggression (the use of expressions such as "dead," "poison," "witch," and "prisoner").
14. Possibility of playing (or practicing) alone (e.g., hopscotch and jump rope).
15. Motor activity involving only parts of the body (e.g., tiddilywinks and spinning top).

---

11. The examples are *not* of boys' or girls' games (we insist that there are very few such games) — but rather of games in which the particular characteristic is present.

16. Multiplicity of rules dictating (almost) all moves (e.g., hopscotch).
17. Competition between singletons (e.g., leapfrog, chess, and marbles).
18. Verbosity (e.g., I spy, fortune-telling games).
19. The use of fine and specialized physical skills (e.g., marbles and jacks).
20. Song and rhyme (e.g., jumping rope rhymes).
21. Multiplicity of well-defined stages (e.g., jacks, Chinese elastic).
22. Rhythm (e.g., hand-clapping and coordination games, ball bouncing games).
23. Taking turns in an ordered sequence (e.g., tops, monopoly, and hopscotch).

Though this ranked list is tentative and neither exclusive nor complete (this chapter, in fact, deals in some detail with equally important factors not mentioned in the above list such as strategic thinking and egalitarianism), it can give us certain insights into the kinds of activities preferred by boys and girls. Numbers one through nine on the list may be said to represent boys' characteristics, that turn out to be related to (a) bodily strength (characteristics 1, 2, 7, and 8); (b) need for achievement (characteristics 4, 5, and 6); and (c) orientation toward the group (characteristics 3 and 9). Numbers fourteen through twenty-three on the list similarly represent girls' characteristics and relate to (a) routine activities (characteristics 23, 21, and 16); (b) individualistic rather than group orientation (characteristics 23, 17, and 14); and (c) specialized skills (characteristics 22, 19 and 15 and, specifically, verbal skills as represented in 20 and 18).

Some Implications of Boys' and Girls' Play Habits

Children prefer, on the whole, to play with members of their own sex. This tendency increases between the ages of three and eight. When playing in mixed groups, numbers are usually relatively large, and there tends to be a majority of girls. Cross-cultural comparisons and even comparisons within a culture show that there are few games that are consistently typical of either boys or girls. There are specific characteristics of games that attract one sex more than another. Typical boys' play characteristics are related to physical strength, need for achievement, and orientation towards the group, as a general rule. Typical girls' characteristics are related to routine activities, individualistic orientation, and specialized skills.

Many games combine boys' and girls' characteristics. The same game may offer different challenges to each sex and appear equally attractive to both sexes, though for quite different reasons. The fact that boys and girls tend to mix mainly in larger sized play groups reflects not only a certain stigma associated with mixed playing in small groups but also, and perhaps primarily, the fact that in larger groups there is often a greater division of roles and an element of group competition. Large groups offer members of each sex a chance to express themselves in their own special ways, and a balance of power is maintained since each sex has some advantages over the other.

TIME SPAN AND GROUP SIZE

The Time Span of Games

Children may spend hours playing, but the span of time continuously spent on one game is usually surprisingly short. The games played by close to 50 percent of all boys and girls observed in the street lasted no longer than five minutes! The differences among age groups were surprisingly small in this respect; 40 percent of the children aged thirteen to fourteen still played for no more than five minutes in succession. Table 2 presents for all schools and for the street the numbers and percentages of children playing for up to five minutes, five to ten minutes, and on up to fifty minutes and over in five minute intervals. (All intervals above fifty minutes included less than 1 percent of all players and were therefore combined.) I have not distinguished between boys and girls in Table 2 because there were no systematic differences between them with regard to time span. Since the school recess lasts for ten minutes, this is the maximum length of time recorded at school. One can see that more children play for five minutes or less in school than in the street. Since the school bell breaks up over 60 percent of the games, this is not really surprising. What is more interesting, however, is that almost two-thirds of children's games are terminated after no more than ten minutes, even when there is no school bell to stop them. Only about 10 to 15 percent of all players are involved in games which last for more than twenty minutes. Our detailed records of reasons for the termination of street play indicate that these reasons were mainly related to the players themselves and were categorized as "quarreling," "starting anew," or "switching to another game"; sometimes the game simply "came to its natural end" or "petered out." Contrary to what may be supposed, games seldom ended because of outside interference, cases in which, for example, the children are called home or when older children disrupt a game of younger players.

Table 2

Number of players in play groups whose games lasted for specified time spans and their percentages out of all players

Play Groups	TIME SPAN IN MINUTES (Number of Players/Percentage)									
	Up to 5 No. %	5-10 No. %	10-15 No. %	15-20 No. %	20-25 No. %	25-30 No. %	30-35 No. %	35-40 No. %	40-45 No. %	45-50 No. %
Street										
Nursery	642	48.1								
First Grade										
Second Grade										
School										
First Grade										
Second Grade										

It might have been expected that games with rules would tend to last longer than games without rules. There is some indication that games with rules do last longer, but the differences are very small.

The Size of Play Groups

Children aged three to eight play mainly in small groups. About 30 percent play in groups of just two children, 50 percent play in groups of no more than three, and between 80 to 90 percent play in groups totaling no more than six players. As might be expected, kindergarten children tend to play in smaller sized groups (two, three and four players) than do school children. We have found (Eifermann 1971a) that the size of play groups is a good indicator of the level of development of the players. The older the children are and the higher their level of school achievement, the more they tend to play in larger sized groups. Our studies further show that in spite of the shortage of time (that gives children less of a chance to get organized in large play groups) children are more apt to play in larger groups at school than they do in the street. Very few children aged six to eight play in groups of more than ten players, even at school. The differences in group size between school and street support the explanations offered earlier in this chapter — the greater extent of age and sex mixing in the street was due to the smaller number of children available there.

Rather surprisingly, we have found (at the ages considered) there is no consistent difference in group size whether children play games with rules or without them and whether they play in mixed groups or in those differentiated either by sex or by age.

In our street observations, we also recorded the number of children who joined or left the group during play without causing the game to come to a stop. In close to 70 percent of all cases no changes in group size occurred. In 20 percent of the cases one child joined or left; in 9 percent there were two children who joined or left, and in 2.5 percent there were three. Children often replaced one another so that the balance of players in the group remained very much the same. In any case, there was no clear tendency for play groups to become smaller if the game lasted longer than the usual period. A considerable proportion of this traffic in players occurred in the larger sized groups.

Conclusions about Time Spans and Group Sizes

Generally, unsupervised play and games of children aged three to eight last for a remarkably short time before being interrupted, usually by the players themselves. Children may soon, or a little later, return to their games, starting anew or starting new games altogether. The impression that children are sometimes "possessed" by their need to repeat the same game over and over again or that they cannot be torn away from the current craze is not necessarily contradicted by the findings on time span. The findings do suggest, however, that because such obsessions are so striking and at the same time so difficult to understand their incidence may have been exaggerated.

We can conclude on the basis of the facts now established that the ten to twenty minute recess period customary at school satisfies the children's needs quite well, even though a great deal of playing is interrupted by the school bell.

The size of natural play groups tends to be surprisingly small; although, the proportion of players in larger sized groups increases with age. Groups of more than six children are rare. However, much *organized* play, particularly outdoors, does involve large groups. In the light of our findings it seems desirable to ask some questions that may not have been taken sufficiently into consideration: To what extent do children enjoy such organized games? What are the characteristics of large group games which children play spontaneously? To what extent can children profit by the introduction of further organized games in large groups?

IN CONCLUSION

My intention in this chapter has been to present certain concrete findings on games, play behavior, and the structures and modes of organization of play groups involving children aged three to eight. I have not assumed that the presentations and discussion of implications are inclusive of all aspects of social play. Important aspects such as the kinds and functions of onlooking at play, verbalization in play, uses of play equipment, and the size of play space were not included. I have tried to focus attention on some of the aspects which have been neither properly observed nor given due weight in discussion in the past. These aspects are age and sex-mixed groups, the time span of games at various ages, the recurrency of games, and egalitarianism in play.

I think it is quite evident from many of the facts presented in this chapter that children's games and play behavior are in many ways a true mirror of their actual (rather than potential) level of development. When children are younger they interact less in their play, play fewer games with rules, play fewer games of strategy, play for shorter periods of time, and play in smaller groups. Most comparisons of the level of play of disadvantaged children with that of other, more privileged children of the same age (Eifermann 1968, 1970a, 1970b, 1970c) indicate that disadvantaged children play at a more advanced level than the more privileged children. What is less clear, however, is whether children who play at a less advanced level do so because of lack of ability or lack of motivation. The question of whether or not children can be successfully encouraged to raise their level of play (and still enjoy playing) is of prime importance. Some of our findings suggest that this may be possible, even without intensive adult interference.

Following her observations, Parten (1943) concluded that children who have had nursery school experience did not differ in their level of social interaction from those who lacked this experience. Our own findings suggest, however, that early experience may be very important. We have found, for example, that kibbutz children raised together in small children's groups tend to play at a level of interaction in advance of their years as compared with their peers who are raised in conventional family groups. How intensive early group experience must be in order for it to be significant is still an open question. I believe the facts presented in this chapter would indicate that we should experiment in constructing games and in directing play in ways that will meet a child's needs and at the same time further his developmental potential.

REFERENCES

Aaron, D., and Winaer, B.P. *Child's Play.* New York: Harper & Row, Publishers, 1965.

Abt, C. *Serious Games.* New York: The Viking Press, Inc., 1970.

Boocock, Sarane, S., and Schild, E.O., eds. *Simulation Games in Learning.* Beverly Hills: Sage Publications, 1968.

Bresnitz, S., and Lieblich, A."The Unconscious Plays Patience." *Simulation & Games* 1(1970):5-17.

Chateau, J. *Le Lou de L'enfant.* Paris: Librarie Philosophique, 1955.

Eifermann, R.R. *Determinants of Children's Game Styles.* Jerusalem: The Israel Academy of Sciences and Humanities, 1971a.

————. "Level of Children's Play as Expressed in Group Size." *British Journal of Educational Psychology* 40(1970a):161-70.

————. "Cross-cultural Comparisons of Children's Games." Paper presented at the Center for Human Development, Founding Fellows International Congress. Jerusalem: July, 1970b.

————. "Social Play of Kibbutz Children: A Comparison with Moshav and Town Children." Paper presented at the Seventh Congress of the International Association of Child Psychiatry and Allied Professions. Jerusalem: August, 1970c.

————. "Cooperativeness and Egalitarianism in Kibbutz Children's Games." *Human Relations* 23(1970d):579-587.

————. "It's Child's Play." In *Games in Education and Development*, edited by E.M. Bower and L. Shears. Springfield, Ill.: Charles C. Thomas, 1972a.

————. "Rules in Games." In *Artificial and Human Thinking*. Amsterdam: Elsevier, 1972b.

————. "Social Play in Childhood." In *Child's Play*, edited by R.E. Neron and B. Sutton-Smith. New York: Wiley, 1971b.

Erikson, E.H. *Childhood and Society* (2nd edition). New York: W.W. Norton & Co., Inc., 1963.

Hegeler, S. *Choosing Toys for Children*. London: Tavistock Publications, 1963.

Inbar, M. "Participation in a Simulation Game." *The Journal of Applied Behavioral Sciences* 6:239-244.

Kepler, H. *The Child and His Play*. New York: Funk & Wagnalls, Inc., 1962.

Lehman, H.C., and Witty, P.A. *The Psychology of Play Activities*. New York: Barnes, 1927.

Matterson, E.M. *Play and Playthings for the Preschool Child*. Baltimore: Penguin Books, 1967.

Opie, Iona, and Opie, P. *Children's Games in Street and Playground*. Oxford: The University Press, 1969.

Parten, M., and Newhall, S.M. "Social Behavior of Preschool Children." In *Child Behavior and Development*, edited by Barker, R.G., Kounin, J.S., and Wright, H.F. New York: McGraw Hill, 1943, pp. 505-525.

Peller, Lilli. "Libidinal Phases, Ego Development and Play." *Psychoanalytic Study of the Child* 9(1954):178-98.

Piaget, J. *Play, Dreams and Imitation in Childhood*. London: Routledge & Kegan Paul, 1962. (First French edition, 1951).

Speeth, S.D. "The Rational Design of Toys." *Journal of Creative Behavior* 1(1967):398-410.

3
Teaching Self-Control and Self-Expression Via Play

Ronald E. Feldman
University of California, Davis

INTRODUCTION

The period between ages 2 1/2 and 6 is an extremely important one in early social and emotional development. During these years young children develop and consolidate a number of basic patterns for social interaction with other children. In this early period of life some children develop interpersonal problems in self-control and are found by playmates to be excessively dominant, overly aggressive, or generally difficult to get along with. Some other children develop problems in self-expression; they have difficulty in expressing their opinions, desires, and emotions, and they let other children dominate them. The majority of young children in this age group, however, tend to express and develop more balanced patterns of social interaction with their peers. They are learning to understand and to respect the feelings, desires, rights, and points of view of their playmates. At the same time they are learning effectively to defend their own rights (with mild forms of aggression, if necessary) and to communicate their opinions, desires, and emotions to their playmates.

This chapter is concerned with the development, identification, and prevention of problems in self-control and self-expression in young children, ages 2 1/2 to 6. The beginning sections of the chapter deal with the development of patterns of social interaction during this period of life and identification of the problems in self-control and self-expression that appear during these years. Special attention is given to the role of aggression in the play of young children. The middle sections of the chapter cover long-term personality studies of children who first exhibit problems in self-control and self-expression between years 2 1/2 and 6. Also reviewed in these middle sections is the research relevant to the question of whether or not young children really benefit from teacher guidance. The final sections of the chapter present suggested practices that teachers might employ in preventing the development of problems in self-expression and self-control in the children who attend their preschools, kindergarten classrooms, or daycare centers. The suggested practices represent *one* well thought-out approach to preventing difficulties in self-control and self-expression among young children. The procedures described are based on my experiences as a teacher, on discussions with other teachers, and on my knowledge and interpretation of relevant research carried out by psychologists and educators. Although broadly based, the suggestions unavoidably reflect my personal values. Many teachers may find some or perhaps most of these suggestions to be relevant, but they may see other suggestions as being inappropriate or totally unacceptable personally. Hopefully the suggestions, in addition, will spark teachers to consider and investigate approaches not mentioned in the text and thereby lead to further knowledge regarding the fostering and development of self-control and self-expression.

THE FORMATION OF PATTERNS OF SOCIAL INTERACTION

In the 3 1/2 short years between ages 2 1/2 and 6 young children learn a number of basic patterns for social interaction. Some of the very substantial changes that take place during this period are described and illustrated in this section of the chapter.

A young child age 2 1/2 knows how to talk and how to walk, run, and to do any of a number of things with his hands. He has spent much time by himself investigating various objects, and he knows how a number of toys work and how to have fun with them. When older people take an interest in him and make efforts to structure his play, he interacts with them in a variety of ways, but social interaction between two young children age 2 1/2 is very primitive in nature. The children understand little about the feelings and desires of each other. Their feelings are mostly centered on themselves.

Suppose four cars were given to two children age 2 1/2. The following episode is typical of what might happen. (The number "1" in parentheses indicates that this episode is the first one described in the chapter.)

(1) Both children grab for the cars. (The idea of equal division of property is quite beyond the limited reasoning capacities of the two children. After all, children of this age cannot even count.) As it happens, each child gets two cars. The children sit next to each other examining their cars. Though they are near to each other, the children do not interact. (This is a form of *parallel* or side-by-side play.) Perhaps the children then go off in opposite directions, pushing their cars across the floor. In the course of this maneuvering the children approach each other once again and bump their cars together once or twice in playful fun. After taking part in this simple episode of *interactive* (playing-together) play, the children once again go off in opposite directions. (No words have been exchanged. The children have not cooperated nor competed. Neither child has led the other. Their play has been very simple, even during the brief period when it was interactive.)

Suppose the same four cars were given to two children who have just turned six years old. The following episode is very typical of what might happen. (For simplicity's sake, the children are given the names "Child A" and "Child B.")

(2) Child A, voluntarily *assuming responsibility* for dividing up the cars, gives two cars to Child B and claims two for himself. The two children then drive their cars across the floor next to one another. Arriving at the other side of the room, Child B sees some pieces of wood. He suggests to Child A that they build a tunnel, and together they build a structure consisting of two sides and a top. Child B says to Child A, "Give your cars to me. You go to the other side, and I'll show you something." Child A, trusting Child B, gives him his cars. As suggested, Child A goes to the other end of the tunnel, and the two children begin rolling the cars back and forth from one end of the tunnel to the other. (The play from the beginning has been *interactive* in nature; cooperation, competition, suggestion, leadership, and a game with mutually agreed-upon rules all have appeared.) (1,2,3,4,5,6,7,8,9,10)

As Episodes 1 and 2 demonstrate, patterns of social interaction develop along two interrelated lines between the years 2 1/2 and 6. First, young children learn a number of ways in which to play enjoyably with one another. Secondly, the children learn more mature methods of handling and resolving the actual or potential sources of conflict that occur as social play becomes more complex. Although our discussion will consider both types of social interaction, we shall place greater emphasis on the trend relating to self-control and self-expression in conflict situations.

SOME GENERAL CHARACTERISTICS
OF CHILD-CHILD CONFLICTS

Young children are inexperienced in life and are immature emotionally and intellectually. Most people who structure programs at daycare centers, preschools, and kindergartens are aware of these facts. Accordingly, programs are planned that allow the children to spend most of their time involved in free play and in structured activities designed to be interesting and fun at the same time. Also, a few relatively easy-to-carry-out responsibilities may be required of the children (for example, cleaning up the table or putting away their own clothes). A staff of teachers, teacher aides, and volunteers is on the scene to protect the children from danger and to encourage smooth and harmonious patterns of play. Often, the classrooms and playgrounds themselves are designed especially for the enjoyment and education of young children.

Despite these factors, the problems of life begin early for young school children. For most adults life is a mixture of frustrations and pleasures — matters are much the same for young children. The average young child, in fact, is frustrated in carrying out his desires some seventeen times each hour in protected playground and classroom settings. (11,12,13) For example, a young child attending school or a daycare center only three hours a day is prevented from getting his way, temporarily or permanently, some fifty times a day or a total of 250 times each week.

The frustrations encountered in the playground and classroom by the young child are normal, everyday ones. They befall all young children, and in somewhat modified form the same varieties are encountered by adults. For the young child about 15 percent of the frustrations result chiefly from limitations in his own capacities. For example, frustrations result from the inability to complete a difficult puzzle or from limitations in the resources of the school or daycare center (the school may not own a softball, clay, or tools).

The remaining 85 percent of the frustrations involve relationships with people. About one-half of the frustrations involving other people result from interactions between the child and teachers or other adults. Probably most typically the adult frustrates the child by enforcing a general school rule: "Mary, you'll have to put away your toys before you can go outside." Sometimes an adult frustrates a child by failing to pay attention to him when the child would like the adult to do so. Other adult-child frustrations result from the adult's intervention in quarrels or other difficulties involving two or more young children. The remaining one-half of the people-related frustrations occur at the hand of one or more of the young child's playmates. Generally, these frustrations occur because one child's desires *conflict* with those of another child. In Episode 1 a conflict of desires between two very young children momentarily broke out, but in Episode 2 two somewhat older children averted a potential conflict situation over the division of limited resources. Two additional child-child conflict situations at different age levels are depicted in Episodes 3 and 4.

(3) (This conflict situation is the most simple and most frequent type. (19) One child wants to possess property with which another child is playing. In this example, two very young children — age 2 1/2 or 3 — are involved in parallel play.) Two children are playing next to each other in the same sandbox. Child B is filling a pail with sand. Child A is pushing a small truck through the sand. Child A who becomes bored with pushing the truck looks up and notices the pail. Wanting the pail (and perhaps not understanding the notion that an object can belong to someone else), he grabs it away from the other child. Child B begins to cry.

(4) (This problem is a more complex one. Two children, ages four or five, are involved in interactive play. A third child, wanting nobody's property, simply tries to join into the fun.) Child B is on one end of a teeter-totter. Child C is on the other end. The apparatus is going up and down smoothly until Child A climbs on between Child B and the middle of the teeter-totter. The teeter-totter no longer works. Child B becomes angry, and he says, "Get off" to the intruder. Instead of getting off Child A does some quick thinking; he moves to the middle of the apparatus. The three children resume play, all showing considerable enthusiasm.

For the average child such child-child conflict situations are frequent and normal events. He encounters them an average of seven times an hour, day after day (11,12,13), responding with patterns that soon develop into habits. Even when variations in the level of complexity of play are taken into account, it may be that friends quarrel with each other more often than do mere acquaintances. (14) Other information indicates that quarrels can occur more frequently when sharing accompanies play than when play is not accompanied by sharing. (15) Apparently these everyday social problems accompany the inevitable exchanges and involvements of human existence. These conflicts generally are more complex than they initially appear to be.[1] If we examine Episode 4 as a case in point, we find that the physical problem (three people sharing a teeter-totter) is too difficult for many young children to solve; that strong emotions (fear and anger) were aroused and may cloud resolution; and that effective conflict resolution requires more ability to see the viewpoint of the other person than many children possess.

As indicated by the emotions displayed by young children, child-child conflicts are important and upsetting experiences in the daily life of the young child. Some 75 percent of crying episodes that occur while young children are at school are due to conflicts with other children. (17) The remaining 25 percent of at-school crying episodes result from all other causes together, including accidental injuries. Anger and aggression are present at least 15 percent of the time as a child's very *first* response in child-child conflict situations. (13) Although the issue has not been studied formally, it appears that aggression and anger occur in a sizable percentage of child-child conflict situations before such episodes are resolved. The next section of the chapter is concerned with the outbreaks of aggression and anger, normal and extreme, that occur when a child's desires come into conflict with those of other children.

TOO LITTLE SELF-CONTROL?
AGGRESSION AND ANGER IN YOUNG CHILDREN

Teachers of young children justifiably are concerned with aggression and anger in their students because during the period between years 2 1/2 and 6 children are learning and consolidating basic patterns of social interaction. In earlier times, many teachers viewed all forms of aggression and anger as being undesirable. A teacher's objective often, but not always, was to teach the young child to *control* his more violent impulses as much as possible and as soon as possible. With today's dual emphasis on control and on expression

---

1. Analysis suggested by passages from D.K. Moore, and A.R. Anderson, "Some Principles for the Design of Clarifying Educational Environments," in *Handbook of Socialization Theory and Research* (Chicago: Rand McNally, 1969).

of feelings, anger and aggression are being seen in a different fashion. Teachers are interested in understanding what forms of aggression and anger are normal and less normal for young children, in how the expression of these impulses changes with age, in determining whether or not the aggression takes a potentially dangerous form, and in understanding the causes of or reasons behind a child's expression of anger or aggression. These issues are covered in this section of the chapter.

The episodes contained in the section are intended to convey my general interpretation of "adequate" self-control without at the same time drawing a hard and fast line as to the meaning of "adequate." Human behavior is too varied and complex for such simple categories; judgments are made most suitably with appreciation of the child's life circumstances, cultural background, individual personality, and life expectations. For our purposes "aggression and anger" include all actions, physical or nonphyscial, with which force, threat, or anger-related emotions are associated. Thus a child can display aggression or anger by hitting or pinching a playmate, by grabbing a toy that belongs to another child, by chasing a child who has taken a toy from him, or by yelling in anger at a playmate "You give it to me."

Some general information concerning aggression and anger in young children may be of interest. Aggressive encounters between young children rarely last longer than one minute, and more often than not the actual quarreling ceases within thirty seconds after the episode has begun. (18,19) During these episodes, pushing, hitting, pulling, foot stamping, pinching, and the throwing of relatively harmless objects are all common and normal behaviors. (19) Not normal, however, are such actions as hitting a playmate time and time again after he has fallen to the ground, frequent loss of temper, physically dangerous actions, or prolonged feuds that last several minutes or even days. (18)

Young boys of this age are generally more aggressive than young girls. This may be due to sexual stereotyping rather than biological predispositions. Aggression, indeed, seems to follow boys around. Boys quarrel more frequently with boys than girls do with girls. In addition, young girls quarrel more often when interacting with boys than they do when playing with other girls. Boys tend to use physical means of aggression. Girls tend to use verbal tactics more frequently. (14,15,18,19)

Aggressive episodes tend to last slightly longer as children become older because the problems that children ages 4 or 5 encounter are more complex than those encountered by children 2 1/2 or 3. (19) Aggressive behavior becomes less physical and more verbal and is exhibited less and less frequently as children mature in years during this early period of life (ages 2 1/2 to 6). *This gradual replacement of aggressive behaviors by other equally effective but less violent conflict-resolving processes is one of the most important changes taking place between years 2 1/2 and 6.* Teachers can play an important role by helping to guide children through the involved set of associated learning experiences.

Spontaneous versus Deliberate Aggression

Child-child conflict situations often arise suddenly, and frequently they are not fully understood by children as to source and meaning. Aggression in such circumstances often occurs because of an involuntary "flooding of feeling."[2] On other occasions a child will employ aggressive behavior for a very practical reason — aggression helps him to get things his way. Quite frequently aggression in child-child conflict situations is in part spontaneous and in part deliberate.

Two episodes follow. The first depicts a situation in which aggression is a result of a flooding of feeling. The second illustrates a situation in which the aggression is premeditated and deliberate.

(5) A jump rope is sprawled out on the ground. Child B is sitting on the ground, and he is examining one end of the rope. Not noticing that Child B is examining one end of the rope, Child A grabs the rope by the loose end and begins to play with it. Believing that the rope was deliberately stolen from him, Child B grabs the rope back in anger. Emotions heat up, and a serious quarrel ensues. (These aggressive behaviors resulted from a misinterpretation of the situation on the part of both children.)

(6) Child A is blowing a whistle. Child B walks slowly toward him and then suddenly reaches out with her hand and grabs the whistle away.

Deliberate aggression is a complex phenomenon that may not always deserve the concern and excitement generated about it in teachers and parents. Very young children (ages 2 1/2 to 3 1/2) have difficulty in understanding the desires and rights of other children and have only limited verbal capacity to express their feelings. (Episode 3) Even though most children employ aggression from time to time, many normally do so infrequently, and few do so in

---

2. From suggestions made by Marilyn Schwartz.

dangerous forms. Aggression can take harmless as well as dangerous forms and can vary in purpose from legitimate self-defense to attempts to gain the property and privileges of other children. These different dimensions of deliberate aggression are illustrated in the two episodes that follow. The aggressive action depicted in Episode 7 is relatively harmless and normal; that described in Episode 8 is worthy of teacher concern.

(7) (Child A is not aggressive very frequently.) Child A who is climbing up the bars of a jungle jim finds that Child B is blocking his way. Instead of going around Child B, Child A begins to push Child B out of his way. Child B who is not particularly frightened but willing to comply moves over to the next rung. Child A climbs to the top of the jungle jim. Both children play contentedly.

(8) (Because Child A has been frequently aggressive other children have been avoiding her. As a consequence, Child A has not begun to learn less coercive methods of resolving conflicts with other children.) Children B and C are playing in the doll house. One child is holding the mother doll, and the other child is holding the baby doll. A third child, Child A, enters the doll house saying, "I want the mother doll." The child who has the mother doll (Child B) says, "I have the mother; you play with the sister." Child A grabs the mother doll. Child B says to Child C, "Let's go play somewhere else." Child A is left alone.

Indirect Causes of Aggression

A sizable majority of episodes of aggression probably stem from various kinds of conflict-of-desire situations like one child's desire to own a toy, to play in a given area, or to carry on play in a certain fashion conflicts with the desires of other children. (Episodes 5-8) On other occasions, however, aggression results from less obvious, more indirect causes or motives. Four such indirect causes are discussed in the paragraphs that follow. The particular events depicted in Episodes 10 and 11 reflect difficulties in self-control and are worthy of teacher attention.

Curiosity and the Desire to Tease

Children are curious about how other children will respond to their actions. Also, children sometimes simply enjoy upsetting other children. In Episode 9 the actions of Child A indicate that he is not *really* interested in possession of the object he wrests from Child B.

(9) Child B is playing with a metal car. Several unused, identical cars are spread out on the floor next to him. Child A grabs the car from Child B, walks a few steps away, and looks back at Child B. Child B picks up another car and begins to play with it. Child A returns, takes the second car away from Child B, runs off to the other side of the room, and looks back at Child B. Child B takes a puzzle down from the shelf. Child A drops the car and runs off to join some children who are building a fort with cardboard bricks.

Social Ineptness and Feelings of Being Socially Rejected

Child A of Episode 9 was not afraid to play with other children. Child A in Episode 10 exhibits very similar behavior for a very different reason. His nursery school experience is his first social encounter with other children. He does not know how to approach other children successfully, and as a result, he has been rejected a number of times. Feeling rejected, Child A becomes angry and vents his hostilities on the other children. At the same time, his actions indicate that he would like very much to play socially with his classmates.

(10) Child B is running around the school yard on her stick hobbyhorse. In order to communicate to Child B his desire to be chased by her Child A grabs the hobbyhorse. Child B falls down. Misunderstanding Child A's actions, Child B hits him with her hobbyhorse. In retaliation, Child A throws sand at Child B and then pushes down several other children.

Desire to Gain Attention

Child A in the following example achieves his objective of gaining attention from his playmates and from the teacher. He may exhibit this behavior because he receives too much or too little attention at home and is either accustomed to being the center of interest or to seeking the individual concern of adults by "causing trouble."

(11) Child B is throwing a ball up in the air, catching it as it falls. During the descent of the ball Child A pushes Child B down, grabs the ball, and stands facing Child B with hands on hips. Several other children gather around, and Child A says, "He won't bother me any more." A teacher scolds Child A saying, "I told you not to push other children down!" Child A giggles and runs off to play on the swings.

Boredom and the Need for Diversion

(12)   The children have been seated on the rug listening to a story for about fifteen minutes. Child A pinches Child B. A minute later he takes a ribbon from Child C's hair. The teacher lets the group go out to play. Child A plays especially vigorously and no longer tries to annoy his classmates.

TOO LITTLE SELF-EXPRESSION?
TIMIDITY AND INHIBITION IN YOUNG CHILDREN

Aggressive actions by a child disrupt the play of other children, produce considerable noise and disturbance, and frequently involve the teacher and occupy her time. Episodes in which children fail to express or to act upon legitimate and acceptable desires are equally important but not likely to receive as much attention. Future adult life can be as unsatisfying for a person who fails to defend his rights or to communicate his feelings or opinions as it can be for a person who is self-centered and aggressive causing others to avoid social contact with him. Between ages 2 1/2 and 6 some young children may begin to develop problems of either type. Several contrasting pairs of examples perhaps will clarify for the reader the author's conception of the meaning of "adequate" self-expression. As was true for self-control, we shall avoid hard and fast guidelines and shall dwell upon general considerations.

Communication of Desires or Opinions

In the first example a child fails to communicate a desire when she has a need and a right to do so. In the second example communication of an opinion by a child results in a needless and avoidable argument.

(13)   Child A and several other children while seated around a table are cutting scraps of paper and pasting the scraps onto individual cardboard backings. A jar of paste is within reach of the other children but is just beyond the reach of Child A. While Child A looks at the paste but says nothing the other children paste their scraps of paper onto their cardboard backings. Noticing the plight of Child A, a teacher encourages Child A to ask that the paste be passed to her.

(14)   Children B and C are each pushing dump trucks loaded with leaves across the school yard. Child A appears on

the scene and says, "Why don't you carry sand?" In response Child B says, "We're making a pile of leaves." Child A dashes over to the sandpile, picks up a handful of sand, and drops the sand into the storage bin of Child B's truck. An argument ensues.

Self-Expression in Defense of Legitimate Rights

In the next two episodes children express themselves in defense of legitimate rights. In Episode 15 Child A defends his legitimate rights, even in the face of the threat of being disliked for doing so. In Episode 16 Child A allows another child to push him around.

(15) Child A is riding a tricycle. Child B attempts to push him off. Child A pushes Child B away. In response, Child B says, "If you don't give me the tricycle, you won't be my friend." Child A, deliberately ignoring Child B, continues to ride on the tricycle.

(16) Child A is hammering together a wooden "airplane." Child B takes the hammer from him. Child A watches Child B use the hammer.

Seeking Teacher Assistance

If a young child depends too much on teachers for assistance, he may not learn how to express his desires to other children. The seeking of teacher assistance in itself is an expression of desires and a way of coping with a problem situation. Contrast the following two examples.

(17) Child B is pulling a wagon around the playground. Child A who wants a ride but is too timid to approach the other child asks a teacher "Will you tell him to to give me a ride?"

(18) Child B is sitting in one wagon and holding on to another wagon. (He is not saving the wagon for a friend.) Child A approaches Child B, points to the unoccupied wagon, and says, "May I have that wagon?" Child B's response is "No! It's mine. You can't have it." Child A attempts to take the wagon, but Child B kicks him. Then Child A seeks a teacher's assistance and says, "He won't give me the other (empty) wagon."

Response to Failure or Disappointment

In childhood as in adulthood, things do not always turn out as one might wish, even after one has expressed his desires and communicated his opinions. In some circumstances failure or disappointment may be undeserved or unjust. In other circumstances a frustrating outcome, as in the following examples, is a just one. Contrast Example 19 with Example 20. In which example(s) does Child A make the best of the circumstances that befall him?

(19) Child A takes a truck away from Child B. Child B grabs back the truck and says, "I'm not finished yet." Child A kicks over a doll and goes off by himself into a corner to sulk.

(20) Child A is swinging on a tire swing. Child B climbs on with him. (In this school two children frequently swing together on the tire swing.) Child A says, "Get off!" Child B ignores him. (A teacher is not nearby.) Child A remains on the swing. Within moments the antagonism disappears, and the two children together manage to propel the tire swing almost into orbit!

THE PROBLEM CHILD:
PASSING PHASE OR LIFE-LONG HABIT?

The majority of young children solve child-child conflicts effectively and without excessive violence or are in the process of learning how to do so. Some young children, however, exhibit considerable difficulty either in controlling or in expressing their desires and appear to be continuing to behave in the same patterns. Are these "problem" children merely passing through a phase, or are their problems likely to become permanent ones?

This question can be answered by studying the same children over a time span of a number of years (longitudinally). None of the longitudinal studies of young children we will consider has been addressed specifically to the question of the persistence of early problems in self-control or self expression, but several of the studies have involved investigations of closely related issues. The findings from the more important studies are all very similar. A particularly relevant study carried out by a psychologist, a social worker, and a psychiatrist is described and discussed in detail in this section. (21) The three professionals reviewed the behavior records of selected children written by the nursery school teacher, and at a different time they reviewed the reports made later by the grade and high school teachers of the same children. They rated each child without knowing the child's name on such behaviors as participation in group activities, ability to share and take turns, and acceptance by other children. The investigators then put the names on the nursery and school records to see whether and in what way earlier patterns remained consistent with those of later childhood. As a result, they were able to answer some questions about the persistence of problems in self-control and self-expression during childhood.

Question: *Some nursery school children have poor relationships with other children; other nursery school children have good relationships with their classmates. Are those children with poor early relationships more likely to have poor relationships with other children in the future?*
Answer: Yes. The children who show poor relationships with other children in nursery school are more likely to show poorer relationships with their classmates when they are older.

Question: Do all *nursery school children who show poor relationships with other children continue to show poor relationships during the later years of childhood and during adolescence?*
Answer: No. Only some of the children continue to show poor relationships with other children during later years.

Question: *Do* all *nursery school children showing good relationships with other children continue to show good relationships during grade school and high school years?*
Answer: No, but the majority of these children continue to show good relationships in future years.

Question: *How do all these facts fit together?*
Answer: The nursery school years are very important ones for the learning by children of how to relate to other children. The child who establishes good relationships with other children at this early age is at a definite advantage when compared with children who have not done so. Some children outgrow their early problems during later years of childhood. Other children do not.

Question: *The evidence indicates that a nursery school child who shows poor relationships with other children has a greater chance than the average child of showing poor relationships with other children in later years. Is this same type of child also more likely to exhibit other kinds of school-related problems in future years?*

Answer: Yes. He is more likely to have problems in his relationships with teachers, and he is also more likely to exhibit various neurotic symptoms such as nervousness, tension, fingernail biting, and fearfulness of injury.

This preceding study concerned a child's general relationship with other children. Longitudinal studies also have been made of the more specific characteristic "aggression directed toward other children." As discussed in a previous section, children become less and less aggressive between years 2 1/2 and 6. During this period of life they gradually learn other methods for resolving their conflicts with one another. Many of the children who are very aggressive at ages three and four, however, continue to be very aggressive at ages four and five. (18,22) Some of the children who show large amounts of aggression at ages three to five continue to do so even at ages ten to fourteen. (23)

What are the implications of these studies for the teacher? First, the teacher should expect young children to show problems relating to the excessive use of aggression, the failure to take turns, and the failure to protect their own rights. These problems are normal. Secondly, a teacher may expect children gradually to grow out of these problems. Thirdly, a teacher may see justification for encouraging the children to grow out of these problems because the problems often but not always linger on in the same or in modified form.

How can a teacher help children to overcome problems in self-control and self-expression and encourage them to learn effective, fair, and nonviolent ways of resolving their problems with one another? In the next section of the chapter we begin our consideration of this topic by examining the question: What do young children learn and fail to learn when teacher guidance is restricted to a very minimal level?

WHAT CHILDREN LEARN WHEN TEACHERS GIVE MINIMAL GUIDANCE

One frequently reads that children are their own best teachers and that children can learn best when they are left to their own devices. Most people agree that adult influence can be harmful to children. Is it true that children do not require adult guidance at all? What happens when children are not given guidance by teachers?

We cannot really ask what happens when children are given no guidance because children are influenced inevitably by the teacher and by the other adults present at daycare centers, kindergartens, and preschools.[3] Adults design and equip the classrooms and playgrounds in which children play. They select and distribute the materials. They encourage certain activities and create shortages and physical dangers. In addition, most teachers are likely to provide some general structure that the children may carry over to other activities and to free play. Teachers also usually prevent children from running away or from hurting one another and set up time schedules that accord with their personal routines. We rarely encounter the *total* absence of rules and guidance procedures.

There are two ways to study what happens when teachers give children only a minimal level of guidance. The first method involves comparing the growth and development of children who are given *minimal* guidance to those who are given *moderate* levels of teacher guidance. The second approach involves studying in the play of children the types of behaviors the children themselves encourage and discourage in one another. Two studies will be described, one involving the first method and the other making use of the second method.

George Thompson, an eminent child psychologist, compared the personality development of two groups of nursery school children attending the same school each day at different times in the afternoon (1:00 to 3:00 or 3:00 to 5:00). (28) One group of children received *minimal* teacher guidance. The teachers were instructed to help the children in case of danger or extreme difficulty but otherwise "to give information and help only *upon the specific request from a child or a group of children.*" These teachers, then, exerted *minimal direct* influence on the personality growth and development of their pupils. As a result of infrequent interaction with the children, the teachers and children probably formed few friendships with each other. Consequently, the teachers probably exerted minimal *indirect* as well as minimal direct influence on the play patterns of the children.

The other group of children received a *moderate* level of *direct* guidance. These children probably received a moderate level of *indirect* teacher influence because some friendships probably were formed between teachers and children. "The teachers were instructed to help the child in his relations with other children and in his use of play materials *within their judgments* as to how each individual child's social and emotional needs might best be met." These teachers were free to guide the children when they saw fit to do so.

The average I.Q. scores and age of the children in the two groups

---

3. From suggestions made by Catherine Landreth.

were almost identical, and at the beginning of the school year the children in the two groups exhibited about the same frequency of problem behaviors in their play with other children belonging to their group. However, by the end of the year the children in the minimal guidance group showed a much higher incidence of problem behavior in their play with one another than did the children from the moderate guidance group. By that time all of the following types of characteristics appeared at least twice as frequently in the play of the minimal guidance children: a child is hit, shoved, or grabbed at by another child; a child is persecuted by another child; a child is threatened by another child.

The findings of a study by Patterson, Littman, and Bricker (17) provide at least a partial explanation of why the children in Thompson's minimal guidance group exhibited so much aggression. Over the course of an eight-month school year, Patterson and his colleagues observed and recorded the aggressive encounters of middle-class children in two preschools. (The teachers in these schools were free to guide the children as they saw fit.) The investigators recorded which children initiated attacks, and they noted the responses to these attacks by the victims. Five important findings emerged from their study.

1. Children vary widely in their frequency of expression of aggression.
2. Aggression is a *very normal* and effective aspect of child play. Most children are aggressive on occasion, and such aggression definitely helps a child get the things he wants from his playmates.
3. A few very aggressive children (possibly exhibiting problems in self-control) find that aggression works for them and continue to remain highly aggressive during the entire school year.
4. A few very nonassertive children (possibly exhibiting problems in self-expression) *fail* during the school year to learn effective methods of defending themselves against attacks from their peers.
5. Children often do not effectively teach one another to overcome problems of self-control or self-expression. There is no assurance that children will outgrow their problems in the realistic exchanges of the school and playground. In the absence of teacher guidance highly aggressive children are rewarded with success for being aggressive. More timid children do not receive support for their initial efforts at self-expression.

These findings regarding the general effects of minimal guidance are illustrated specifically in Episodes 21 and 22.

(21)   Child A is playing with a doll. Child B grabs it away from her. Child A begins to reach for her doll but stops when Child B glares at her.

(22)   Child A has been playing with a tricycle for a long time. Child B grabs the tricycle and says, "It's my turn." Child A says, "All right. Can I have another turn in a few minutes?" Child B says, "Yes." Child A leaves and when he returns in a few minutes for the tricycle he is pushed away by Child B. Child A is probably not apt to offer to take turns again.

On the other hand, young children frequently resolve child-child conflicts quite effectively on their own. The following example illustrates such an occasion. Other illustrations can be found in Episodes 2,4,7,8,17,22, and 23.

(23)   Child A takes a block from the top of the fort being built by Child B. Teasing his playmate, Child A runs away with the block. Child B chases and catches Child A and takes the block away from him. (In this example, Child B defends himself vigorously but without excessive violence, "keeping his cool" in moderately stressful circumstances. The very experience is likely to assist him to successfully handle the stressful situations he encounters in the future.)

What are the implications of these findings for the teacher? If children are given minimal guidance they can develop and perpetrate in one another potentially long lasting problems of self-control and self-expression. At the same time, children can learn much of benefit from uninterrupted social play experiences with other children. The teacher's role is clearly one of charting a course between extremes, to provide guidance and yet to provide opportunity for independent learning. In later sections of this chapter, we shall present some guidelines teachers might employ to promote a combination of self-control and self-expression. Before doing so we shall examine the philosophical bases and reasoning that are behind the application of these guidelines.

The remaining sections of this chapter are organized around a series of issues. The first issue concerns "when to intervene"; the second issue "the child with serious problems in self-expression"; the third "the child with serious problems in self-control"; and the fourth "flexible but consistent teaching of play traditions." Under each issue we examine alternatives, present our resolutions, and give a series of illustrative episodes.

Issue I: When to Intervene

Children benefit considerably from uninterrupted play experiences with other children. For this reason very frequent teacher intervention can interfere with the normal, independent development of patterns of play and conflict resolution in young children. In general, teachers should intervene only when assistance or participation is requested by a child or when they can justify their intervention on the basis of some general teaching goal. Some relevant guidelines on when intervention is appropriate are described and illustrated in the discussion that follows.

Top priority should be given to protection of children from possible significant physical injury. (27) All other considerations are secondary to this one. Teachers should use whatever reasonable method is quickest and most efficient in stopping harmful behavior, even though the stopping procedure may not teach the children new patterns of self-control or self-expression.

(24) Child A who wants a turn on the swing pushes Child B off of the swing. Child B who is justifiably indignant picks up a handful of sand to throw at Child A. The teacher immediately grabs the hand of Child B, preventing his throwing of the sand and a possible eye injury to the other child. Child B becomes very angry at the teacher, but that consequence cannot be avoided. After tempers calm down, the teacher explains that sand can injure the eyes of another person and then guides the children toward a solution to their problem.

A teacher should respond in some manner to a child's verbal or nonverbal request for assistance. Ignoring the child completely communicates lack of interest and respect. The teacher's response, if possible, should be one that teaches the child to become less dependent on her for assistance. In Episode 25 the teacher suggests a solution that gives Child A the responsibility for carrying out the action.

(25) Child A: "Teacher, I want to swing on the tire." (Child B is on it.) Teacher: "Perhaps you might ask B if you can. If he says no, maybe you can tell him that you want the tire when he is finished."

Intervention can occur prematurely and without sufficient justification. Teachers can first give the children a chance to solve the problem on their own and to grow from this valuable learning experience. An inventive solution arrived at by young children without teacher assistance is illustrated in Episode 26.

(26)   Child A takes a car from Child B. Child B says, "Give it back!" Child A says, "No!" Child B goes to the shelf, takes down a truck, and plays contentedly.

Although teachers should not intervene prematurely, on certain occasions quick intervention can prevent the occurrence of unnecessary trouble.

(27)   Several children are playing with dolls in the doll house. While the children are looking in the other direction Child A enters the doll house with a pail of water and prepares to pour the water on the dolls. The teacher who employs a stopping procedure says to Child A, "Don't do that." Child A turns around and goes back outside.

Teacher intervention can be justified if a fairly serious situation appears to be worsening without sign of improvement. Intervention in such circumstances is especially appropriate if an opportunity is available for teaching the children how to resolve a conflict in a new way, or to understand the feelings of a playmate. In Variation "a" of the episode that follows the teacher stops a dispute but fails to take advantage of the opportunity for teaching the children an alternative pattern of behavior. In Variations "b" and "c" the teacher leads the children toward discovery of a solution to their mutual problem.

(28)   Child A is "painting the wall of the school with a brush wet with water from the pail at his side." Child B who also wants to "paint" grabs the pail away from Child A. Child A grabs the pail back, and the two children engage in an increasingly violent tug-of-war over the pail. The teacher first stops the difficulties by taking the pail.

(a)   Then the teacher says, "No more painting. Since you can't get along, you can't play with the pail."

(b)   Then the teacher says, "I have a question. Can anyone figure out how both of you can reach the pail at the same time?" Child B, showing great delight, places the pail closer to himself than to the other child. Child A, realizing that he can reach the pail, wets his brush and resumes painting the wall. Seeing that difficulties have been resolved, the teacher leaves.

(c)   As in Variation b, Child B places the pail closer to himself than to the other child. Child A protests, "The pail is too close to him." The teacher waits to see if the children can resolve difficulties without further guidance. Child B voluntarily moves the pail somewhat closer to Child A. The teacher leaves.

Children with minor problems in self-expression or self-control, with the assistance of occasional teacher guidance, normally grow out of their problems. The general guidelines described to this point apply to children falling into this minor-problem category. Children who display more serious problems in self-expression or self-control generally have acquired their problem behavior as the result of numerous learning experiences spread over a considerable period of time. These major-problem children often require a sizable number of experiences for unlearning the deeply rooted problem behaviors and for learning the alternative patterns with which their problem behavior can be replaced. Accordingly, intervention is more appropriate and justifiable with a child who displays a major problem of control of expression.

Issues II and III cover extensive programs of intervention for major-problem children. By way of introduction, Episodes 29 and 30 illustrate teacher intervention after a dispute has already ended and when the possibility for physical injury is almost nonexistent. In the first episode the teacher employs a teaching procedure for teaching a major-problem child a new pattern of self-control. In the second episode the teacher makes use of a similar procedure for guiding another problem child toward the performance of a new pattern of self-expression.

(29) Child B is pushing a truck across the floor. Child A approaches him and says, "Let me have it." Child B refuses to give over the truck. In response, Child A folds his arms and begins to glare at the other child. The teacher mentions to Child A that a similar truck is located on a shelf across the room, and then she leaves so as to avoid giving Child A the impression that he is being pressured into doing something against his will.

(30) Child A has just asked Child B for a ride on the back of his tricycle and has been refused. As is his usual habit in such situations, Child A goes off by himself for a long crying spell. Understanding that Child A's feelings are ones of personal rejection rather than ones of disappointment at not being able to play on the tricycle, the teacher points out several "fun" ongoing activities in which *other children* are involved. The teacher leaves, and perhaps in a few minutes Child A approaches and enters into one of the play situations that the teacher has brought to his attention.

Issue II: The Case of a Child with Serious Problems in Self-Expression

Child C displays a major problem in exhibiting self-expression. Her history exemplifies a fairly common pattern. By nature Child C is not an assertive child. Her initial experiences with other children of her own age were frightening. At first she attempted a variety of actions to express herself, but her efforts were inept and she often met with humiliation, rejection, and failure. Rebuffed, she ceased her efforts at self-expression and did not make herself visible and known. Now at age four, she is easy prey for other children and chooses to spend much of her time in solitary play.

At the beginning of the school year Child C's teachers notice her problem and regard it as a major one. In response, they make a concerted effort to help her develop her abilities in self-expression. The teachers seek out opportunities for using leading procedures and at other times look for occasions for stopping actions and for developing alternative patterns of behavior. (Episodes 31, 32, and 33.) In the first two episodes that follow (31 and 32) the teacher intervenes when the only justification for doing so is that Child C can be taught new patterns of self-expression. In Episode 33 the teacher encourages Child C to be less dependent on her teachers for assistance.

(31)   Child C asks Child B very timidly, "Can I swing?" (on the tire). Child B briefly glances in her direction and says, "No," and then continues to swing on the tire. Child C is discouraged and begins to walk away. At that moment a teacher stops the child's strategy of retreat. In Variation "a" the teacher encourages Child C to express her desire in a manner that results in failure. In Variation "b" however, the teacher encourages the child to use a procedure that works for her. As a result Child C is more likely to ask for her turn in future social play.

(a)   The teacher suggests to C, "Why don't you tell him you want to play." Child C approaches Child B and says, "I want to play." Child B says, "No." The teacher has gone elsewhere. Child C walks away, even more discouraged than before.

(b)   The teacher approaches Child C and suggests, "Maybe Child B is not finished playing with the swing. Perhaps you can tell him that you want the tire when he is finished. I bet he'll give it to you then."

Child C follows up on the teacher's rather open-ended suggestion and solves the problem of what to do while she is waiting by playing in the nearby sandbox. As soon as Child B begins to leave the tire swing, Child C rushes over to assert her privilege to be the next one to swing.

(32) On another occasion, one teacher notices that Child C, although quite upset, does nothing when Child B deliberately takes a pail from her. The teacher stops Child C's strategy of conflict avoidance and in a supportive manner teaches Child C to express the legitimate desires she feels. (If Child C were not upset, the teacher would not have intervened. Even though Child C displays a major problem, the teacher is careful not to impose her own needs and interpretation upon the child.)
The teacher asks Child B to give back the pail, and at the same time suggests to Child C, "You can take it back now." On another and similar occasion the teacher simply suggests, "You can tell him you want it back."

(33) Young children are just forming their self-images. A teacher has a strong influence on a young child's beliefs about himself. One study, in fact, has demonstrated that young children are less likely to be able to carry out a task if a teacher says "I don't think you can do it" or if a teacher discourages a child only with the tone of her voice. (32) In this episode the teacher encourages Child A and helps to give her confidence to perform an action without teacher assistance.

(34) Child A: "Teacher will you ask Child B to let me use the scissors?" Teacher: "Why don't you ask her yourself?" Child A: "No. She won't give them to me." Teacher: "Yes, she will. She likes you very much." (This information is true, not merely possible or pseudosupportive.) Child A asks for the scissors.

Issue III: The Case of a Child with Serious Problems in Self-Control

Child D is a spoiled young boy. At home he has learned to get his way by yelling, hitting, and complaining. He transfers to other situations the aggressive, self-centered behavior taught to him unwittingly by his parents. At school he characteristically takes instead of asks, frequently imposes his desires without consideration for the other party, and often unjustifiably becomes angry in frustrating circumstances. Because of the continuing influence from Child D's parents the concerted group teaching effort on the part of the teachers does not immediately succeed, but after several weeks Child D begins to relate to his playmates in a more balanced manner. Some procedures used by Child D's teachers are illustrated in the discussion that follows. The discussion itself is divided into three segments, each of which illustrates some generalizations regarding effective child-centered teaching.

Point 1

Stopping procedures are appropriate for ending difficulties and occasionally for purposes of making teaching possible; by themselves, however, stopping procedures usually do not teach new patterns of behavior. (28) In Episodes 24 and 27 (described previously) the teacher employed a stopping procedure appropriately for purposes of ending unnecessarily destructive behavior. In Episode 28, Variations "b" and "c" (also described previously) the teacher stopped difficulties so that she could effectively employ a teaching procedure. Well-intentioned attempts at guidance, however, do not always stop or teach. In Episodes 35 and 36 teachers employ teaching procedures that fail to teach.

> (35) Child D is running up the sliding board. Child D's behavior is causing considerable disturbance because the other children are running down the sliding board. The children do not seem to be able to solve the problem by themselves. The teacher intervenes saying to D, "Will you go down the sliding board like the other children do?" Child D ignores her plea. Then she says, "All right. Will you go down the sliding board after you get to the top?" Child D climbs to the top, climbs down the ladder, and then climbs up the sliding board again. The teacher says to the other children, "Why don't you let Child D by? Then everybody can be happy." (Greater firmness and consistency and less pleading would be desirable on the part of the teacher.)

> (36) Child A is on the teeter-totter. Child D tries to push him off. Child A hits Child D. The teacher intervenes by *explaining*, "Child A was here first. The seat on the teeter-totter belongs to him." The children ignore the teacher and continue to quarrel. (The teacher should have separated the children first.)

Point 2

Aggressive and angry young children often are willing to try out and to learn more reasonable methods for expressing their desires. Whatever the cause for their behavior, children are more likely to respond in a sincere, reasonable manner if the teacher accepts the child's feelings and approaches him with tact.

Episodes 37 to 40 illustrate this general point. In Episode 37, Variation "a", the teacher moralizes and indicates to the children that she does not view them as human beings capable of voluntary goodwill. In contrast, in Variation "b" of this episode the teacher accepts Child D's anger and helps him to understand its origins. In the same context she teaches the other child a valuable rule of social play. In episodes 37 to 40 the teachers in other ways encourage Child D to develop voluntary patterns of self-control.

(37)   Child D has built a road in the sandbox. Child B who is chasing a ball runs through the sandbox and accidentally destroys the road built by Child D. Child D hits Child B, and the children become embroiled in a violent fight. The teacher, stopping difficulties, *separates* the two contestants.

(a)   Then the teacher says, "We don't yell and fight! Why do you have to be so bad?" The children who feel shamed and intimidated leave the immediate area of play.

(b)   Holding the children until both of them calm down, the teacher then says to Child D, "Can you explain to Child B why you were angry at him?" Child D remains silent. The teacher then says to Child B, "Child D thought you did it on purpose. That's why he was angry. Am I right, D?" Child D says, "Yes, I thought he meant to do it." The teacher continues, "You should run around the sandbox, B, if someone is playing in it. A child who is playing in the sandbox might be making something."

(38)   Child B is playing with a box of blocks. Child D says, "Let me have some." Child B consents and hands Child D several blocks. The teacher says, "That's a good idea, Child D. Now you both have blocks to play with."

After receiving frequent encouragement from his teacher, Child D begins to ask for things more frequently. However, this after-the-fact encouragement does not teach Child D ways of adapting to the inevitable situations in which "asking" will not work for him.

Teachers should feel free to a certain extent to express *their natural feelings* to children. However, I personally do not believe it is necessary or of value to yell at, shake, or hit a child or to cause him to feel guilty for minor or accidental incidents of "undesirable" behavior. In Episode 39, the teacher expresses her natural disapproval to Child A for his *potentially injury-causing* action. In this way she tries to teach Child D to hold in his excessively violent impulses of aggression. At the same time the teacher clearly communicates to

Child A that she still very much *accepts him as a person* and effectively leads Child A into practicing another method (waiting) for getting what he wants. In Episode 40 Child D expresses anger in violent modes. In this instance the teacher accepts Child D's expression of anger and helps him to understand its causes. Then she teaches him a less violent means for *expressing* his anger or leads him to redirect his impulses toward a constructive solution to the difficulties.

(39) Child D and Child B are at the sink washing their hands. Both children reach for the soap at the same time, but Child B secures it first. Child D kicks Child B. Child B cries. The teacher comforts Child B and tells Child D, "I understand that you wanted the soap, too. That's why you became angry. But you really hurt Child B. Shoes are hard, and they hurt." To Child B, "It's all better now. Can you hurry up with the soap so that Child D can use it?"

(40) Child D has just carefully set the table for four other children. A big ball lands in the middle of the table, scattering dishes, milk, vegetables, meat, and baby bottles in all directions. Child D begins to hit the child who threw the ball. Since this aggression serves no necessary purpose, the teacher intervenes and uses the episode for teaching purposes. She separates the children and while holding them both says to Child D, "I understand why you are angry. Your dishes have been scattered everywhere, and you just have finished working hard to arrange them so neatly. I would be angry, too, if that happened to me. Would you like the dishes to be the way they were before?" Child D says, "Yes." The teacher replies, "All right. Let's all make the dishes look as pretty as they looked before."

One topic remains. Some educators recommend encouraging an especially aggressive child to hit dolls, to throw bean bags, or otherwise to "let out" his aggressive energy. This strategy is useful in the case of children who are bored or who require physical exercise. However, these "letting out" procedures do not teach young children to understand or constructively to redirect their angry and aggressive impulses or to resolve their conflicts by alternative, less violent methods.

Point 3

A close and trusting relationship between teacher and child is very important. The use of coercive measures can create a teacher-child relationship based on fear. However, special procedures are required for dealing with children who, with full understanding of their actions, repeatedly insist on spreading disruption in the school setting. Some teachers, in such circumstances, feel that punishment (a type of stopping procedure) is necessary. I favor the mild but usually effective procedure of removing a disruptive child from an activity or from the room or playground. Some teachers may regard this procedure as being too severe. Others may feel at times a necessity for *threatening* a child with deprivation of some privilege (for example, no snack at "snack time") if he does not mend his ways. Probably relatively few teachers resort to physical punishment (spanking or hitting, for example). In any event, punishment by itself does not teach children what else to do or how to do it. In order to effectively deter behavior, punishment should be employed in conjunction with teaching procedures such as those described in Episodes 37b through 40. (29,30)

The removal of Child D from the room is illustrated in Episode 41. In Variation "a" the teacher accomplishes the action firmly and swiftly. In Variation "b" the teacher inadvertently rewards Child D with special attention and also causes him to feel that he is a bad and unacceptable person.

(41)   Child B is playing with a truck. Child D walks up to Child B, pushes him down, kicks him, and takes the truck away. Child B who is justifiably afraid of Child D does nothing. The teacher intervenes by saying, "Child D, can you give the truck back to B? There is another truck over here (points) that you can play with." Child D hits the teacher with the truck and actually hurts her.

(a)   The teacher takes the hand of Child D and says, "We are going into the other room." Child D tries to resist, but the teacher, paying no attention to him, keeps on walking. She leads him into the kitchen (where an aide is working) and says, "In a few minutes I'll come back and let you out to play again." Keeping her promise, the teacher returns shortly and says, "OK." Child D runs out to play.

(b)   Child D resists as the teacher is leading him to the kitchen. The teacher stops and says to some nearby children, "See what a bad child D is. He hits people, and now he won't come into the kitchen where bad children go." Then the teacher grabs Child D up in her arms and takes him screaming to the kitchen, admonishing, "If you try to get out, I'll make you go back again." The teacher returns shortly and says, "You can come back now, but you better be good."

Issue IV: Flexible but Consistent Teaching of a Minimum Number of Play Traditions

Social traditions and laws, when restricted to a reasonably small number, can contribute to the smooth functioning of an adult group and to the security of the individuals belonging to it. For example, the traditions of driving on the right side of the road and stopping at red lights can facilitate the safe flow of automobile traffic. Similarly, a minimal number of child-tailored rules and traditions can contribute to the creation of a harmonious play environment, facilitate the development of feelings of trust and security, and give the children a basis for resolving some otherwise ill-defined situations. Teachers can transmit these traditions and enforce them at the same time by explaining to the children why they have intervened and by intervening in a manner that is consistent (although, hopefully flexible) from occasion to occasion. The discussion that follows covers some suggested basic rules and traditions and contains some illustrations of consistent yet flexible enforcement and transmission of these conventions.

Area 1. The Taking of Turns and Determination of Ownership

Children quarrel more frequently over the possession of property and other privileges than for any other reason. (18,19,28) The high incidence of quarrels in these circumstances indicates that some relevant rules and traditions are needed.

Some teachers believe that a child should be able to use a given object until he has "finished playing with it." They contend that causing him to take turns involves imposing adult notions of time and scheduling on the free-flowing play patterns of the young child and, in addition, fosters the notion that property belongs either to oneself or to someone else. Other teachers feel that children should be induced to take turns with items that are popular or in short supply, especially when the school itself is short on toys. Such teachers may also feel that a tradition of turn taking can teach children to share possessions and can prevent children from spending all their time with one toy (such as a swing).

The issue is a difficult one. In the majority of cases young children can be allowed to play with toys until a given indoor or outdoor period of play has ended. However, many special circumstances arise. The item may be the only one of its kind available, and a second child may request its use during the next given period of play. In such circumstances the teacher may wish to require that the item be given over to the second child. Some items (such as wagons) can be enjoyed by two or more children simultaneously. Teachers may wish to require children to share such items if demand runs especially high or if the material is in short supply. Children can be allowed only short turns on one-to-a-school items (such as rope swings) with which many children simultaneously happen to want to play. (In such cases lines may prove to be of value.) If two children race for an item at the same time, the child reaching the item first can be allowed "to keep" it. Items that a child has made or brought from home comprise a special class. A child should not be required to share such items; though, of course, he is free to do so. Some teachers believe in avoiding trouble by placing such items in "cubbies" or high on shelves.

Four relevant illustrative episodes follow. In these instances the teacher respectively teaches the "first come" rule, leads a child into an experience of sharing, brings the attention of a child to the needs of a playmate, and makes a special effort to establish a relationship of trust between herself and a child.

(42)   In this episode two children race for a swing. One child reaches the swing before the other one. Note the two courses of events and teacher responses that are described respectively in Variations "a" and "b."

(a)   Two children run to the swing, and Child A reaches it first. Child B pulls Child A from the swing and throws dirt at him. Seeing no end to the trouble and a possibility that one child will be injured, the teacher separates the children and explains, "Child A gets to swing because he reached the swing first. Would you like a swing when someone's finished, B?" If B replies in the affirmative, the teacher tells the children who are swinging that B gets a turn when one of them has finished. Perhaps no other child gives up his swing before the play period has ended. If it is the teacher's custom to do so, she may tell the children before they go outside that Child B gets a swing. In the process she teaches Child B to wait for a turn by leading him to wait and then allowing him to find out that waiting "works."

(b)   Two children run to the swing, and Child A reaches it first. Child B pulls Child A off the swing and gets on it himself. Child A (who is not a child with serious problems in self-expression) runs off to play on the tire swing. The teacher stands by but does not intervene.

Whenever another child wants to play with Child A, he discourages the other child's gesture of friendship. In Episode 43 the teacher interprets the school's ownership tradition *flexibly* but does not act in a manner inconsistent with that tradition. As things turn out, Child A is not forced to do something against his will, and yet he learns a new and rewarding pattern of behavior.

(43) Child A is swinging on the tire swing. Child B gets on the tire swing with Child A. Child A calls to the teacher, "He's on my swing. Make him get off." The teacher comes over and says, "Let me show you something that is a lot of fun." (Child A has been sitting inside the tire swing.) She picks up Child B and places him on top of the tire swing. Then she pushes both children on the tire. The children giggle and otherwise show that they are having fun. Then the teacher calls over another child to push the two children. (If Child A had protested vigorously, the teacher would have suggested to Child B that he take a turn later.)

In this episode note how the teacher explains a school tradition and at the same time shows Child A that her (the teacher's) promises can be believed.[4]

(44) Child B is playing on one of the three rocking horses in the school. The other two rocking horses are occupied by other children. Child A tries to get on the rocking horse, but Child B pushes him away. Child A complains to the teacher, "She won't let me ride the horse." In response, the teacher explains, "It's her turn. She can ride until she gets tired of riding. I tell you what; I'll mark your name down on my list. If no one leaves his horse before we go in, you can have a horse when we come out to play after snack time." During the next play period the teacher follows up on her pledge.

Area 2. Exclusion from Play
Conflicts also frequently occur because one child is excluded by other children from play in which a group is involved. (19,28) One possible solution to such situations involves establishing a tradition that a new child *must* be included if there is enough room for him. Teachers should respect the group's rights to exclude another child when there is no room for an additional child *or* when the entrance of an additional child would seriously disrupt some play pattern that has already "set in." In other circumstances either intervention methods (when intervention is necessary or desirable) that encourage the group *voluntarily* to accept the child or methods that encourage

---

4. From suggestions made by Marilyn Schwartz.

the child to approach the group in a more successful manner should be used. This philosophy of intervention is illustrated in Episodes 45 and 46.

(45) Child A tries to enter a cardboard box into which Children B, C, and D have already squeezed. Child B screams at Child A, "Get out!" Quite upset, Child A begins to cry. The teacher comforts Child A by saying, "The other children didn't want you to come in because there was no room for you. See how little room there is. They still like you. In a few minutes why don't you come back? Maybe there will be room for you then."

(46) Children B, C, and D are "playing store." One child is a storekeeper, and the other children are buying toys from her with "make-believe" coins. Child A says to them, "Can I play?" One of the children replies, "No!" Child A takes his case to the teacher, complaining, "They won't let me play." "I tell you what," says the teacher. "Here is some play money. Maybe you can tell the storekeeper that you want to buy something."

Area 3. Disputes Involving "How to Play"

Conflicts frequently arise because children disagree in regard to how play is to be carried on. (19,28) The occurrence of such conflicts indicates that the children have a need for some guiding traditions in this area. In Episode 47 the teacher transmits a "majority rules" tradition while intervening in a dispute arising in a game originated by the children themselves.

(47) The teacher has made a new playground toy for the children. She has put a small table out in the yard and has slanted a board from the ground to one end of the table so that the children can climb up. The children have begun a simple game. They climb up the board, stand in line on top of the table, and then jump off. One child, however, consistently runs up and down the board pushing off any child who happens to be in his way. The other children become angry, but they are unable to control Child A because he is more assertive than they. Play is being disrupted constantly, and the children are beginning to quarrel with each other. Child A is being rewarded with success for his antics. For these reasons the teacher intervenes. Knowing Child A well and realizing that he understands the situation, the teacher is rather firm with him. The teacher, however, does justify the decision with an explanation.

The teacher says to Child A, "The other children are all going up the board. The board is too skinny for people to go down at the same time. Can you climb up the board like the other children are doing?" If Child A persists in his disruption, the teacher removes him from the activity.

Area 4. Prohibited Behavior

One of the important trends taking place between years 2 1/2 and 6 is the replacement of excessively violent behavior by less violent but equally effective responses to conflict situations. Teachers can help children to learn to discriminate permissible from nonpermissible aggressive behavior by consistently prohibiting and responding to occurrences of excessively violent or dangerous behavior. A list of nonpermissible behaviors might include the following: Holding sticks; throwing sand, rocks, or other dangerous objects at other children; hitting other children with dangerous objects; pushing down other children in the vicinity of hard objects or concrete; and placing anything in or near to the eye of another child. In Episode 48 the teacher prohibits dangerous behavior and explains her reasons for doing so.

(48) Child A is hitting Child B with a stick. The teacher takes the stick away from Child A and *tactfully* explains, "Nobody, not even teachers, can play with sticks because sticks can accidentally hurt other people." Child A picks up another stick. The teacher without hesitation takes the stick away. Child A yells to the teacher, "My big brother will beat you up." The teacher ignores Child A.

SUMMARY

Between the years 2 1/2 and 6 the social play of young children rapidly becomes more interactive and complex in nature, and young children usually develop a number of basic patterns for social interaction with other children. Not surprisingly, the passage through this period is not an easy or smooth one for all children. Children's play can be very rough and difficult to understand, and sudden conflicts frequently arise as the children interact in normal patterns with one another. In this context some children develop potentially long lasting problems in maintaining self-control; these children fail to learn effective methods for handling, constructively redirecting, or expressing without excessive violence their impulses of anger and aggression. Some other children develop potentially long lasting problems in exhibiting self-expression; these children experience considerable difficulty in learning to express their desires and in defending their legitimate rights and privileges.

The play situations of young children can be very complex, and problems of children in maintaining self-control or in exhibiting self-expression are not always easily differentiated from the host of patterns that characterize the "normal" play of children. In an attempt to convey to the reader a sense of such problems, a number of interrelated issues has been discussed and illustrated with detailed examples of children's play. Particular attention was given to distinguishing from one another the various causes and circumstances of aggression and anger and to differentiating the normal from the excessively violent expressions of such impulses. Considerable space was also given to discussion of the circumstances and consequences associated with various forms of communication of desires.

A review of the relevant studies indicates not only that children can develop considerable self-reliance when left by teachers to their own devices but also that teachers can assist certain children in breaking out of otherwise self-perpetuating and contagious problems in self-control and self-expression. In the process of providing guidance, however, teachers can very easily impose adult patterns of behavior and interpretation on young children or can fail to be effective at all. I have described a philosophy of teacher guidance combining elements from the "future-oriented" and from the "child-centered" schools of educational thought.

In the course of their everyday functions, teachers have many opportunities at hand for helping to prevent in young children the development of problems in self-control and self-expression. These problems are less likely to develop if the play climate is one that encourages the development of trust and the formation of friendships. Teachers can help to create such a climate by means of thoughtful choice, distribution, and introduction to the children of toys and other items of equipment. In their day-to-day routines some children fail to discover that other children can be trusted, enjoyable companions. Some children perhaps fail to learn effective methods for approaching other children in play. Teachers can help to break children out of these patterns by leading (not forcing) these children into some interpersonal experiences that they might not create for themselves without guidance. Many spontaneous opportunities arise for teaching children new patterns of self-control and self-expression. Teachers can take advantage of these opportunities by employing effective yet child-centered "stopping" and "teaching" intervention procedures. With the assistance of occasional teacher guidance offered in appropriate circumstances, children usually outgrow minor problems in maintaining self-control or in exhibiting self-expression. However, major-problem children often require frequent teacher guidance that is given in a child-centered yet effective manner appropriate to the circumstances of their play.

REFERENCES

Appel, Madeleine Hunt. "Aggressive Behavior of Nursery School Children and Adult Procedures in Dealing with Such Behavior." *Journal of Experimental Education* 11(1942):185-99.

Bandura, Albert. *Principles of Behavior Modification.* New York: Holt, Rinehart & Winston, 1970.

Berk, Laura E. "Effects of Variations in the Nursery School Setting on Environmental Constraints and Children's Modes of Adaptation." *Child Development,* in press.

Dawe, Helen C. "An Analysis of Two Hundred Quarrels of Preschool Children." *Child Development* 5(1934):139-57.

Eifermann, Rivka R. "Social Play in Childhood." In *Child's Play,* edited by R.E. Heron and B. Sutton-Smith. New York: Wiley, 1971.

Graves, Elizabeth A. "A Study of Competitive and Cooperative Behavior by the Short Sample Technique." *Journal of Abnormal and Social Psychology* 32(1937):343-61.

Green, Elise Hart. "Group Play and Quarreling among Preschool Children." *Child Development* 4(1933):302-7.

————. "Friendships and Quarrels among Preschool Children." *Child Development* 4(1933):237-52.

Greenberg, Pearl J. "Competition in Children: An Experimental Study." *The American Journal of Psychology* 44(1932):221-48.

Heathers, Glen. "Emotional Dependence and Independence in Nursery School Play." *The Journal of Genetic Psychology* 87(1955):37-57.

Honig, Alice S., Caldwell, Bettye M., and Tannenbaum, Jordan. "Patterns of Information Processing Used by and with Young Children in a Nursery School Setting." Paper presented at the Convention of the Society for Research in Child Development, Santa Monica, California, March, 1969.

Jackson, Philip W., and Wolfson, Bernice J. "Varieties of Constraint in a Nursery School." *Young Children* 23(1968):358-67.

Jersild, Arthur T., and Markey, Frances V. *Conflicts between Preschool Children.* New York: Teachers College, Columbia University, 1935.

Johnson, Marguerite Wilker. "Verbal Influences on Children's Behavior." *University of Michigan Monographs in Education,* 1, 1939.

Kagan, Jerome, and Moss, Howard A. *Birth to Maturity.* New York: Wiley, 1962.

Landreth, Catherine. *Education of the Young Child.* New York: John Wiley, 1942.

————. "Factors Associated with Crying in Young Children in the Nursery School and at Home." *Child Development* 12(1941):81-97.

McKee, John P., and Leader, Florence B. "The Relationship of Socio-Economic Status and Aggression to the Competitive Behavior of Preschool Children." *Child Development* 26(1955):135-42.

Muste, Myra J., and Sharpe, Doris F. "Some Influential Factors in the Determination of Aggressive Behavior in Preschool Children." *Child Development* 18(1947):11-28.

Parten, Mildred. "Social Participation among Preschool Children." *Journal of Abnormal and Social Psychology* 27(1932):243-69.

Patterson, Gerald R., Littman, Richard A., and Bricker, William. "Assertive Behavior in Children: A Step toward a Theory of Aggression." *Monographs of the Society for Research in Child Development* 32(1967):5, Whole No. 113.

Sibley, Frances Kelley. "A Comparison of the Social Techniques of Younger and Older Nursery School Children." Unpublished Master's Thesis, University of California at Berkeley, 1945.

Sibley, Sally A., Abbott, Martha S., and Cooper, Bettye P. "Modification of the Classroom Behavior of a Disadvantaged Kindergarten Boy by Social Reinforcement and Isolation." *Journal of Experimental Child Psychology* 7(1969):203-19.

Stone, L. Joseph, and Church, Joseph. *Childhood and Adolescence.* New York: Random House, Inc., 1968.

Thompson, George G. "The Social and Emotional Development of Preschool Children under Two Types of Educational Programs." *Psychological Monographs* 56(1944):5, Whole No. 258.

Westman, Jack C., Rice, Dale L., and Bermann, Eric. "Nursery School Behavior and Later School Adjustment." *American Journal of Psychiatry* 37(1967):725-31.

Wolfson, Bernice J., and Jackson, Philip W. "An Intensive Look at the Daily Experiences of Young Children." *Research in Education* 2 (1969):1-12.

4

Building Self-Esteem in the Classroom

Stanley Coopersmith
University of California, Davis

During the past few years I have become increasingly involved with school programs that are seeking to raise the self-esteem of their children. Although most of my initial reactions to questions from teachers and principals were based on previous ideas and findings, I quickly became aware of the large number of people who were seeking various ways to build self-esteem. I also became aware of four questions that made it difficult for many people to get seriously interested and committed to building self-esteem in the classroom. The first question is "Why should the school get involved in the issue of building self-esteem?" The underlying and important issue raised by this question is whether the schools, that are supposed to educate children, should take on the task of building self-esteem which is more properly the duty of parents or mental health professionals. A second, related question that is frequently raised is "Should schools that seek to build esteem do so at the cost of improving the child's skills and knowledge?" Underlying this question is the concern that in helping the child to feel good about himself we may be reducing the amount of time and effort given to reading, writing, and other academic skills. This question is often raised in the form of a choice — "Do we want children to think they're good or do we want them to know more?" The third question, generally pessimistic in its conclusions and implications, asks "What makes you think the school can overcome the effects of the home?" This question assumes that we cannot raise self-esteem in the classroom because of the earlier and greater effects of parental treatment, financial position, race and ethnic memberships, and other powerful social influences. The fourth question proceeds on the premise that the goal of raising self-esteem has long been recognized and can easily be achieved. It is expressed by the query "What's new about changing self-esteem — we've been doing it for years?" People who ask this question have concluded already that teachers know how to raise esteem, i.e., by helping the child get good grades and make friends and by indicating encouragement. Taken together, these four questions of the necessity, appropriateness, interfering consequences, and feasibility of raising self-esteem in the schools represent sober concerns of teachers, parents, and the public at large. My own experience leads me to believe that these questions must be openly and directly discussed and answered before schools will enter seriously upon programs to build self-esteem.

If we turn to the first question of why the schools should get involved in building self-esteem, we can note that literally dozens of studies (e.g., Bledsoe 1964; Bodwin 1957; Brookover and Thomas 1964) indicate that children with high self-esteem perform better and will do less poorly in their school work. It appears that children who feel better about their own ability to perform and expect to do well actually do better in their studies. There are indications that the kindergarten child's feelings about himself are a better indication of his reading readiness than is his score on an intelligence test (Wattenberg and Clifford 1964). Other studies indicate that students who are unsure of themselves or who expect to fail are inclined to stop trying and just give up on school (Quimby 1967; Shaw and Alves 1963). These research studies indicate that feelings of confidence and self-respect are as important in school performance as they are in other areas of life. Athletic coaches tell us about the importance of the will to win and the belief that we can be victorious. Parents know how a fearful youngster withdraws, becomes ashamed, and drops out of activities. It turns out that self-esteem is not something separate from performance; it is an important, integrated part of performance itself. Self-esteem is one of the attitudes and beliefs that a person brings with him when he faces the world. It includes his beliefs as to whether he can expect success or failure, how long he can put out effort, whether he will be hurt by failure, and whether he will become more capable as a result of his experiences. In psychological terms, self-esteem provides a mental set preparing the person to respond according to expectations of success, acceptance, and personal strength. Since a child's attitudes about his abilities and expectations of success and failure are an integrated part of his school performance, it does not make much sense to treat these attitudes as something separate and unrelated to school. The reasons for building self-esteem in school are very practical and directly related to the child's efforts and motivation to learn and succeed.

The second question, whether the schools should take time from teaching academic skills and information to help foster self-esteem, is basically a question of the school's priorities and responsibilities. Phrased as a choice it seems obvious that skills have priority over esteem until we ask whether the choice is real, necessary, or sensible. As we have already indicated, self-esteem is not something separate from achievement, but it is an important and integral contributor to effective performance. The question of choosing esteem *or* skills ignores the most important and constructive question — how do we develop procedures that increase skills *and* at the same time increase esteem. We can seek methods that help to improve both the child's competencies and his feelings of success and confidence rather than separate methods and processes. An alternate way of looking at this issue is that we are employing affectively toned procedures as a means of gaining increases in cognitive skills. Another important answer to this question is that we find that traditional methods of focusing solely or largely on skills and knowledge are not proving to be very effective in producing high levels of learning or keeping the students interested in school. Frequently, we hear parent and student complaints about lack of motivation and noninvolvement in learning and student disinterest with what occurs during school hours. Absentee rates are climbing markedly, and disciplinary and drug problems are becoming increasing sources of parent and teacher concern. If traditional procedures worked, there would be some practical basis for continuing their use. Since they are proving to be ineffective, there seems to be little reason to advocate their continuation or to further develop procedures and materials based on the ideas they employ. Part of the answer of what to focus on appears to be greater attention to some of the feelings and motives associated with learning. Positive feelings about oneself appear to be one of the feeling states that increases involvement and successful performance. As such, esteem is not a secondary, luxury option in the school's program, but it is more of a basic component of a program geared to motivate learning.

The third question as to whether the schools can overcome other influences that reduce feelings of self-worth can be answered on a factual level. There now seems to be abundant evidence that the general social influences on esteem are not as strong as popular opinion often assumes. Several studies (e.g., Rosenberg 1965; Coopersmith 1967) have revealed that social status, income level, education, and occupation are not related very closely to feelings of personal worthiness. It appears that although social status and monetary income play some role in whether people feel favorably toward themselves, that role is not as important as more specific direct interpersonal treatment. Money may make people more comfortable, but it does not necessarily make them like themselves better. It turns out that the kind of treatment that children receive from other people in their immediate personal lives is more important in determining how they feel about themselves than are more abstract conditions of status and wealth. It is more important for the growing child's esteem that his parents accept him and establish clear guidelines within which he can explore than that his parents earn a thousand dollars more or get a new car. Parents can and do make a difference in developing feelings of self-worth, and their influence lies largely in how they treat their children directly rather than in where they are in the social system. Another important issue involved in the question of whether the schools can overcome previous destructive influences is the nature of the relationship between the schools and parents. From the vantage of recent studies in building self-esteem it seems that a partnership between parents and schools is not only desirable but also necessary if the child's self-esteem is to be maintained at a positive level (Brookover 1965). Parents are involved in the initial formation of self-esteem in the home. They give the child the emotional support and feedback that he is lovable. Schools can help the child gain a sense of confidence in his skills and competencies and foster esteem in the classroom. Building esteem in children, particularly in children who already think poorly of themselves, requires collaboration between parents, school, and child. We have evidence that their collaborate efforts can increase the child's feelings of self-worth. Thus the question of whether the schools can overcome the effects of home or poor cultural conditions that have already produced feelings of unworthiness can be answered with a generally affirmative response (Brookover 1965; Coopersmith 1970). Programs to overcome other influences require collaboration between parents, child, and school; development of new types of school programs; specific parent education and parent participation activities; and training for teachers and parents in how to affirm themselves and other people (Satir 1955; Otto and Mann 1968). Cooperative efforts to increase esteem involve a reinterpretation of the boundaries and responsibilities of the school and home. Through much collaborative efforts educators and parents strive to do what they can to give their students (and themselves) a sense of worth and motivation to succeed. In sum, the schools can raise self-esteem that results from prior difficulties and mistreatment. One of the ways in which they can raise self-esteem in students is to seek greater parental involvement in schools and provide guidance and training on effective parenting to their communities.

To the fourth question "Haven't we been involved in raising self-esteem all along?" we can only reply that most schools are set up in such a way that they may more often produce feelings of failure than success. Traditionally, most schools have employed competition, grades, and fear of failure as means of motivating students. They have recognized verbal intelligence as the major, if not sole, basis for determining who is capable and likely to succeed. These schools have set up a system that virtually guarantees that the majority of children will feel they have not succeeded and are constantly being examined, and they are anxious about how well they will do in the future. If schools, as organizations, are likely to produce more negative than positive feelings, it also appears that teacher and parent ideas on how to raise self-esteem are generally incorrect. It appears that if we tell children they are successful, encourage them to persist, flatter them, and reward them, we are not necessarily going to increase feelings of worth (Brookover 1967; Weiner 1971). Conditions of permissive treatment or complete democratic equality are not likely to increase feelings of worthiness (Coopersmith 1967; Baumrind 1967). Recent educational innovations that focus on maintaining an open classroom or allowing the child complete expressiveness and exploration are likely to result in uncertain or low self-esteem rather than feelings of self-competence and self-respect. Most popular ideas on how to increase a child's feelings of self-esteem are either wholly or partially wrong or so vague as to be virtually useless for practical application.

My point in discussing these questions at the outset has been to confront some underlying issues that might cause resistance or cloud examination of the reasons and feasibility of building self-esteem in the schools. Many people believe that they have sufficient knowledge of psychology and education in general and of self-esteem in particular, and they are not open to other, more research-based findings. The building of self-esteem is receiving more attention now than at any previous time, and research studies in the past ten years, for example, are far more numerous than those conducted in the preceding fifty. In the remainder of this Chapter, I shall present a brief resume of major findings on building self-esteem in the school. I will include a way of thinking about the processes involved in forming and changing self-esteem and also some practical, specific guidelines and practices that are likely to raise self-esteem in the home and classroom.

GENERAL CONDITIONS FOR BUILDING SELF-ESTEEM

The child who comes into the classroom has had many experiences already that have led him to develop certain ideas about his worthiness, rights, powers, and responsibilities. Children are not born with concerns of being good or bad, smart or stupid, lovable or unacceptable. They develop these ideas about themselves largely on the basis of the way they are treated by the significant people (parents, teachers, and peers) in their own world. To the child these ideas of self are expressed by his statements about who he is, what kind of person he is, whether he can do things, and whether he is accepted and loved. When the psychologist talks about self-concept and self-image he is talking about the child's ideas and picture of the object he refers to as "I" or "me." The very young child first develops the ideas about what kind of "me" he is on the basis of whether his parents give him love and physical attention; whether his mother and father want to be with him and stay with him when he is in need and difficulty; and whether they are willing to exert themselves for his welfare. A child is able to interpret the treatment he receives. He feels rejected when he is ignored for long periods, punished in a severe physical fashion, and unappreciated for what he has done and contributed. For the young child (up to three years) it appears that his opinion of himself is quite similar to the opinion his parents hold of him (Morris 1954). What they see as valuable he will probably see as valuable; what they see as the right way for him to behave he will probably mirror; what they see as the behavior of a "good boy" he will probably see as the way for him to behave if he wants to be "good" and accepted by them. Parental actions and words are the first — and at that time only or major — way of thinking about themselves that young children have available to them. Their picture of themselves and the judgment of whether that picture is good, lovable, acceptable, or successful comes largely from the treatment, perceptions, statements, and expectations of parents. Parents are the first looking glass from which we learn to see ourselves. They give us our earliest assumptions of who we are and whether we can and will succeed (Davidson and Lang 1960). They do this first by their physical actions and then by the language and ideas they teach us to employ and direct toward ourselves.

Peers also play a role in developing the way in which we see ourselves. Their influence comes through the informal social and play activities in which they select playmates, invite each other to birthday parties, follow some youngsters, and completely ignore others. Preschool and school influences affect the way in which we see ourselves, but the influences occur later than those of peers and parents.

In the school experiences the child learns how he is viewed and treated in the world of ability, skills, and performance — a new, different, and important part of his self-picture. The picture that the child forms of himself — the self-concept or self-image — is the picture that he carries around as a guide to his actions and indications of how he may expect to be treated. This self-image is the content of his perceptions and opinions; his self-esteem represents the attitudes, values, and evaluation he places on his self-image. An example of the difference between self-image and self-esteem is that a child may see himself as mischievous, active, and moderately capable (his self-image), and then he may conclude also that he is a popular, competent individual who feels positively and approvingly about himself (his self-esteem). Another child with the same image of himself might come to negative conclusions about himself. Self-image and self-esteem, the self-picture and its evaluation, are not tied together since different children can make different evaluations about the same self-image on the basis of how they have learned to regard certain features of the image.

Children (up to the ages of six to seven) lack the language and conceptual skills required to express, describe, and communicate their self-concepts and self-judgments. Generally, they are incapable of verbally expressing the pictures they have of themselves, partially because they lack the tools of description and partially because the picture seems so natural that it is almost too obvious to examine. The self-concept of the child is somewhat like water is to fish — it is there, it is real, and it is hard to consider any other way, medium, or form. Given the child's limited ability to communicate the most effective way of gauging his picture of himself is to observe how he acts under particular conditions. A child who is fearful and reluctant to explore a play area or who moves away from other children and adults is communicating that he is uncertain about what to do and afraid that he will not handle himself well. Self-images of uncertainty or incompetence might also be expressed in refusing to do new things or crying readily. The pictures that children (and adults) hold of themselves act as guides and blueprints to their actions. Children use these pictures to determine which actions, clothing, and activities "fit" and which are not right for them. The child who believes that he is lovable, fun, and acceptable to adults is likely to approach adults in a direct and friendly manner. The child who pictures himself as a clown and joker is likely to try clowning when he comes to school. The youngster who sees herself as a "little doll" will be apt to dress and act in such a way that her self-image will be projected to others.

Children do not always act consistently with the ideals and

behaviors their parents admire and reward. There are many instances, particularly in children over six to seven years who have explored the world beyond their home, where they develop pictures of themselves that are different than those held and advocated by mother and father. Some of the sources of varying self-images are differences between the images held by the father and mother; inconsistencies due to parental changes of opinion; differences between parent images and peer images (for example, parents see a strong, aggressive child as delicate, peers treat him as an intrusive bully); characteristics that are rewarded or rejected differently by parents and peers; and particular periods of developing powers during which new self-images are being explored and developed. An example of this last source of inconsistency is a three-year-old's display of stubbornness or negativism that apparently reflects explorations of power and control that parents find difficult to accept from their previously compliant child. Children who resist or reject the images their parents hold of them are likely to feel some tension or self-rejection. Although these children may be asserting, clarifying, and defining their self-images for themselves, they are shedding at the same time an important external source of definition and reward. Children also strive to ignore and shed those parental images imposed upon them that are rejecting, severely restraining, or unfitting to their physical capacities. Thus they may feel active, although their parents see them as passive; they may prefer to eat lightly, although their parents prefer them to eat heavily; they may see themselves as having *some* good features, although their parents see them as being totally unlovable; and they may see themselves as expressing their needs, although their parents see them as selfish and demanding. The child plays an active role in forming his self-image of himself. Whereas parents lay the early foundations of self-image through their attitudes and treatment, the child subsequently engages in peer and school experiences that provide alternative perspectives on who he is and what are his strengths and notable characteristics. After a while the child becomes capable of selecting and rejecting those opinions among the opinions of others that he regards as most "fitting" to his prevailing self-image. The process by which the child develops his concept of himself follows the same stages of formation and change as are involved in the formation of concepts regarding external objects.

The negative images imposed upon children can exert a heavy burden on the healthy development of the child. A child's rejection or redefinition of such images can help his growth. It is worth noting that most parents do not deliberately and consciously impose a negative or destructive image upon their child. Parents do tend to repeat the patterns and views of children under which they themselves were reared. It appears that most parents (and teachers) do what they believe is "the right thing" for the welfare of their children. If they err, it is because "that right thing" is based on a particular, mistaken view of how a child in general, and *their* child in particular, can grow up to be an effective and accepted adult in that society.

The question of what the conditions are that lead children to see themselves favorably has been answered in considerable detail (Brookover, *et. al.* 1965; Coopersmith 1967; Baumrind 1967; Rosenberg 1965). There appear to be three major conditions that seem to be associated with the child's development of positive feelings about himself. The first and major condition is *acceptance* of the child as he is, with his capacities, limitations, strengths, and weaknesses. That acceptance is expressed by interest in the child, concern for his welfare, involvement in his activities and development, support for him in his times of stress, and appreciation of what he is doing and can do. Acceptance is also expressed by recognition of his frailties and difficulties and by the awareness that he can only do so much and be his particular kind of person at this time in his life. Such acceptance is a recognition that there are certain realities that are part of the child and that he presently can be nothing more than what he is. Such acceptance does not mean that the parent or teacher approves of all the child's qualities, but it does mean that the teacher or parent can see the child for what he is without being confused by his own feelings of dissatisfaction and desire to change him. Without this previously defined acceptance the child is not perceived as he is but as someone else wishes him to become. Without such acceptance he cannot be viewed for his strengths as well as his limitations. Without such acceptance he can be ignored readily and rejected until he totally complies. Without such acceptance the child does not have the emotional support to change and try new ways of behaving. Finally, without such acceptance he must deny those very parts of himself that may be causing him difficulty and that must be confronted if he is to change. Acceptance is not necessarily indicated by the amount of time the teacher or parent and child have together but by the feelings and attitudes expressed during that time. As in so many human relationships, it is the quality of expression rather than sheer quantity that is critical. Children can sense concern, interest, and appreciation and are not easily fooled by words of praise and affection or demonstrations of physical affection. Acceptance from others is a basic condition for accepting oneself, and the teacher who forgets that in a desire to move children along is actually hindering the very process she seeks to promote.

The second major condition associated with feelings of self-esteem is a clearly defined set of *limits* that is spelled out early in a relationship with parents and teachers. These limits are the boundaries of what is permissible and acceptable to the teacher or parent, and they define the rules by which life in the school (or home) is to be conducted. To be effective limits have to be focused on specific actions, firmly presented, and consistently enforced. They have to be based on realistic and reasonable grounds that are open to examination and discussion. Thus a teacher may set limits on actions that are likely to result in physical harm to oneself or other children or require all students to take a brief rest period or insist that no child can take more than one turn when other children are waiting. In order to have significant meaning to the children limits must have significant meaning to the teacher; in order to have behavioral consequences for the child, limits must be firmly regulated; and in order to have the psychological force of "reality," the teacher must genuinely believe and expect that the limits she sets will be observed. It appears advisable to set a relatively small number of limits that can be maintained without making enforcement into a burdensome and tension building way of life for the teacher and child. Since children are inclined to test limits wherever they are, it is almost inevitable that the limits set will be clarified and elaborated over the course of time. Limit testing creates an important reason for teachers to establish limits that are reasonable and not very constrictive. Limits that are based on vague, abstract consideration are likely to be tested heavily in the realities of the classroom and may have to be overly defended or abandoned. Such limits are likely to reflect the teacher's anxieties or need for control rather than situational realities or the principles of child development. Limits are the boundaries of the classroom structure that define what the child can and cannot do, what the rewards are for doing well, and what the penalties are for doing poorly. Studies on building self-esteem indicate that effective and constructive enforcement of limits is nonphysical and does not threaten loss of love. Enforcement tends to be directive — spelling out what is expected and the consequences of disobedience. Enforcement also provides alternatives to the inappropriate behavior for which the child can be rewarded. In enhancing environments, enforcement focuses on the rewards given to the child who stays within limits, and enforcement stems from an acceptance and concern for the child. As such, enforcement is basically a question of management and not a conflict of wills between teacher and child.

Limits are important to the child because they provide him with clear guidelines, standards, and expectations by which *he* can determine whether he is performing successfully according to the rules of that situation. Without limits and guidelines there are no rules or ways of judging what is acceptable; without rules and standards the child cannot know whether his actions and performances are successful and acceptable. Limits indicate what is forbidden and regarded as undesirable; standards indicate behavior that is encouraged and the desired or acceptable level of performance. Without limits the child is uncertain as to where he stands and whether he is progressing; with limits he can make decisions and recognize the rewards he may receive and penalties he may have to pay. It appears that children interpret limits as indications of concern and interest, use them to define standards and dangers, fight them to explore and assert themselves, and internalize them as guides to conduct themselves.

The third condition for building self-esteem is revealed by *respectful treatment* for children who observe limits and play by the rules of the family and classroom. In many ways this condition for building esteem is like having a bill of rights for children who live within the framework of the classroom constitution. A bill of rights that builds self-esteem allows questioning, differences of opinion, and privacy and recognizes the individual child's unique needs and style. A bill of rights approach allows children latitude for expressing their opinions and interests as long as they follow the general rules and guidelines that have been set down by their teachers. It is important to note that these rules are set up by procedures that are *not* democratic in the popular meaning of that term. The research evidence indicates that conditions for building esteem in children require some authoritative direction and leadership by adults (Baumrind 1967; Coopersmith 1967). Young children reared in esteem-enhancing environments are not given a full and equal voice in making rules, establishing limits, or deciding how money, time, and space should be distributed. The parents or teachers play the definitive role in establishing the rules. They also enforce them in a decisive manner and thereby establish clear lines of decision making and authority. This procedure is similar to democracy as it is practiced and not as it is considered in abstract or ideal terms. In a democracy a set of guiding rules are established. There is considerable freedom for people who observe those rules, and certain people are given the power to enforce and modify regulations. The citizens can and do express their views and can change laws and introduce new ones. Citizens have power, but power derives from operating within and through the established rules and responsibilities. The family that produces children with high self-esteem is characterized by parents who assume direction, who do not give children full and equal voice in rule making (although giving them a voice and some influence), and who are clear about their own powers and responsibilities. One of the factors that makes the above conditions work to produce positive effects is the marked parental (or teacher) acceptance of their children. Such acceptance leads these parents to make rules based on concern for the child's welfare rather than their own needs for power or the reflected glory obtained from the successes of their children. Accepting parents also listen and communicate with their children; although, they do not necessarily do what their children ask. Another constructive factor is parental tendency to set up rules that are reasonable, realistic, and flexible enough to change as children develop greater powers and knowledge. These parents are as committed to the freedoms within rules and the rights of children who observe boundaries as they are to the rules themselves. Parents who enhance self-esteem in their children are authoritative but not authoritarian, decisive but not dictatorial, and committed to both the freedom and responsibilities of their children.

The conditions of acceptance, limits, and respectful treatment appear to produce high self-esteem by providing personal concern from people who are important to the child, by providing standards that he can use to guide his progress, by defining what is acceptable, and by setting up stable and secure boundaries within which he can safely roam and explore. Children are not born with standards, rules, or definitions, and they apparently require them if they are to make judgments about themselves or other objects and issues. Without standards there can be no definitions of success, without rules all behaviors become possibilities, and without standards and rules there is unlikely to be sufficient confidence in the conduct of other people to permit the development of a broad bill of personal rights. Children who lack standards cannot develop high self-esteem because they remain uncertain of how to determine their capabilities and performance. Adults who talk of children finding and doing their "own thing" fail to recognize that children find their "thing" by selecting among the alternatives available to them, by getting immersed in working with their "thing" and making it theirs, and by gaining standards and skills with that "thing" so that it becomes a source of esteem and personal satisfaction. If we look at the backgrounds of children who are self-reliant, exploratory, competent, and self-accepting, we find that their parents make maturity demands, enforce limits firmly, and are responsive to reasonable and valid objections and suggestions (Baumrind 1967). It appears that the way to help a child become self-managing, self-motivating, and self-enhancing is to provide an early framework that is real, reasonable, and respectful.

The conditions that result in positive self-images generally are established and maintained by teachers and parents who are themselves relatively confident and secure. These parents or teachers tend to have relatively clear ideas of the actions and goals that are important to them, and they try to express their values in their lives. These individuals tend to be decisive, aware of what is important and valuable to them, and capable of acting on their beliefs. They appear to have sufficient self-esteem for themselves; so, they do not seek further esteem by controlling and dominating their children or students. These teachers affirm themselves through expressing their own abilities as teachers rather than gaining feelings of worthiness through the activities of others. Thereby they attain success through their own competencies. In the classroom these teachers tend to focus on producing an environment that would increase learning and help youngsters develop confidence in their abilities, rather than on controlling the actions and growth of their students. Teachers who devalue a child by focusing on his limitations and placing continual attention on grading, competition, and classroom control cause a child to defend himself against the fears and pressures their actions raise. To defend their self-esteem, children in such situations withdraw their interest and attention, conform passively, attack a routine that induces stress, doubts, and fears, and lose their enthusiasm for learning in a situation that penalizes them for being aware of their feelings. Teachers with high self-esteem are more likely to explore alternatives that lead to increased learning and less likely to accept traditional or popular methods as being necessarily proven and superior. They are likely to be expressive, self-accepting, and self-assured, and they are quite realistic in their assessments of their children, schools, and themselves. Teachers with high self-esteem set up a classroom as a learning situation for children, establish realistic and reasonable limits and standards in which they believe, and maintain those standards in a direct and nonpunitive manner. Teachers who esteem themselves and focus on the task of student learning often have a positive effect on the self-esteem of their students (Aspey 1969). They apparently accomplish this by serving as models for their children on how to gain skills and express competencies and also by maintaining a style in which they examine questions and make decisions. Teachers who accept themselves are more inclined to accept others (Trent 1957); teachers who reject themselves are more inclined to reject others (Omwake 1954). A teacher's attitudes toward herself are an important part of her manner in dealing with children as well as adults. Teachers who have positive attitudes about themselves and feel confident about their abilities as teachers are able to relate better to others and express their competencies in the classroom (Fey 1954; Luft 1966). Studies by Arthur Combs and his associates have revealed that effective teachers hold more favorable and realistic attitudes toward themselves than do teachers who are less competent (Combs 1963, 1969).

School staffs that wish to foster self-esteem can make several administrative decisions that would promote that goal. The school administrators involved should look at their procedures to determine whether these procedures tend to devalue the role of the teacher and resist practices that enhance student esteem. One very direct manner of promoting the self-esteem of children is to promote the self-esteem of the children's teachers. Practices that devalue the teacher often have devaluating consequences upon the child. For example, the school policies might tend to emphasize grading, control, and quiet at the expense of teacher and student explorations of new personal sources of success. It is ineffectual as well as hypocritical for schools to advocate that their teachers learn how to build self-esteem while the school's policies contradict or subvert that end. In all too many instances, I have observed supervisors and principals who come out in favor of building self-esteem for the children in their schools but who are dismayed when they find out that such building cannot be achieved by having the teachers learn a few simple techniques and procedures. The school administrator who wants to build self-esteem in the schools he supervises should recognize that there is no simple, superficial, safe shortcut to achieve that goal. If an administrator is serious, he will recognize that some of his present administrative procedures may have to be altered if the esteem of his staff and students is to be raised and that some of his basic assumptions and beliefs may be challenged in the process. For example, he may face the issue of how to circumvent, retrain, or replace those members of his teaching staff who are rejecting and dictatorial in their attitudes and actions. Preventing the destruction of self-esteem is, in its own way, as constructive an action as enhancing its development. Reducing negative influences that appear in the form of destructive teacher characteristics and devaluating classroom practices can have constructive consequences for the esteem of the children in a particular school. Another administrative method for fostering self-esteem is to provide training programs for teachers who wish to work toward developing self-esteem in their students. The new and different concepts and procedures involved in building self-esteem cannot be learned and mastered by reading a chapter or text. Some clarification of the reasoning, methods of dealing with such problems of discipline, grading, and appropriate materials, and specific resolutions of complex issues are clearly in order if the teacher is to feel confident that she is indeed pursuing program goals effectively. Training programs to build esteem might benefit from in-service group counseling for teachers, aides, and administrators (Combs 1965; Jersild 1965). Teaching staffs could explore their ideas and attitudes towards teaching, children, and educational procedures and could also develop more effective and expressive ways of relating to one another. There are already several programs in affective education that provide group counseling as a means of increasing staff effectiveness by changing attitudes and facilitating communication. The Louisville program, which is perhaps the largest and most intensive, innovative program in America, reports that such training effectively helps teachers utilize their abilities in a more flexible and constructive manner (Foster and Henning 1971).

CLASSROOM CONDITIONS AND MATERIALS THAT HELP BUILD SELF-ESTEEM

One of the underlying goals of programs that seek to build self-esteem is to help the child use himself as the major focus and resource of his learning experiences. These programs recognize that the only long-term solution to the problem of children's motivation and involvement in learning is to give them more acceptance and room for initiative within the school. These programs attempt to introduce the conditions that generally facilitate self-esteem, i.e., acceptance, limits, and respect, and then to add features that are specifically geared to increasing learning skills and competencies. Programs that seek to build self-esteem appreciate and accept the importance of the child's attitudes and feelings in the learning situation. The recognition that the child's senses and affect, as well as his abilities, are major resources in education is certainly not new or specific to programs that build self-esteem. Maria Montessori, the perceptive and concerned physician who founded the schools that bear her name, clearly recognized the importance of the child's senses and actions in early learning. New today are the acceptance and refinement of Dr. Montessori's ideas and a broader array of procedures and materials to heighten the child's awareness of his role in the learning process. What is also new is the recognition of several practices that increase the likelihood that a child will become aware of his strengths and be able to confront his fears, failures, and frustrations. The reasoning underlying the above procedures is that by providing conditions in the classroom that allow the child to recognize and appreciate his interests, abilities, reactions, and impact upon materials and other people we increase the likelihood that he will become involved in learning and thereby using his energies and abilities more fully and effectively. This results in greatly increased focus on (1) the process of gaining the learner's participation, (2) greater concern that the child have positive expectations in the classroom activities he pursues, and (3) greater efforts to help the child deal with his difficulties. Traditional programs in schools have focused on learning as being a process that is applied *to* children. Programs that build self-esteem focus on a child's particular resources as a means of increasing learning *by* children. The difference between the two approaches is a matter of emphasis and initial preference and is by no means absolute. I believe that programs to build self-esteem, generally, place a high priority on the perceptions, beliefs, attitudes, and individual strengths of their students as the major method for gaining motivation and increased learning. In a very real sense, motivation is built into these programs since their goal is to develop a child who will seek out activities and demands that involve him and a child who can gauge his own progress and who can reward himself for a task well done.

A considerable number of classroom conditions contribute to building self-esteem, not all of which can be considered here.[1] In this section we shall discuss three major types of classroom practices that help build self-esteem. The three classroom conditions to be considered are the responsive environment; student beliefs and expectations of success; and the ability to cope with failures and frustrations.

THE RESPONSIVE ENVIRONMENT

The central idea behind the responsive classroom environment is that a school should be designed to respond to the learner. By so doing, the school can give the child an awareness of his own powers and help him to recognize that he can make a difference in his own life. According to Glenn Nimnicht, John Meier, and Oralie MacAfee who developed the responsive environment as a means of building

---

1. Although most of these findings are only recently beginning to appear in the literature, there are several books that offer useful ideas and summaries. These include: *Self-Enhancing Education* by Norman Randolph and William Howe; *Educational Implications of Self-Concept Theory* by Wallace LaBenne and Bert Greene; and *Self-Concept and School Achievement* by William Purkey.

self-esteem, such an environment helps the child to perceive that what he wants is important. In designing that environment Nimnicht, Meier, and MacAfee assumed that children have different interests and needs and are not all ready to learn the same thing at the same time. They also assumed that the child's sense of competency and power in a situation that he can explore and influence is an important source of his motivation and involvement. They assumed that an environment that provides feedback and helps children learn how to seek and use such feedback encourages autonomy and initiative. Among the basic conditions of this information-giving, responsive environment are:

- allowing the child free exploration among several activities;
- giving the learner immediate information about the consequences of his actions;
- self-pacing: the rate of activity and progress is determined by the child;
- free use of materials so that the child can make his own discoveries of how events are related.

A major idea of the responsive environment is that the child can engage in activities that are self-rewarding. The rewards, punishments, and information about the progress of the activity come from the games, toys, tapes, and similar materials themselves rather than from other children or an adult. In a responsive environment the child learns to listen to himself, use his sense and judgment, and self-evaluate his progress rather than seek confirmation from other people. This "autotelic" environment provides *feedback* to the child that he learns to use as information to determine what *he* likes, how *he* is doing, and whether *he* is satisfied. The reward, satisfaction, and information come to him from his actions in that situation and not from external sources. It is not against the grain of this program for teachers to praise the child but rather that such praise be given *after* the child has begun his explorations and gotten some initial feedback from the activity. In any event, teacher rewards are given secondary place to feedback from the materials and activities themselves.

To set up the responsive environment effectively the teacher has to make a number of decisions. Although the environment may permit free exploration and pacing, the teacher does establish the limits of that environment, the activities and materials it will contain, and the way in which it will be organized. Thus, the teacher determines how many activities will be available (generally four to six); whether the activities will be individual, small, or large group (a choice is usually available); what types of materials will provide the most information and feedback (varying by activity); and within what limits the child can explore (generally broad and clear). The teacher, in effect, plans the environment to achieve the objectives she would like to accomplish. If preparation for reading is a major goal she sets up an environment of materials to promote that goal, such as letter blocks, books, typewriter, chalk, and other materials, that would provide activities. The basic assumption is that if the child can explore among the available activities and reading activities are as interestingly presented as are others, he will likely pursue and discover reading acitvities by his own choice. Arranging the environment so that the child is likely to make discoveries and pursue activities related to teaching objectives is an important part of the teacher's contribution in the responsive environment.[2]

If we examine a typical day in a classroom set up according to responsive environment principles, it provides some concrete idea of the activities and the program. If we observe the children as they enter the environment, we find that they are free to choose from among such different activities as looking at books, listening to records, building with blocks, working with puzzles, playing with manipulative toys, or painting. They may stay with an activity as long as they like, or they may move on as often as they feel. As the day progresses, small groups play games (that are learning episodes) with the teacher or assistant; others will ask the teacher to read to them. The teacher and assistant are available as resources, and they respond to the children rather than initiate and have children respond to them. Child-initiated conversations and activities are encouraged with the teacher providing supportive service by reading, playing, and participating in their activities. There are large group activities each day such as planned lessons, singing, or listening to the teacher read a story, but the child does not have to join in any of these activities. If he prefers to pursue some other activity in the classroom, then he can work by himself as long as he does not disturb the group. Once each day in kindergarten and first grade classes that have learning booths an aide invites the child to come to a booth that has an electric typewriter. Children who accept the invitation are taken to the booth and taught basic reading skills through use of the typewriter. The child begins by playing with the typewriter, and whenever he strikes a key the aide names it. The

2. Dr. Nimnicht has developed a comprehensive training program in the Responsive Model Follow Through Program. That program is now available for children from ages three through eight. (Grade three). The program is administered through the Far West Laboratory for Educational Research and Development, 1755 Folsom Street, San Francisco, California.

child moves from these first explorations through matching, discriminating, combining, and producing his own sounds and words. At each phase the emphases are upon making his activities self-rewarding and allowing him to discover the rules and regularities of reading and other actions. In the case of reading, the electric typewriter with teaching aide alongside enables the child to begin individualized reading and writing well before his own fingers and senses could achieve those goals. The child gains a sense of competency and control and is able to use his own actions as a basis for guiding his learning efforts.

The responsive environment seeks to have the child become his own source of praise. The teachers' praise is placed in a secondary position to the praise he gives himself. In addition to the emphasis on gaining information and satisfaction from the work itself, the child becomes the organizer and source of his experience and rewards. In all too many cases children who learn to respond to external rewards have little interest in what they are learning. By putting the focus on the child's rewards to himself we help the child to gain greater awareness of his own curiosity, exploration, and satisfaction in learning. By focusing on self-rewards we allow and encourage the child to use not only those abilities that have been traditionally valued in schools but also all of his abilities and survival skills. For many children from disadvantaged backgrounds there are skills of a nonverbal or different cultural background that can help him succeed by being all of himself. Such a focus also means that the teacher's role is shifted to that of facilitator rather than disciplinarian, changer, or imparter of information. This role gives the child more control of himself in the classroom, and it also means that he must assume greater responsibility for his own learning.

STUDENT BELIEFS AND EXPECTATIONS

Since the student tends to act consistently with the attitudes and beliefs he holds about himself, classroom practices that foster positive and constructive beliefs are likely to have favorable consequences for achievement. The student who believes he can do well in school is inclined to strive harder since he assumes he can succeed. A child who is convinced he will fail sees no point in extending himself. Student beliefs about their capacities and what other people expect — teacher, parent, and peers — lead to personal definitions of what is appropriate and desirable. The beliefs that "I am capable" and "I can learn" are apt to be associated with expectations that "I will succeed" and "I will do well in school." These beliefs set up a way of thinking about what is normal and desirable that can raise us up to greater efforts, lead us to persist, or convince us that there is no reason to continue (Diggory 1966). The teacher who tells the child that he is not bright and convinces him that she is correct need no longer be concerned about his performance. The moment the child accepts her judgment that he is likely to fail his efforts will sharply decline. The teacher who can instill in a child the expectation that he is capable of learning provides him with an important long-term asset that he can use to achieve the goals set by the teacher and accepted by him.

The major forces of student beliefs and expectations about their capacities are the teacher's beliefs, classroom practices, and parental expectations. There is clear-cut evidence that teachers who expect children to learn and believe they are capable of succeeding produce marked increases in student performance (Rosenthal and Jacobsen 1968; Brookover, Erickson and Joiner 1967). In the study entitled "Pygmalion in the Classroom" teachers in a public elementary school were told that about 20 percent of the children in their classes had been classified as "high potential" on the basis of previously administered ability tests. The teachers were given the names of these students and told that they had the capacity to make large improvements in academic performance during the coming school year. Although these names were randomly chosen (the children were not, in fact, of greater potential than other children in the classes), tests administered toward the end of the school year indicated that the selected students had made significantly more improvement than students who had not been labeled as "high potential." At year's end when interviewed by the experimenters, the teachers also indicated that they felt that the "high potential" students were more likely to be successful in their future lives than were other children, and they were also more exploratory and personally interesting. The teachers apparently translated their more favorable beliefs about "high potential" students into more demanding and attentive behavior. It seems that the children who were the recipients of such attention and expectations changed their own opinion of themselves and in turn made more demands upon the abilities that they possessed. The chain of events seems to be that the labeling of students as "high potential" caused the teachers to raise their expectations of these students, and these teachers' expectations were then translated into more support for the children as well as greater respect, attention, and reward for the children's efforts (Good 1971). The students who received such attention apparently became more aware of their own possibilities and became more motivated to live up to the demands and goals they had set. It appears that the teachers' acceptance and warmth toward students who put out efforts may have made it easier for the children to internalize the teachers' standards and expectations.

Other studies indicate that teacher attitudes have a significant impact on the academic success of their students. When students believe that their teachers feel favorably toward them, they are far more likely to be successful in the classroom and also more pleasant and constructive in their academic and social activities (Davidson and Lang 1960). There appears to be a number of steps involved in translating such positive teacher and student expectations into more successful achievement. We should note that expectations are part of the person's assumptions about what is appropriate, likely, and desirable for him. A person who expects to do poorly structures the situation in such a way that he is likely to fail. This means if a child believes that he cannot and will not do well, there is little point in making an effort. The student who makes such an assumption is quite reasonable in not seriously trying since there would be no point in efforts that are doomed to failure. Along this same line, we might note that expectations lead people to make choices and decisions that are consistent with what they believe to be the likely outcome of their actions. The child who assumes he will do poorly in math or reading and whose judgment has been confirmed by poor grades in these areas is apt to choose other subjects that are more rewarding and in which his chances of success are greater. In those subjects or areas of life where the child assumes he will fail, he is likely to pay greater attention to activities that might yield success than to the range of activities he sees as likely to produce failure. Stated in terms of the child's rational decision making, the issue is whether the efforts he makes will provide a good "payoff" in terms of successful attainment. Expectations evoke behaviors by setting up goals and possibilities that previously may have appeared impossible or unlikely. In effect, more positive expectations change the odds as to what will "payoff" if effort is exerted. The child who previously believed he could not learn how to read and decided not to put much effort into reading may make a marked change in his belief when he has reason to believe that reading is within his grasp and that his efforts will "payoff." This capacity of expectancies to evoke behavior by altering the person's perceptions of the probabilities of success and failure is perhaps their most notable feature. The capacity to set up psychological odds as to probable outcomes underlies the whole notion of a self-fulfilling prophecy. The child who has an image of what is possible strives to make that possibility real; the child who believes that certain areas of study or levels of success are beyond him stops trying and goes on to something with greater possibilities of satisfaction.

An extended study by Brookover, Erickson, and Joiner (1967) provides some other ways in which expectations directly affect action. Their study reveals that many students who think they can do well in school do not think that other people expect them to make an extended and serious effort to attain high levels of success. They also found that many children do not believe that it is considered appropriate to put out great effort in the school situation. It is possible that the schools in their efforts to reduce extreme competitiveness between students also may have lowered demands and expectations of excellence. Another way in which expectations may affect actions is the student's perception of what is considered desirable and valuable in the classroom. For effort to be expended the child has to value the goals and behaviors that are regarded as desirable by the teacher. If the goal is not valued, the limited rewards that he obtains (grades) may not be sufficient to lead to sustained effort and involvement. Teachers and parents often talk of the importance of schooling, reading, and other aspects of education, but they do not always live out their values. It is not always clear to parents and peers how important and disastrous nonperformance is. How important is it to be a good reader if you want to be a good student in the class? What are the penalties in terms of other people's definition of him if the child does not live up to that role performance? Expectations may be altered if the child believes that nonperformance may have serious consequences in the way in which he is viewed — particularly if attainment is within his grasp. This aspect of expectations is part of the student's role definition of how he is supposed to act and perform in the classroom. Students may not know how to play that role very well without having their specific duties, conduct, and responsibilities spelled out in detail. Orne (1962) talks of the expectations placed upon playing out a role as its characteristics demand. Orne means that a clearly stated role carries with it expectations as to whether a person is behaving appropriately. There is a sense in which the student has to become obligated to perform his role if as a student he is to take his work seriously and personally. To facilitate the sense of obligation it is necessary for the teacher to define the role in terms of duties, time to be spent, and effort without at the same time imparting a sense of guilt, burden, and compulsiveness. This is no easy task, but it is important if the child is to see himself as a student who has the obligation of using his school time to gain skills and knowledge.

Another way in which beliefs affect school performance is the kinds of opportunities that the school provides or fails to provide to students. Teachers may often take away choices from children because they believe that these children are not ready for or capable of attainment in that particular area, e.g., reading, mathematics. For example, in the early part of the twentieth century it was assumed that there was no point in coaching black children in track since they were obviously unable to run fast. This assumption on the part of the schools took away a choice from the black child in the area of track. Other assumptions still may eliminate choices in areas of learning.

There have been a variety of studies made on the ways in which personal beliefs of success can lead to improved performance (Goldstein 1966; Cook 1962). Studies indicate that where greater expectations of success are provided by the teacher, employer, or researcher, the workers or students are generally more productive and successful. Examination of these studies indicates that improved performance occurs not by means of statements of expected success but by several changes in the conditions of work. Among these changes are introduction of novelty into the learning or work situation; the greater knowledge of results that is given to the student or employee; the greater respect and range of choices given to the student; and the more frequent interaction between the teacher and student in such situations. Another reason these procedures are effective is that the student may come to accept and believe that the powers of the teacher have a serious impact upon his performance. Students who believe that their teachers can really help them learn and gain valuable skills are more willing to follow their requests and standards. Teacher expectations of performances produce effects by a series of commitments. The teachers become committed to their students, to helping them develop, and to having the students become committed to goals that they think are reasonable, desirable, and attainable. The students who sense the teacher's commitment to learning and to them are likely to internalize that commitment.

The recognition that teachers and parents influence a child's expectations should not lead us to believe that the process is easy or to expect too much too soon. Expectations are translated into actions by careful and reasonable procedures applied in small steps over time. Following such a procedure Brookover claims that "very few students fail to perform at expected levels if they feel that parents or significant others consider their performance important and that the other has them under . . . surveillance."

COPING WITH FEARS, FAILURES AND FRUSTRATIONS

In the ordinary course of a child's early home and school life, he inevitably encounters experiences that are beyond his capacities, markedly different from those with which he is familiar, or inducive to conflict with other children or adults. Such experiences are not only normal and inevitable in the life of all children, but they are also part of the way in which the child's capacities to deal with life are shaped. The issue is not whether or not a child will experience feelings of fear, failure, and frustration but whether and how he can deal with them. Since children cannot avoid demands and differences with other children, their proper development requires that they gain skills and competencies to deal with their feelings and external difficulties. Among the factors related to such competencies are a positive self-concept and high self-esteem. The child who has a negative self-concept and believes that he is incapable and unable to deal with his feelings or external events is likely to take a passive and defeatist attitude when faced with difficulties and pain. He is likely to be overwhelmed by feelings of helplessness and weakness when demands for performance or personal conflicts occur. The child's concept of himself is related to the way in which he deals with the world because the child who believes he is powerless fails to perceive the strengths he does have and establishes a self-defeating prediction of failure. The child who has a positive self-concept starts with the conviction that he is capable of dealing with problems and is likely to take a more optimistic, direct approach to confronting his difficulties. The child's self-concept is an important asset in determining how he deals with his inner world of feelings and outer world of events, demands, and interactions. That asset is expressed in the child's manner of perceiving, judging, and responding to the events of his life. We will consider how the teacher can help the child gain and develop skills to cope with his fears and difficulties. In this function the teacher can serve the child best by helping him gain new ways of perceiving and responding to the problems of his life. Our discussion will be limited to ways that appear appropriate for teachers and parents and that do not go into the possible deeper sources of the child's fears. Teachers who are faced with children who experience extensive and persistent fears should advise their principal and the child's parents rather than deal with such feelings by themselves.

Children with a negative self-concept tend to demean their own capacities and thereby make themselves vulnerable to their own doubts and the demands of other persons. The negative self-concept is associated with a lack of faith that the person can effectively deal with himself or other persons. In traditional psychological terms that lack of faith in oneself to deal with threats and problems is termed anxiety. Anxiety is the feeling of helplessness, uncertainty, and dread that a person experiences when he perceives a situation or event that he believes is beyond his powers. The threat is basically a threat to his self-esteem since it forces the person to recognize the limits of his powers to deal with and control his life. Viewed in terms of self-concept there are four major difficulties in self-concept that lead to feelings of helplessness and dread. The first difficulty is represented by a child whose self is *divided* and who feels, in part, that he can and in other ways cannot deal with the problems that confront him. Such a child would say that he might be able to dress himself and then ten minutes later indicate with equal certainty that he could not. A second difficulty is represented by the child who is *uncertain* of whether he can deal with even minor problems. This uncertainty is represented by a shrug of the shoulders or a statement that "Maybe I can do it," but there is a persistent, underlying doubt that success can be achieved. A third type of difficulty is represented by the child who has internalized high standards from his parents and who feels that he should perform at certain levels but who finds that he is unable to do so. A child with such *should-am* feelings may feel that he should be able to finish his homework at a certain time or be able to run as fast as other children, but since he is incapable of doing so he is a failure. The fourth difficulty that is associated with feelings of helplessness is represented by the child who concludes he is worthless, weak, and without redeeming features or strengths. Such a child has defined himself as *helpless* and defeated, and he acts according to that self-definition.

Several conditions have been associated with the child's development of feelings of helplessness and uncertainty, some of which have been discussed in earlier sections of this chapter. Among conditions that have been associated with high levels of childhood anxiety are severe punishment and restrictions, extremely high parental standards, harsh negative evaluation, and frequent or intense changes in parental or teacher mood and reaction to children (Ruebush 1963). The greatest source of feelings of inadequacy occurs in situations where the child feels he is going to be evaluated and judged by other persons. In such situations, many children feel that they cannot live up to the standards that have been set by either the parent or the teacher since they lack the capacities and skills to reach acceptable, much less successful, levels of performance. Another condition that increases the likelihood of anxiety and uncertainty is sudden, unexplained change. Children in general, and particularly those who are unsure of themselves, have difficulties in knowing how to react in novel situations that do not have anchors of familiar people or objects. Anna Freud's study (1946) indicated that children who lived in cities that were being heavily bombed were more anxious about separation from their parents than they were about bombs themselves. Children are, after all, dependent upon others for survival and relatively helpless (as compared to adults) in terms of physical skills, knowledge, and problem solving. Under certain circumstances, separation from parents and a familiar environment may lead the child to believe that he has lost the source of his emotional and physical security. The early school years are often a trying period precisely because they represent the first separation of the child from his parent as well as being the first situation in which the child's competencies will be publicly evaluated. The fears and uncertainties of separation and evaluation are a real and objective feature of the young child's venture into the academic world.

Each child develops his own methods for dealing with the tensions, frustrations, and other unpleasant feelings that accompany separations, evaluations, and other difficulties. He protects himself in a variety of ways. These ways have been traditionally called "defense mechanisms" (A. Freud 1946) or "coping mechanisms" (Murphy 1962). Defense mechanisms are methods of reducing the negative feelings that occur in the child's mind but that do not involve changes in the real world. They are psychological processes that enable the child to change the meaning of a situation or to reach a less upsetting meaning that may, however, be distorted and unrealistic. The defense mechanisms remove, reduce, or change the threat to the person's self-esteem, or they change the picture of the self so that it is more capable and lovable. Since the defense mechanisms operate only in the world of the person's ideas they do not involve or require any action on his part. Defense mechanisms are to a certain extent functional since they provide at least temporary relief from feelings of helplessness and solve the immediate problems of psychological pain and distress. In the long run, overuse of defenses may lead to problems if they prevent the person from dealing with the concerns and difficulties of his life. The child who is psychologically convinced he is brilliant despite his poor performance will someday have to confront the realities of his limited abilities and skills in the classroom. At a theoretical level, defense mechanisms represent an attempt by the person to maintain a picture of himself by hiding certain feelings and actions that may detract from the views that he currently holds. When the child's self-image is directly and openly threatened, he is said to become "defensive" which means that he becomes very sensitive and apprehensive and may even become strongly antagonistic. Defensiveness is associated generally with a clear attack upon self-esteem followed by overreaction, sensitivity, and an inflexible position of self-defense. It seems clear that direct attacks upon self-esteem, e.g., telling children they are not smart or not worthy, leads them to be defensive and forecloses further communication. Children who feel attacked do not reveal themselves to the attacker and cannot move beyond the fortress they feel compelled to erect. Such children have to protect the self-image they have already expressed and cannot alter it while the attack proceeds, or they may be left totally exposed. Such defensive postures come from poor communication with parents as well as from direct attacks. Parents who do not openly show their feelings toward their children discourage the children from being curious and emotionally expressive (Ruebush 1963). The result of such limited communication is that the children fail to develop motivation and skills in communicating their feeling to other persons or to themselves. They they do not talk about such topics as failure, sex, death, and anger that might be upsetting to the parent, and these children remain largely unaware and impassive about their own feelings on these issues. They have, in effect, closed themselves off from themselves as well as from other people.

There are several ways of dealing with anxiety that are particularly common among young children. These defense mechanisms include (1) *regression,* acting in the manner of a much younger child, as for example thumb-sucking or baby talk; (2) *denial,* when the child refuses to accept the existence of a threatening event or situation such as the refusal of the child to accept the birth of a baby brother and insistence that such an event has not occurred; (3) *withdrawal,* one of the most frequent defenses of young children that involves avoidance of situations in which the youngster feels he will fail or be rejected; (4) *projection,* a defense in which the youngster attributes to someone else his own negative feelings, thoughts, and fears, as in a case when a child claims that another youngster does not like him when, in fact, he does not like the other child; (5) *repression,* the most complete exclusion of threat, such as when the child who represses an event cannot even recall the event and is not aware that he has forgotten it. These defense mechanisms are not the only ones that young children employ to defend their self-esteem, but they appear to be widely and frequently used for that purpose.

Coping mechanisms represent a more active approach than do defense mechanisms in dealing with harm, novelty, and threats to self-esteem. Among the direct action tendencies are preparation against harm, various forms of attack, avoidance, and apathy. Through use of coping procedures the person attempts to gain some mastery over the sources of threat and discomfort rather than to deal with them solely in his mind. The study of coping has been pursued most vigorously by Lois Murphy and her colleagues (1962). They studied how healthy, normal young children dealt with the demands and stresses of such conditions as novelty, sickness, moving, beginning school, and conflicts. Murphy studied the same children from infancy through childhood and found several procedures that were employed often to solve childhood problems. She also studied the home backgrounds and parental treatment these children received and sought to establish which home conditions were associated with different patterns of coping. Murphy reports that children develop characteristic ways of coping that remain fairly consistent over childhood, e.g., impulsive attack or withdrawal. Children may vary somewhat from these consistent coping procedures, but such variations are generally part of an overall strategy in which the long-term pattern is a stable feature. She also finds that all children cope in some ways and develop coping strategies that are particular and individual to them.

One of Murphy's major contributions has been the idea that people not only defend themselves against anxiety, but they also assert themselves and deal with the world in an active manner. Through this idea she has sought to express the positive notion that people deal with life as well as hide from it by building defensive walls. There are two classes of coping: direct actions and indirect, holding actions. Direct actions are aimed at direct elimination or reduction of harmful conditions. These direct actions involve examining the source of harm, judging the actions suitable to deal with it, considering alternatives, and selecting the most effective way of removing or weakening it. To prepare against physical harm a child may learn to protect or defend himself; to prepare against failure he may study at home; to prepare against his sloppiness with paints he may wear old clothes or cover his clothing. Children often do not know the alternatives open to them nor are they able to anticipate consequences without some initial guidance. Another method of coping is to directly injure, remove, or otherwise attack the person considered responsible for the threat. Attack may be verbal or physical, accompanied by emotion or expressed without feelings. Another coping strategy frequently found among children is avoidance of harm. When a child is faced with a person who is considered overwhelming and dangerous, avoidance or escape is his reasonable solution. Murphy views this avoidance as retreats that make sense psychologically and physically because the child apparently feels that there is no other direct action that will be effective with that person. In the immediate situation, the child can save his esteem by avoidance until he develops his capacities to deal with the particular individual or situation more actively and directly.

SOME SPECIFIC ADVICE ON BUILDING SELF-ESTEEM

1. *Accept Feelings as Real and Support Their Expression*

It is important for teachers to recognize that the child's fears are extremely real to him; although, they may seem trivial or nonsensical to an adult. By accepting the child's negative feelings as a legitimate part of him, the teacher helps the child become more aware of parts of himself that he may have previously denied. Adult acceptance of negative feelings of fear, conflict, and rejection makes it easier for the child to express himself more openly since the child and teacher can accept the fact that all people sometimes experience such feelings. This recognition and its open communication provide emotional support in a period of stress and enable the child to have a companion who shares but does not lose respect for him because of his misery and apprehensions. Such acceptance of negative feelings and support in their expression is probably the basic condition in helping the child to confront his fears and problems. The recognition that it is all right to show disappointment, apprehension, and weakness liberates the child from having to hide himself from himself as well as others. A positive and constructive self-concept requires that the child accept all of himself, not only the positive, optimistic parts.

2. *Realize the Individual Differences in Coping*

As we indicated earlier in this section, the work of Lois Murphy has shown that children differ markedly in the ways in which they deal with adversity and the time and pace with which they handle it. Some children confront adversity head-on; others withdraw. Some children are more apt to withdraw initially and then come back strong shortly afterward. Teachers and parents should seek to establish what coping procedures are employed generally by a given youngster and observe that youngster over a period of time. Even though the youngster is not employing a method that the adult thinks is appropriate and reasonable for a given problem, it does not mean that the child lacks coping strengths. Assessment of the particular strengths is important since the teacher may decide that it would be advisable to teach a child alternative strategies and broaden the options open to him in confronting problems. It is essential to know the strengths he currently has and to move from that point to broaden his strengths.

3. Avoid Drastic Sudden Changes

One way in which the feeling of uncertainty can be reduced is to provide an environment that is relatively well-structured, stable, and predictable. Children are uncertain enough in their own self-image, and uncertainties in the outside world often cause them to be apprehensive and emotional. Teachers can help prevent feelings of distress and uncertainty by announcing shifts and changes in schedule, personnel, or rooms as early and as clearly as possible and by keeping such changes to a minimum. Outside of the school parents can do much the same regarding separations necessitated by child illnesses that require hospitalization, parental absence, or by parental work conditions. Children can cope with novelty and change within great limits provided they are given sufficient explanation of and experience with such changes and are given clear and consistent sources of support. Examples of such support would be a continuity of teacher if the school environment changes; temporary mother presence in the classroom if the child shifts schools; and mother sleeping in the hospital if the child requires medical treatment.

4. Adopt a Problem Solving Approach to Difficulties.

Children who feel overwhelmed and helpless in the face of demands cannot mobilize themselves to use their energies effectively. They lack the ability to put events in perspective; they are unable to analyze situations to see what courses of actions are open to them; and they often lack sufficient perspective upon themselves and their problems to see how they can best employ their strengths and abilities. Teachers can help the child by adopting a problem-solving approach in which difficulties are seen as both problems and opportunities. To be dealt with effectively difficulties must be examined from different points of view and broken down into manageable parts; then a definite course of action must be established. Teachers can help clear up the ambiguities and uncertainties that the child may be imposing upon the situation that are fogging up the search for a solution. A child may believe that he does not have the right to ask the teacher for help, that he does not have enough time, that if he misses part of the instructions he cannot ask the teacher to repeat them, that he cannot be partially right but must be altogether correct, and that speaking up for himself is bad or wrong. Teachers can be helpful by indicating that explanations are not a waste of time, that problems can be broken into parts, and that there are many ways of being correct. On a more immediate level teachers can also help the child to learn what his particular strengths and abilities are and how they can be applied in a specific situation that confronts him.

5. *Provide a Model of Effectiveness*

Teachers who are themselves fearful and apprehensive are likely to communicate their uncertainties to the children in their classrooms. Teachers who express confidence in their abilities and deal with the issues of their own lives may bolster the child's assurance and help him to recognize that problems can be successfully confronted. Children may also gain confidence from other children, and a child will often try a new or risky action with his peers that he would hesitate to do alone or with an adult. The teacher who expresses a coping orientation — who indicates that something can be done rather than accept outcomes passively — serves as a model of how to act and is thereby able to help the child mobilize his own energies. Such models also can make the child aware that even serious events have their humorous sides. Difficulties often cause people to limit their visions and pay attention to only the troublesome and unhappy features of their life. Teachers who are composed and organized in the face of difficulties, who can express humor as well as doubts, and who indicate that troubles are only a part of life show a child how fears can be dealt with as well as indicating they *can* be dealt with.

6. *Help the Child Develop Constructive Ways of Dealing with Difficulty*

Children (and most adults) characteristically employ a limited range of procedures for dealing with their difficulties. An important way of helping youngsters is to increase the range of procedures open to them and thus broaden the strengths they can bring to bear. Teachers also can provide some outlets by which the child can express his apprehensions in order to release tensions and gain awareness of his feelings. For example, physical activity may help the child to relieve his tensions. A talk about feelings with a friend may provide support, and fantasies about methods of dealing with his problem may open up new, alternative courses of action that are not part of the child's usual strategy. It may also be helpful for the child to play out different roles that reveal how else he might act in the face of difficulty or try out several different behaviors that offer varied approaches to the same problem. Breaking a problem down into its component parts so that they can be dealt with separately rather than as a total mass may be more effective, particularly if the child is overwhelmed by the total experience. These breakdowns increase the range of alternatives since each part can be looked at and explored separately. In general, it is advisable to accept the child's negative (and positive) feeling, encourage expression of feelings and actions, put the problem in perspective, and then adopt a problem-solving approach. A problem-solving approach requires not only talk but also an exploration of behaviors in which the child considers and confronts various courses of action. Some of the behavioristic methods of reconditioning and habituation by which the child gradually learns that the objects he fears are not as deadly as he believed may be effective in such an exploration. These methods can help reduce the level of fears and enable the child to respond to his difficulties more directly and confidently. When the level of fears is reduced to a manageable level it may be possible for the child to see the problem as being within the range of his capacities.

7. Maintain Self-Respect in the Course of Increasing Coping Strengths

Teachers and parents should recognize that the child is coping as well as he can even when he is not doing well from their vantage. It is self-defeating to strip the child of his self-respect in the process of helping him go forward. Accordingly, teachers and parents who wish to help the child develop improved methods of coping should do so in privacy and confidence whenever possible. They should always proceed in a manner that indicates respect and concern for the child rather than pity or rejection. In short, coping strengths are not developed by beating down defenses or by rejecting and antagonizing the child. All too often the teacher or parent is upset at the slow pace at which the child is developing his strengths and becomes impatient at the pace of his progress. This slow pace is a problem for the adult, but generally it is essential and reasonable for the child. Adult impatience often leads to destructive actions such as ridiculing the child for his fears, ignoring his fears as unreal or trivial, or forcing him to stay in a situation he finds stressful even though he is markedly distressed. Such actions generally subvert rather than accelerate the child's ability to confront problems. A more constructive approach would be to give the child a clear, constructive role to play in either his school work or social play. Clear roles provide social support, a clear indication of what is expected, and leeway for the child to be exploratory on his own. Children who have difficulty coping are apprehensive and sufficiently self-critical that they need clear indications of support rather than brave speeches or shoves into the sources of their fears.

8. Parent Education and Cooperation in Developing Coping Strengths

There are many children who report sizable differences between the standards and expectations of their teachers and parents. Living with such differences produces tension and so do efforts to reduce them. Children may also be confronted by parental expectations that exceed their capacities to achieve and by lack of parental support for methods of dealing with school problems. In other cases, children may have parents who expect them to fail and who see no point in encouraging them to succeed. Some recent studies have indicated that parent education and training can often help the parent provide the child with direct and indirect support for dealing with his problems (Alexander, Chess, and Birch 1968; Brookover 1967). Such parent education can be initiated at a conference between parent and teacher or of parent, teacher, and child. Some schools provide parents with a list of relevant reading; others provide or suggest programs that may help parents increase their abilities to communicate and assist the youngster. It appears that enlistment of parental cooperation is a major avenue for increasing coping strengths, and it clearly increases the speed and effectiveness of efforts to increase the child's capacity to cope.

Helping children learn how to deal with the problems and threats of their life requires that we help them learn how to psychologically defend themselves and actively cope with threats to their well-being. Increasing psychological defenses requires that we help children to gain a more complete, consistent, and complex view of themselves. As the person gains a self-picture that incorporates his positive and negative characteristics and that recognizes his weaknesses and strengths and begins to accept his real capacities rather than those that have been imposed upon him, he has less need to defend a self-picture that has serious limitations. Another psychological defense requires that the child learn to reject insults, failures, and rejections that are not due to his own actions and standards or for which he is not responsible. In this way we help the child to become less vulnerable to outside stress and his own negative feelings. Coping skills can be increased by helping the child to take a problem-solving approach to his fears and difficulties. A problem-solving approach requires appraising the child's situation and his own strengths, breaking the problem down, viewing it from various perspectives, and then selecting a course of action. The child needs support to begin moving forward, and an effective model and clear-cut role of effectiveness are helpful in that regard.

SUMMARY

In this chapter we have examined the significance of self-esteem for the educational process and indicated some of the methods by which teachers and parents can help build self-esteem. The question of the relevance of self-esteem in the classroom is most directly answered with the recognition that self-esteem is significantly involved in student motivation and that several studies have indicated that self-esteem is a major factor underlying academic achievement. From the available evidence it appears that many of the previously accepted ideas and procedures on how to raise children's self-esteem are not effective, e.g., praise and popularity. However, newly developed procedures appear to be capable of increasing the child's feelings of personal worth. Among the general conditions that produce high self-esteem are warmth and acceptance of the child; well-defined, consistent, and enforced limits and standards; and expressions of respect and appreciation for the individual child's wants, interests, and opinions. The teachers and parents of children with high self-esteem tend to be authoritative rather than authoritarian, are relatively clear in their own values, and tend to be decisive in the actions that they take.

The chapter considers three conditions that have been found to help build self-esteem in the classroom. The first of these is the responsive environment in which the teachers and classroom materials are designed to respond to the learner. In such an environment the child gains an awareness of his own powers and learns that what he wants is important. He also learns to take initiative for himself and is thereby encouraged to take responsibility for his actions. The second condition considered is building student beliefs and expectations of success and competence. Following the line that teachers and students who believe that the child can succeed establish a self-fulfilling prophecy of success, the chapter considers how much expectations are translated into teacher and pupil behaviors. Among these behaviors are increased, but reasonable, demands, teacher commitment, and increased range of student choices. The third method considered is developing methods of coping with the child's fears, failures, and frustrations. These methods are broken down into defense mechanisms that represent psychological processes in the child's mind and coping mechanisms that involve a more active approach to problems. Teachers are given some guidance in how to increase coping strengths through taking problem-solving approaches, providing a model of effective performance, and avoiding procedures that may arouse defensiveness.

The chapter provides a theoretical framework and considers how the child's self-concept and self-esteem is formed, defended, and altered. Parents, peers, and teachers play a role in being the significant figures in the child's world, and their opinions play an important role in forming and maintaining esteem, particularly in the early years. The teacher is given some theoretically based procedures on how to help the child by developing skills and competencies that focus on developing academic skills rather than serving as a parent surrogate or therapist.

REFERENCES

Alexander, T., Chess, S., and Birch, H. *Temperament and Behavior Disorders in Children*. New York: New York University Press, 1968.

Aspey, D.N. *A Study of Three Facilitative Conditions and Their Relationships to the Achievement of Third Grade Students*. Dissertation Abstract, University of Kentucky, 1965, 1853-A.

Baumrind, D. "Child Care Practices Anteceding Three Patterns of Preschool Behavior." *Genetic Psychology Monographs* 75(1967):43-88.

Bledsoe, J.C. "Self-Concepts of Children and Their Intelligence, Achievement, Interests, and Anxiety." *Journal of Individual Psychology*, 1964, 20.

Bodwin, R., and Bruck, M. "The Relationship between Self-Concept and the Presence and Absence of Scholastic Underachievement." *Journal of Clinical Psychology* 18(1962):181-82.

Brookover, W.B. et al. *Self-Concept of Ability and School Achievement. II: Improving Academic Achievement through Students' Self-Concept Enhancement*. U.S. Office of Education, Cooperative Research Project No. 2831. East Lansing: Office of Research and Publications, Michigan State University, 1965.

Brookover, W.B., Erickson, E.L., and Joiner, L.M. *Self-Concept of Ability and School Achievement. III: Relationship of Self-Concept to Achievement in High School*. U.S. Office of Education, Cooperative Research Project No. 2831. East Lansing: Office of Research and Publications, Michigan State University, 1967.

Brookover, W.B., Thomas, S., and Patterson, A. "Self-Concept of Ability and School Achievement." *Sociology of Education* 37(1964):271-78.

Combs, A.W. *The Professional Education of Teachers*. Boston: Allyn and Bacon, Inc., 1965.

Combs, A.W., and Soper, D. *The Relationship of Child Perceptions to Achievement and Behavior in the Early School Years*. U.S. Office of Education, Cooperative Research Project No. 814. Washington, D.C.: Department of Health, Education and Welfare, 1963.

Combs, A.W. et al. *Florida Studies in the Helping Professions*. University of Florida Social Science Monograph No. 37, 1969.

Cook, D.L. "The Hawthorne Effect in Educational Research." *Phi Delta Kappan*, 1962, pp. 116-22.

Coopersmith, S. *The Antecedents of Self-Esteem*. San Francisco: W.H. Freeman and Co., 1967.

Davidson, H.H., and Lang, G. "Children's Perceptions of Their Teachers' Feelings toward Them Related to Self-Perception, School Achievement, and Behavior." *Journal of Experimental Education* 29(1960):107-118.

Diggory, J.C. *Self-Evaluation: Concepts and Studies.* New York: John Wiley & Sons, Inc., 1966.

Fey, W.F. "Acceptance of Self and Others, and Its Relation to Therapy Readiness." *Journal of Clinical Psychology* 10(1954):226-69.

Foster, C., and Henning, J. *Personal Communication,* January 1971. Evaluation Report 1970-71 prepared by Dr. Larry Barber, Department of Research and Evaluation, Louisville Board of Education, Louisville, Kentucky, 40202.

Freud, A. *The Ego and the Mechanisms of Defense.* New York: International Universities Press, 1946.

Goldstein, A. et al. *Psychotherapy and the Psychology of Behavior Change.* New York: John Wiley and Sons, 1966.

Good, T.L., and Brophy, J.E. "Teachers' Communication of Differential Expectations for Children's Classroom Performance: Some Behavioral Data." *Journal of Educational Psychology* 61(1970):365-74.

Jersild, A.T. "Voice of the Self." *NEA Journal* 54(1965):23-25.

LaBenne, W., and Greene, B. *Educational Implications of Self-Concept Theory.* Pacific Palisades, California: Goodyear Publishing, 1969.

Leventhal, T., and Sills, M. "Self Image in School Phobia." *American Journal of Orthopsychiatry* 34(1964):685-95.

Luft, J. "On Nonverbal Interaction." *Journal of Psychology* 63(1966):261-68.

Morris, D., Soroker, E., and Burrus, G. "Follow-up Studies of Shy, Withdrawn Children: I. Evaluation of Later Judgments." *American Journal of Orthopsychiatry* 24(1954):743-54.

Murphy, L.B. *The Widening World of Childhood.* New York: Basic Books, 1962.

Nimnicht, G., MacAfee, O., and Meier, J. *The New Nursery School.* New York: General Learning Corp., 1969.

Omwake, K.T. "The Relation between Acceptance of Self and Acceptance of Others Shown by Three Personality Inventories." *Journal of Consulting Psychology* 18(1954):443,446.

Orne, M.T. "On the Social Psychology and the Psychological Experiment with Particular Reference to Demand Characteristics and Their Implications." *American Psychologist* 17(1962):776-83.

Otto, H., and Mann, J. *Ways of Growth.* New York: Grossman Publishers, 1968.

Purkey, W. *Self Concept and School Achievement.* Englewood Cliffs, N.J.: Prentice-Hall, Inc., 1970.

Quimby, V. "Differences in the Self-Ideal Relationship of an Achieved Group and an Underachieved Group." *California Journal of Educational Research* 18(1967):23-31.

Randolph, N., and Howe, W. *Self Enhancing Education*. Palo Alto, California: Sanford Press, 1966.

Rosenberg, M. *Society and the Adolescent Self Image*. Princeton, N.J.: Princeton University Press, 1965.

Rosenthal, R., and Jacobsen, L. *Pygmalion in the Classroom: Teacher Expectation and Pupils' Intellectual Development*. New York: Holt, Rinehart & Winston, Inc., 1968.

Ruebush, B. "Anxiety." In *Child Psychology*, edited by H.W. Stevenson (62nd Yearbook National Social Studies Education). Chicago: University of Chicago Press, 1963.

Sarason, S.B. et al. *Anxiety in Elementary School Children*. New York: Wiley, 1960.

Satir, V. *Conjoint Family Therapy*. Palo Alto, California: Science and Behavior Books, 1967.

Shaw, M., and Alves, G. "The Self-Concept of Bright Academic Underachievers: II." *Personnel and Guidance Journal* 42(1963):401-3.

Trent, R.D. "The Relationship between Expressed Self-Acceptance and Expressed Attitudes Toward Negro and White in Negro Children." *Journal of Genetic Psychology* 91(1957):25-31.

Wattenberg, W.W., and Clifford, C. "Relation of Self Concepts to Beginning Achievement in Reading." *Child Development* 35(1964):35,461-67.

Weiner, B. et al. "Causal Ascriptions and Achievement Behavior: The Conceptual Analysis of Effort." *Journal of Personality and Social Psychology*, in press.

5

Serving Intrinsic Motivation
in Early Education:
With Particular Emphasis on Science Education

By Robert E. Samples
Environmental Studies Project, Boulder, Colorado

INTRODUCTION

Once you enter the classroom and close the door you have three things going for you: your training, the materials you must use to teach with, and your basic personality. Strangely enough, these three aspects of teaching skill are currently woven together in such a fashion that they tend to reflect the classroom of the past rather than of contemporary America. The people responsible for teacher training and the construction of instructional materials have tended to emphasize the ideas and personality of students who lived in a less changing, less mobile, and less direct society. As a result of this focus on the more stable past, teaching materials and teacher training styles generally have advocated a set of standardized procedures and techniques for each classroom. In industrial terms, traditional practices have focused on efficiency of classroom management and concluded that standardization is the most effective solution. In that sense schools are treating children in the same way that other industries treat their products and consumers.

Let us take a closer look at the problem. Most current teaching practices stem from two basically different models of instruction, a didactic model and a process model. In a didactic model of instruction, that has earlier historical roots, a certain body of content is chosen out of the total environment and is structured by scholars.

Once the scholars have put the material in order, prospective teachers are expected to be trained to teach and test for that content. According to this model the teacher is supposed to act as a *transmission* belt of accepted and valuable information. Efficiency in this model is determined by the speed with which the teacher is able to transmit the content to the students so that the students can in turn repeat almost exactly what the teacher said. The responsibility for those educators in teacher preparation is to provide experience and specific information to the teacher that falls exclusively within the boundaries of the content that they are expected to teach. Materials produced for the teacher following this model of instruction contain the specific elements of the lessons they are to transmit to their students.

The second model of instruction focuses on the process of instruction and represents quite a shift from the didactic model. In this model of instruction the primary emphasis is on the interaction between content and student. The materials used for teaching purposes, rather than being created by scholars in the various fields of history, language, and science, are usually the products of scholars working with specialists in psychology, education, and communication. In fact, this model represents the major effort in curriculum revision. Through funding primarily by the National Science Foundation, many programs have been produced to reflect this process model of instruction. In this model the most important feature of the teaching environment is that the teacher encourages and arranges an interaction between student and materials. To use process model materials the teacher must be trained on how to increase and use such interactions as learning experiences. For example, rather than being trained solely in physics, the teacher would be trained in the process of getting students to interact with physics materials. The teacher's job then would be primarily to keep the student involved in such interactions.

The difference between these two models of instruction should be apparent. In the didactic model the teacher is trained via courses that emphasize content to become a specialist in certain facts, ideas, and theories. If a teacher takes courses in biology the training is geared to get the information that she can then transmit to students who will be in her classroom. Since the important issue is specifically *what* is learned, the technique and style of teachers following this model is lecturing and direct information giving. In the process model, the fundamental elements of the same teacher's training would be to gain an understanding of *how* biologists do their work. The introduction of the procedures used by actual investigators in the particular field has been the hallmark of process-oriented curricula developed during the last few years. A considerable number of new materials, particularly in the sciences, have been developed in support of the process model. Teachers following this approach attempt to encourage students to use these materials in the way specialists in those areas — physics, biology, or math — use them in their work. The emphasis in the process model is on methods employed in organized laboratories; the emphasis in the didactic model is on information presented in lecture form.

At this point, however, we are proposing a third model that is more suited for today's students and today's society. This intrinsic model differs from the didactic and process models in that no specific, predetermined laboratory experiences are selected out of the environment for the students. In fact, neither what the student will study (content) nor how he will study (process) comes directly from the teachers or the materials. Instead the *total environment* becomes the arena for inquiry. Our job as teachers in this environment is to provide a much richer and more diverse environment in which the students can inquire. Thus when the responsibility for choosing content goes to the student, we must shift our postures in order to be able to serve the student's need for sources of information; when the responsibility for the choosing process goes to the students, we must be prepared to provide materials and guidance in accepted practices. *In such an instructional environment the majority of the control for learning goes to the student.* This is in contrast to the didactic model where the majority of control for learning goes to the scholar and in contrast to the process model where the majority of the control goes to the scholar and behavioral scientist who created the teaching materials. In an intrinsic model the students choose not only the content but the way they go about inquiring. Their needs, interests, and perceptions are the point of departure for teaching, and the teacher, scholar, behavioral scientist, and materials are resources that the students use in their search for knowledge. The intrinsic model requires that the teacher be more flexible, imaginative, and open to the individual interests and needs of her students. Since students are intrinsically different from one another, the teacher who employs the intrinsic model must recognize and respect those differences if her students are to be involved and motivated.

The three things that the teacher brings into the classroom, training, materials, and personality, still provide the richest elements of the instructional environment. The instructional materials, geared to serve a specific and precise purpose, are also created according to this same premise. As a result, our training and the materials with which we arm ourselves prejudice us — the teachers — into making the decisions in classroom instruction. An intrinsic model is designed to encourage students to make decisions. If we follow an intrinsic model, we recognize that the point of departure for student learning is *their* interests and perceptions and not ours or scholars' with specialized skills. If we are concerned with the *student's* motivation, we can no longer go into the classroom with the bias of our training and the bias produced by the materials and expect students to engage in activities and searches that are not interesting or meaningful in their lives. The intrinsic model of instruction deals directly with the central issue of how to motivate today's student.

Motivation is an intrinsic quality in human beings. How many times have you heard people speak of motivating children? Motivate is a verb, and it is a verb that must be activated by the person being motivated. *I cannot motivate you* (although I can move you to action), and *you cannot motivate me* (although you can arouse my motivation). Motivation may or may not exist in the didactic and process models of instruction. However, in the intrinsic model of instruction motivation is the fundamental quality that sustains the entire enterprise. This bring us to an intriguing question.

WHAT IS MOTIVATION?

If I can't motivate you and you can't motivate me, how do we turn each other on? For quite a long time psychologists had the answer to this question, but we as educators have tended to muddle their explanations by using improper terminology. What school teachers generally think of as motivation is what psychologists call stimulation. Stimulation is an extrinsic quality. It is something I can do to you and you can do to me, but in terms of motivation the actual inner drive that is created in each one of us and that provides us with the impetus to do something has to come from within ourselves. The cues or invitations might come from the outside, but the drive must come from within us. It is easy to see that didactic instruction and process instruction employ primarily extrinsic stimulation for motivation. In both, the choices are made from outside the student as to what is going to happen to him with stimulation that is going to be provided to induce the student to perform the chosen exercise. The stimulation is much more subtle in the process approach than it is in the didactic because the student is more active in the process approach but relatively passive in the didactic approach. However, whether or not the student really gets involved from the standpoint of *his* own interest is something that is left primarily to chance and the student's own needs and activity pattern outside the classroom situation.

The difference between stimulation and motivation is illustrated in the two following sentences:

"All right, class, everyone get the microscopes out and put them on the table in front of you."

"Would someone please tell Jack where the microscope is? He says he needs it."

Both of these sentences were overheard in elementary school classrooms with thirty-five children in them. However, the difference between the two classrooms was profound as was the difference in the environments in which the statements were uttered. The first sentence was heard in a classroom in which the teacher was using materials produced by the program for elementary science instruction. The unit that was being examined was entitled "Small Things." According to the procedures presented in this unit all of the class members were expected to do the same thing at certain specified points. As a result, the request reflected in that statement was perfectly legitimate in light of the materials and the environment created by them. All of the students were asked to get out the microscopes and look at some cells from the skin of an onion. Children are generally delighted to do such things and excited by the kind of environment that is created by doing things instead of just listening to teachers. Yet, to be absolutely brutal in our distinction between stimulation and motivation, we have to acknowledge that the teacher's sentence was uttered within the context of stimulation. There may or may not have been a large number of students that did not want to look at onion skin cells, but nonetheless they had no choice — they were going to look at onion skin cells. The instruction manual said so, the teacher's training said so, and finally the teacher said so.

The second sentence was said in a room that had the same number of students as the first (thirty-five), but the room had been organized to utilize and develop intrinsic motivation. This classroom had the same materials for the elemenary science study unit on small things as did the first, and it also had beads, books, crayons, hand tools, pieces of wood, construction paper, art objects, typewriters, carpets, pillows, growing plants, a cat, a dog, a guinea pig, one rabbit, a bird, a stuffed bobcat, and several additional pieces of science equipment. This classroom was not as tidy or organized as was the first, but it was filled with children doing a variety of activities of their own choice. The teacher uttered the sentence in our example to a student who had felt the need to look at something small and had approached the teacher with the request for a microscope. The teacher's question, "Would someone please tell Jack where the microscope is?" thus reflects the child's motivation; whereas, the teacher's request that the students get the microscopes out reflected the teacher's desire to pursue a given topic.

Motivation has prevailed almost always in classrooms. However, it has seldom been the intrinsic motivation of the students. It has been the motivation of the teacher, a supervisor, or some administrative official who tends to have more say in instruction than does the student for whom the schools are supposedly designed. The reason that intrinsic motivation should prevail in classrooms is quite simple. The future for all of us holds within it the promise of more complexity rather than more simplicity. In the face of the complexity of tomorrow, schools must assume the responsibility of providing citizens who are capable of dealing with this complexity, much of which must be handled from *within* each of us. The most important quality that any of us can exhibit is a positive equilibrium in dealing with our environment. A motivated population will be better able to rise to the needs of tomorrow than a passive population waiting for some external stimulus to trigger them into action. If these statements are true, then how can highly intrinsic, highly motivational environments be created in classrooms?

WHAT IS INTRINSIC AND EXTRINSIC IN THE CLASSROOM?

In most classrooms the extrinsic prevails. The teacher tends to dominate the action; although, the students are actively involved in such things as growing seeds or looking through microscopes or playing with beam balances. The teacher tends to feel compelled, in response to the training he has received, to require that the children all do essentially the same thing at the same time. As soon as this tendency toward common, simultaneous activities begins to dominate, then you can be sure it is your bag that is involved rather than the student's.

The mere fact that a student seems to enjoy an activity does not mean that he is intrinsically motivated. Once I asked a student who seemed to be terribly engrossed in charting the course of a mealworm across a piece of graph paper what he was doing. He answered pleasantly enough that he was trying to find out how many blocks on the graph paper the mealworm could walk across in a given length of time. I then asked him why he was doing it. His answer was "Because it's 10 o'clock, and we always do science at 10 o'clock." The pleasantness that the child displayed, not only in his behavior but also in his general attitude toward what he was doing, was quite disarming. I realized at that time and have reflected later that *I very often confuse the capacity of a child to submit to my interests as being indicative of his interest and involvement.* I often assumed that because he rushed to pick up things like mealworms and microscopes that he was in fact highly motivated. Only lately have I come to realize that the child's activity did not necessarily mirror his enthusiasm or motivation but might only have indicated that his particular choice was a more pleasant alternative in the spectrum of things that I set out for children in that classroom.

An activity pattern in which children do different things does not necessarily indicate that they are intrinsically motivated. General classroom practice is for all the children to do the same thing at the same time. Psychological principles indicate that children differ markedly in abilities and interests. To account for these differences teachers resort to what they call individualized instruction. Although such instruction is said to serve the needs of the child, a more honest position would compel us to admit that we are serving the needs of the teacher who designs the assignments for the students. These teachers are somewhat nervous about the fact that students cannot perform their assignments at the same rate. As a result, they alter the nature of the materials or the procedures in using them so that all of the children can still do the same thing but at their own (different) rates. *When the rates differ, it appears that the children are not doing the same thing.* However, rate differences are not necessarily an indication that children are responding to intrinsic motivation. Such differences may instead mirror a totally extrinsic kind of control on the children. Intrinsic motivation requires freedom for the child to explore activities of his choosing as well as to determine the rate of progress. Intrinsic motivation requires self-selected activities as well as individually different rates.

In one classroom I was impressed by the fact that children were apparently doing very different sorts of activities related to science. One group of children was clustered around the aquarium, another group hovered over a few microscopes, another group of children was playing with pendulums, and another group was building structures out of soda straws. Aha, I though, I have finally found an intrinsic environment, but, upon talking to the children, I found that the five groups of children that I saw working had each chosen the area of their inquiry from a list that the teachers had put on the board. Teachers often feel that when children choose among alternatives they are in effect doing their own thing. *However, the teachers seem to fail to realize that if they limit the alternatives, they are effectively coercing the children to do what it is that the teacher wants in the first place.* I suppose the best example of this behavior is the college course in which after the professor has assigned a term paper on the topic of your choice and assured you that this is your course and he wants you to pursue avenues of interest to you, he then begins to lecture for fifteen weeks.

Teachers who establish classroom environments in which students predominantly do their own thing are constantly questioned by colleagues, administrators, and children's parents. Most of the teachers have a sense of inner competence and inner strength that allows them very cogently to deal with the kinds of questions that are asked. The questions range from "Will my son learn his multiplication tables?" (from a parent) to "How will your students perform on the standard tests?" (from an administrator). Most of these teachers answer on the basis of their perceptions of what is happening to the students in their classrooms. They seem to sense that once a child begins to accept a responsibility for his own actions, he will be more involved in gaining the skills and competence that make school more meaningful and rewarding to him. *Teachers in these programs generally conclude that children fundamentally want to learn.* Children *want* to communicate and become familiar with the society they have inherited. Children are curious and want to explore what the schools have to offer provided that the schools give them some freedom to explore in their own way. These teacher impressions of children are supported by the objective evidence presented in the Plowden Report. This report, and the later studies it inspired, examined teaching practices that served the child's intrinsic motivation in the infant schools of Great Britain. Children exposed to classroom practices that permit them to explore their own needs and interests accomplish as much in terms of basic skills and achievement as do children taught by more formally organized, extrinsically motivated procedures. The children learn basic skills such as multiplication tables, and they end up scoring well on standardized tests. To the parent and to the administrator who raised questions earlier in this paragraph, the answer is that children who follow intrinsic motivation *"do as well as anyone else"* in terms of traditional competencies. They do, in fact, gain one advantage over their classmates in traditional settings. Students taught in classrooms that serve intrinsic motivation were found to be significantly higher in self-esteem and self-image than were students taught with procedures that employed extrinsic motivation. Inasmuch as self-esteem appears to be associated with academic success (Chapter 4, "Building Self-Esteem in the Classroom" by Coopersmith) the use of intrinsic motivation seems to have indirect as well as direct benefits for learning in the classroom.

Earlier, I mentioned three things with which teachers are armed as they enter the classroom: their teacher training, the materials that they have available to them, and their basic personalities. To summarize, the kind of teacher preparation that each of us is exposed to tends to provide us with a rationale for the extrinsic. We are taught how to make bulletin boards; we are taught how to organize children; how to manage discipline; how to reward and punish certain kinds of behavior; how to quickly standardize certain kinds of procedures in the classroom; how to organize and preserve the materials of instruction. The materials that we bring into the classroom are also dominantly extrinsic. Our professional organizations provide us with materials that have been preselected by experts as useful and appropriate for teaching children of a certain age and ability. We are taught how to present these materials and get children to use them. Thus with two factors against the intrinsic we come to the personal area that can still overcome the dominantly extrinsic qualities of training and materials — our personality.

HOW DO PERSONALITY CHARACTERISTICS
RELATE TO MOTIVATION?

The old saying "What you *are* speaks so loudly that I cannot hear what you say" is at the very core of this third and last resource that we can bring into the classroom, namely ourselves. Each of us knows we have a personality and that our personality can be read by other people. However, because we are so involved with ourselves it is very difficult for us to really understand how our basic personality characteristics affect others. O.J. Harvey has demonstrated recently at the University of Colorado that children are more capable of characterizing a teacher's personality than are trained psychological observers. In the work that Harvey has been doing over the last several years he has developed methods of categorizing certain personality characteristics that underlie personal biases and prejudices. It became obvious that these categories could also be used to study how teachers with those characteristics affect the children in their classrooms.[1]

According to Harvey's classification there are three fundamental personality types: authoritarian, dependency, and freedom. Although the characteristics of each of these personality types are exhibited by all of us, Harvey's studies lead him to conclude that people under stress resort to the personality type that is most consistent with their basic disposition. It might be protested that teaching is not a stress situation, but I believe that only people who have never taught would maintain that position.

Authoritarian Personality

There are two kinds of authoritarian personalities, a positive and a negative. The positive authoritarian is *attracted* to prevailing authority. He tends to go completely with the status quo. If there is a high point on the curve that describes what is preferred by people of power and influence, you will find the positive authoritarian accepting and advocating that view. The positive authoritarian tends to be most compatible with a didactic model of instruction. He believes in authority; he believes in the voice of status, tradition, and scholarship. The positive authoritarian often feels that his belief systems are so strong that those who do not agree with him are somewhat immoral. His style is rational and logical, and his thinking pattern has a high degree of internal consistency. The positive authoritarian will follow curriculum instruction and his value system supports the established procedures and materials. A negative authoritarian is *repelled* by prevailing authority. He often feels that the accepted scholars are wrong. He is often antagonistic toward prevailing authority; he opposes strongly and almost on instinct. Different at the surface, the general tactics and strategies of the negative authoritarian are identical to those of the positive authoritarian with the exception of the fact that one is positive and one is negative. Both sides of the authoritarian personality have a strong sense of external fate in control. What this means is that they believe conditions outside themselves tend to govern whatever happens to them. In the case of the positive authoritarian, his belief supports the external system; in the case of the negative authoritarian, his belief attacks the external

---

1. The category system discussed in this paper reflects Harvey's findings but has been slightly modified for the purpose of clarity. In addition, it should be noted that Harvey measured these personality characteristics when his teacher subjects were under stress. Harvey believes that the posture exhibited by a person when subjected to emotional stress situations tends to give a more true portrait of what his core personality is like than when he is relaxed and poised.

system. Despite the difference between attack and support, positive and negative authoritarians alike are largely guided by external stimuli.

Dependency Personality

Like the authoritarian personality, the dependency personality also seems to have a positive and a negative side. It is more difficult to determine the positive and negative aspects of this personality because the dependency person tends to operate much closer to himself. A positively dependent person sets up situations in which you need him. *His payoff is to be needed.* He wants very much to be the indispensable man. If he were working for a company, he would want to make sure that no one else could do his job. In the classroom, teachers with this sort of personality tend to provide instructions for students that are much too difficult in detail; thus, *their role is fulfilled by being forced to answer the student's need for help — a need they have created.* In a sense we can say this kind of person manages a classroom and the rest of the environment around him in response to his own inner need to be needed. The negative dependency personality very badly needs other people. He sets up situations in which he becomes very dependent upon others, and then he informs them of his dependency upon them. The result is that he forces other people into a position of knowing how much they are needed. He might confront a class with the statement, "After all I've done for you, why do you treat me in this way?" For example, he might constantly remind the class of how much he does for them, when in reality he couldn't live without them as an audience. The dependency personality, like the authoritarian personality, primarily responds to external stimuli, but unlike the authoritarian personality he does it because of his need for people rather than his concern for authority. In a sense, the authoritarian is primarily dependent upon *ideas,* whereas the dependency personality is primarily dependent upon *people.*

Freedom Personality

The fundamental characteristic of the freedom personality is the compulsion to do that which interests him. In turn he expects you to do that which interests you. The result is that if a person with his personality goes into teaching his primary goal is to create an environment in which his students can do things that are of fundamental interest to them. His goal is to support his students in this process of achieving their personal freedom. His fundamental strategy toward his students is to create a situation in which he effectively *eliminates any managed authoritarian control* over them. In addition, he also attempts to *eliminate those conditions that make them dependent upon him*. This person is primarily driven to create a situation of independence for the student and himself. To use a biological comparison, he creates a symbiotic relationship where two organisms can live together for the *mutual benefit of each other but not at the expense of each other*. People with these freedom personality characteristics are not interested in coercing people to any particular doctrine. They may have strong beliefs and strong drives of their own, but they fully accept the fact that these are their own drives and beliefs and need not be shared by their students. In classroom situations they tend to use the curriculum as a loose guideline around which they create environments in which the students can go in their own directions.

Although we have created personality types for the purpose of describing teacher influences, we must be careful not to create a new trap. It would be quite easy to conclude that the types could be graded according to that which we regarded as desirable and effective because these different types exemplify portraits of teacher behavior. Since the major trend in current education, at least in words, is to move away from the authoritarian posture to a more permissive environment in which freedom prevails, it would be easy to say that teachers exhibiting the freedom personality characteristics should get an "A" and that people exhibiting the authoritarian personality should get an "F." Certainly, although each of us has some characteristics of each of these personalities, the purpose in bringing up these personality traits in this chapter is simply to point out that the type most compatible with an intrinsic instructional environment is the freedom personality. School systems that favor didactic or process models of instruction might be more effective with teachers that have authoritarian or dependency personalities. The aim is to fit personality type and teaching model into a consistent and compatible package. As we view the last of the three things the teacher can bring to the classroom, the training, the materials, and the personality, we find that the freedom personality has the greatest potential for creating an intrinsic environment. Since it is within intrinsic environments that motivation dominates and it is up to the teacher to create such an environment, the teacher must be alert to the role that his basic personality plays in the classroom and how his personality actually fits with the teaching model he is using.

WHAT DOES THIS MEAN IN CLASSROOM MANAGEMENT?

Motivation is an elusive human quality. Only the person who possesses it can harvest it. However, environments can be created that will allow motivation to prevail. Since the teacher is in control of the classroom, he is the one who must create this type of environment. The students will respond to the kind of control that the teacher exerts. In this sense we are still talking about stimulation; however, stimulation can very quickly give way to a true kind of intrinsic motivation on the part of the students if the teacher allows, permits, and encourages such actions. If motivation is to prevail, teachers must assess (1) the difference between stimulation and motivation, (2) the difference between intrinsic qualities and extrinsic qualities, and (3) the role of personality characteristics in the learning environment. The teacher must first recognize he must elicit intrinsic motivation in children rather than assume that such motivation will appear by itself. Second, the teacher must realize that he cannot force the classroom environment to fully comply or conform in order to satisfy his own personality. Third, the teacher must be aware that his basic personality is read by the children who are quite perceptive and sensitive in such matters. The dichotomy that may exist between what the teacher says they can do and what they actually do can create an important credibility gap in the school situation. The prerequisite and necessary ingredient to go from a classroom marked by external stimulation to one in which intrinsic motivation prevails is the development of an atmosphere marked by personal trust between teacher and student. In the following paragraphs, I want to suggest some techniques that have been tried by many teachers and that appear to effectively create an environment of trust. Given enough time such an environment results in a dominance of intrinsic motivation in which students learn by seeking to explore their interests and satisfy their curiosity. To get such motivation to flourish, the teacher must (1) create intrinsic attitudes, (2) create ambiguity, and (3) reward divergence.

WHAT IS THE NATURE OF THE NURTURE?

The Intrinsic Attitude

The classroom is the fundamental container in which the children are to exist. It will come as no surprise to most teachers that the classroom conditions they establish and the way such conditions are perceived by their students structures the motivation of their students. For too many children the classroom *is simply a container that houses an attitude or environment of the extrinsic.* Students in such an environment tend to perceive all of the materials contained within the classroom as being weapons that will eventually be aimed at the student. The fundamental reason for such an attitude is that in most students' experiences, such weaponry is precisely what they experience. The students seldom have an open, convincing invitation to treat the prevailing materials as tools of inquiry until they have been specifically directed to do so from the teacher. Not only are the materials extrinsic but also the access route to using them usually follows an extrinsic command.

There are a variety of ways of breaking down this prevailing attitude in classrooms. Judging by my experience, this closed, extrinsic attitude can be broken down within two days and then heightened during the rest of the year. The best way to do this is as follows: At the beginning of the school year, before the students are actually present in the classroom, the teacher can set out a remarkably different plan of action than is usually followed. According to this plan the teacher pays less attention to putting the books in order, making sure all of the supplies are available, and completing all of the paper work necessary to maintain the sanity of the school's central office. If a teacher is committed to the notion of creating an intrinsic environment in the school, then the time could far better be spent looking up all of the *home phone numbers* for each child's parents. Then a personal call should be placed to each of the parents. At this time the teacher should express his interest in the child and invite the parents to contact and meet with him at any time they desire. An additional gesture can be to give the parents the teacher's private home phone number. Not only does this save time for the parent when something significant comes up, but also it is a gesture of good faith that provides the parents with a feeling that you as a teacher care for their child twenty-four hours a day, and not just the six hours in school. After this has been done and almost as an afterthought to the conversation with the parent, the teacher should ask the parent to help the child prepare his very first assignment in school. The assignment is that the child bring *a brown grocery bag full of junk* on his first day of school. Undoubtedly the parent will ask for some clarification of this assignment. The best tactic for the teacher to follow is to be slightly coy and just say "Any kind of junk that you don't want around the house, that is no longer useful to you, and that you think might be useful in the classroom." Again, before the conversation is over, remind the parent to have the child bring this bag of junk on the very first day of school.

It is quite an experience to see thirty-five second graders walk in your front door with thirty-five brown paper bags full of junk. As if the bags of junk are not enough, the students will be very surprised to find that the classroom does not look neat, orderly, and tidy as most classrooms have in their experience. Instead, all of the desks are pushed back against the wall so that there is a great, *hollow, empty arena in the middle of the room.* Since the children cannot get into and around the desks, they have to walk into the middle of the room with their brown paper bags. The teacher then introduces herself and suggests to the students that they empty all of their brown paper bags in the middle of the floor. This action initiates the first of many moments of tension that the students are going to feel on the very first day of school. Even the heartiest of teachers and students will be bewildered after the bags are emptied. No one can possibly imagine the fantastic array of materials that are brought into the classroom with such an assignment. The parents apparently engage in a silent competition as to who can provide the most worthwhile junk to the school. There are electric clocks, regular clocks, irons, knives, forks, plastic containers, glass containers, cardboard containers, milk cartons, aluminum foil, toothpicks, combs, brushes, screwdrivers, magic markers, pencils, old magazines, books, hammers, hair dryers, buttons, pennies, marbles, etc. When the children seem to be milling around this pile of junk, in the most bewildered fashion the teacher should then say, "I've got a lot of work to do for the principal today; so, I want you people to take that junk and *put it in order and put it away on the shelves.*"

The second of the student's moments of tension and confusion has just arrived. Attempts to figure out what the teacher meant by "putting that junk in order," how to put it away, exactly who is supposed to do it, and, most importantly, why the teacher gave the assignment usually occupy the student for most of the day. The timidity with which the students begin to make decisions as to what should take place usually exemplifies the fact that the students have seldom before had an opportunity to make significant decisions. Although the assignment is definitely extrinsic and came from the teacher, the attractive nature of the materials themselves and the nature of the task at hand is usually enough to intrigue the students to action. Before an hour has passed most of the children have learned each other's names, many of them have specified tasks to perform, but most importantly they have expressed their personalities to each other. Upon doing so in an apparently unschool-like task, the students have begun to relate to each other in a lifelike work situation. The result is that they are beginning to "live" together.

Eventually, out of the chaotic mountain of junk heaped on the floor, the children begin to produce some pattern of order. The most significant feature of the order that is achieved is that it derives from the students rather than the teacher. The first step toward an intrinsic environment has been taken. As the students classify and organize the material into a variety of categories, many of which have intrinsic worth to students but not to teachers, the materials find their way to shelves. Depending upon the classification and category system used, the students may choose to divide objects up on the basis of their use or function. In such a classification, containers will go in certain places, and marking instruments will go in others. A shelf of happy items often can be expected. Items on this shelf seldom have any noticeable function at all, but they are delightful bits of material to use and with which to play.

In the course of these deliberations there will undoubtedly have been some shouting, pushing, pulling, and arguing — undoubtedly these arguments will result in a group of students coming to the teacher asking for resolution. A response by the teacher that I have found very successful is *"Children, understand that in this room and in this school this year you will not hurt anyone or anything intentionally."* If elaboration is needed the teacher can say, "Think of all the things that can be meant by 'hurt' and then follow our rule." In this very first day the teacher should establish the notion that most conflict must be resolved internally, by the members of the group themselves rather than outside persons. If the conflict cannot be resolved by the group members themselves, then it should be resolved individually by and for each individual child. Since it will be the students' responsibility to create resolutions regarding personal crises, the teacher establishes at the outset the awareness and recognition that they are going to have to make certain decisions in the class. In addition, the children quickly learn that they will have influence upon the manner in which the class will be run throughout the year. The procedure we suggest for the first day is markedly different than the assertions authoritarian teachers usually express on those occasions. Armed with the rationale that students want to know the specifics of classroom behavior, teachers establish an attitude of the extrinsic on the first day that is difficult to reverse by later actions.

After the first phase of this joyous junk effort has taken place, the teacher can begin the second phase. This does not necessarily mean that the second phase begins on the second day; although, it is important for the teacher to know that this second phase is the most difficult for the teacher to contend with. *Phase two of joyous junk requires that the teacher treat the materials that the school has provided for the students in the same manner as the students have treated their junk pile.* Everything from the supply closet, the science cabinet, under the sink, up on the bookshelves, in the file cabinets, in the shelf on the closet, and in the desk should be taken out and heaped in the middle of the floor in exactly the same fashion that the students did with their joyous junk. When all of these materials are heaped up on the floor in the middle of the classroom, the teacher should repeat the previous assignment to her students, "Put this material in order and put it away so that we can get to it and be able to use it throughout the year." After giving such an assignment, most teachers will turn gratefully toward their desk, wipe tears away from the corners of their eyes, and begin to pray.

Since the students are now experts in organizing junk and putting it away, they begin quickly to work on this new school pile. The school pile of junk gradually disappears and moves back into a variety of places on shelves, in drawers, and under sinks. Since most of the materials that the school brings to bear in the learning situations are materials that have been designed for rather specific purposes, the students tend to organize these in much more specified fashions. The result is that they tend to go almost where the teacher would have put them anyway, but the real benefit is that the students know where all of these things are. The quickest test to determine whether or not the classroom has become an intrinsic environment comes when the teacher needs some particular device, such as a stapler. The odds are that the teacher will have to ask the students. From the standpoint of the distribution of materials within the classroom, the entire center of authority has been shifted. Rather than the teacher being the manager and the "supply sergeant," the students are the ones who not only know where the materials are but also have invented a rationale for putting them where they are.

The most important aspect of the attitude that has been created in the classroom is that decisions were made by means other than teacher rules and consensus. Some of the decisions undoubtedly were reached by consensus; that is, the students got together among themselves and resolved in small groups where certain materials should be placed. In other instances some children made individual and very specific decisions about where things should go. This is in almost direct opposition to standard classroom practice. In normal situations the teacher would tend to be most actively engaged in directing activities toward consensus. Within itself, consensus contains the seeds of extrinsic attitudes. By organizing children together into a speaking group and then requiring that the group set itself up in such a fashion that single decisions be reached, the individuals give up their identities and the authority they have created takes over. We have often been taught to believe that the so-called democratic form of behavior is our way of life. In situations where the only acceptable resolution is a common single decision, teachers often engineer the class into a position in which the teacher's initial point of view is the one that is being served. The children actually act as instruments of coercion and become convinced of the teacher's position; although, their own self-images and feelings of self-worth may be diminished in the process. From the very first day of class, if a teacher avoids any of these exercises to achieve consensus and avoids stepping into the role of consensus manager, a more highly intrinsic environment often will be created.

The intrinsic atmosphere of the classroom can also be heightened by a variety of other techniques. One of the most productive techniques seems to be the replacement of standard, institutional school furniture with materials that are much more like home. Surprisingly enough, except for very specialized furniture such as laboratory tables, potter's wheels, artist benches, drafting tables, sewing tables, and the furniture needed in woodworking and crafts, there is very little reason for the use of the kind of classroom furniture that prevails in schools. *Desks offer no particular benefits in most elementary school situations.* In fact, the existence of a desk provides a first-order kind of territorial claim to be established by the student. A child's attempts, then, to protect the particular trivial territory of his desk tend to result in a great deal of disciplinary hassle. Most elementary school teachers are fully aware of the fact that one of the greatest crimes committed against humanity is the bumping of one student's desk by another. The private ownership of desks in classrooms tends to create containers within containers. This in itself is a reinforcement of an extrinsic environment. To create an intrinsic environment the room must be thought of as a *single, unified environment* in which living and learning can take place. The elimination of the territorial characteristics of owning a desk makes the students seek out those particular places in the room in which they feel most comfortable at a given time. Those territorial places turn out to be useful to the student only when he is engaged in performing certain activities. He realizes that a space in the room does not belong specifically to him, it belongs to everyone; yet, he makes an internal decision to be able to go to that space whenever he needs to. In dozens of experiences that we have had with classroom furniture, we have concluded that a fluid, informal position makes for a more effective activity pattern and less tension and dispute between students.

Another method of serving and developing intrinsic motivation is through display areas that are essentially decoration centers run by and for the students. These specified areas, formerly called bulletin boards, can turn out to be anything that the students want them to be and can be different things at different times. Traditionally, teachers are so compelled to provide information on the bulletin boards that they have taken the full responsibility of selecting and displaying items that they — the teachers — regard to be of interest. We cannot judge the teachers too harshly on this subject since many of the methods courses that they were exposed to in college suggested that it is a grave crime against children for a teacher not to put up colorful and well-designed bulletin boards. However, the result is that another space in the already overly structured classroom is given to the teacher, and less and less belongs to the student. The "intrinsic" way to approach the general issue of space in the classroom is for the teacher to look at the entire area and find out how much of it can now be given completely to the students. The acts of putting away the junk, rearranging the school junk, and eliminating much of the furniture turns most of the area over to the students. Why not go one step further and turn the display area over to the students as well? This does not mean that the teacher assigns to the students the responsibility of putting up a display on the bulletin board because that would be virtually the same thing as the teacher making another extrinsic assignment. If an intrinsic attitude is the goal, then student responsibility for the display area should be treated in a manner consistent with that goal. Following such a strategy, the teacher can inform the students that the bulletin boards are available to them and that they can be used for anything that would foster communication with each other and the people who come into the room as long as it does not destroy the bulletin boards themselves. After this general announcement has been made and followed by a few encouraging remarks, the teacher should sit back and relax and wait all year, if necessary, before anything goes up on the bulletin board. Of course, the teacher should also be prepared to explain to any outsider who might wander in and look in bewilderment at what supposedly constitutes a classroom, the reasons for the lack of traditional bulletin board materials.

Decision making is a process that generally gets better the more you do it. In school, usually the only kinds of choices that most children make are whether or not to obey the teacher — a simple yes/no activity. Classically, in most elementary school classrooms virtually the only decision open to the children is whether they accept or reject a particular decision already made by the teacher. Then, when faced with the kind of freedom necessary for survival in secondary school (limited though it may be) the children very nervously portray to junior high school counselors that they are incapable of such simple activities as finding their lockers, picking up the proper books, or going to specific classes. Unfortunately, many educators who observe this adolescent apprehension feel that what is needed is more specificity and more precise training in the elementary school. It should be obvious from this discussion that such environmental detail and control is precisely what is *not* needed. *When children have never been allowed to make significant decisions, it is highly unlikely that they can make significant decisions.* Because of a lack of experience in decision making children often tend to defend the simplest and most limited area of personal control with a zeal that bewilders any adult who has attempted to communicate or influence that choice. The same zeal appears in older children who sense their lack of experience but nonetheless realize that it is impossible for adults to prevent them from making decisions. These children tend to make choices and then defend them with an almost blind tenacity. When adults judge children's choices, they speak of maturity, rationality, and appropriateness in such terms that they are really evaluating whether or not the children's decisions agree with theirs. Adult's concerns are based far more on the child's decision being in agreement with their own than on the validity of the child's decision in terms of his need, interests, and perceptions. In many regards they are concerned more with the child being "right" than in his learning how to make judgments.

It is obviously important for students at an early age to make significant decisions. The teacher interested in developing intrinsic motivation should provide an environment in which students make significant decisions concerning their course of action in school. One important way to facilitate such decision making is for the teacher to avoid developing situations in which simple yes/no, on/off, black/white or go/no go decisions can be made. All the teacher must do to facilitate decision making is be *ambiguous*. Although we know that this sounds like education heresy at this time when all quarters are calling for teacher accountability, we must keep in mind how students customarily act in the face of demands and structured assignments. Consider the following analogy. Imagine the difference between giving the students a canvas, some paints, and a brush and asking them to paint a picture and giving them a paint-by-numbers kit and asking them to paint a picture. Two different sorts of human involvement result. One requires invention within the constraints of the materials provided; the other requires obedience within the constraints of the materials provided. Invention is a very different quality from obedience. *Specificity nurtures obedience; ambiguity nurtures invention.*[2]

In a sense we are asking the teacher to take the significant portion of risk in the classroom and reduce the risk that the students have to take. In a classroom in which *extrinsic* control is imposed upon the students, the *teachers establish a very low risk situation.* The risk is low primarily because the teacher is in control and thus must do very little to accomodate to the needs and interests of students in her classroom. If a student is not performing in accord with her schedule and expectations, the teacher simply exerts a bit more pressure. Since the student has to comply or suffer the consequences, he is vulnerable and has to bear the risk of failure according to teacher demands. In an intrinsic classroom the risk is almost evenly divided; so, the students who share control with the teacher are also sharing the risk. When the risk is distributed in this fashion, the children are each taking much less risk than they did in the previous situation, and at the same time they are assuming greater responsibility.

Almost all of us tend to be able to perform much more effectively and creatively and much more happily when risk situations are moderate or low. Certainly high risk increases tension and anxiety and interferes with optimum performance. Since the benefits of moderate-to-low risks are true for adults, why not extend the same reasoning to children? Making a decision is a risk-taking enterprise (see Alschuler, Tabor, and McIntyre, chapter 8). The risk is heightened if the teacher behaves in an extrinsic fashion and evaluates and judges not only the student's decision but also the process by which he accomplishes the tasks related to that decision. To reduce the risk for the student the teacher must be able to sacrifice her preconceptions about what is right, good, and appropriate for the student. Instead, the teacher must operate as a helpful witness in the evolution of the student's maturity as he pursues the goals inherent in his own decision. The following anecdote portrays a situation in which the teacher simply followed the course of a specific decision made by the student. Note that the teacher never attempted to put the student back on his original track when he began exploring arenas of profound importance to him.

Vic seemed noticeably apprehensive when he blurted out, "We haven't written a report all year." It was October and school had begun only a month ago. The teacher with careful

---

2. Alternative approaches to the issue of structure and ambiguity are presented in Chapter 3 (Feldman), Chapter 4 (Coopersmith), and Chapter 2 (Eifermann).

deliberation said, "Well, write one if you want."

"About what?" the boy countered.

"What do you want to write it about?"

The question was the clincher. Before, Vic had always written reports because he was told to. Since he had not been told to, he assumed the teacher was derelict in her responsibilities. After asking the question about the report, his suspicions were confirmed. Once confronted his mind raced back into last year and dredged up a topic he had been assigned before. "Oil."

"Fine" the teacher said. "There must be plenty of information here." With that she waved her hand toward the bookshelves that lined the room and turned her attention to two younger girls contemplating a handful of pine cones in various states of disrepair.

Vic's interest in the report diminished, but his interest in oil grew with each resource book he checked. He discovered from a college chemistry book that oil is a hydrocarbon, that is, it is composed of hydrogen, carbon, and oxygen. Later the same day Vic waited patiently as the teacher finished helping two girls identify some flowers they had found on the campus. When she finished, Vic announced the chemical makeup of oil to the teacher. Then he told her he was "going to get some carbon, hydrogen, and oxygen and make some oil."

During the next several days he contacted a professor of geochemistry at the Colorado School of Mines and obtained a guarantee that he would be given the materials to embark on his chemical adventure. When the materials arrived, Vic was surprised to find labels on the bottles that read, "Mossy Zinc, Diluted Hydrocloric Acid, Candle," etc. Upon looking up each of these materials in the library, he found that in fact he did have everything he needed. All he had to do was separate them. Vic read a lot in the next week and spent much time trying to invent the needed laboratory apparatus out of baby food jars, plastic straws, and olive bottles. All the while he received sage consultation from the other class members who ranged in age from four to twelve. Vic was nine. Then, as was agreed upon by his research team, the separation of the chemicals was initiated. The teacher handed out safety glasses and work began. Younger children with spoons, knives, and spatulas gathered carbon out of the candle flames. Vic and others separated the hydrogen and oxygen out of acids and metals. As the materials began to accumulate, Vic decided that by mixing hydrogen and oxygen he could make water. Then by adding carbon to the water he could obviously make oil. The work feverishly continued. Soda water was made according to the text, *Fundamentals of College Chemistry*. The water was then triumphantly mixed with the carbon scraped from the spoons and spatulas. But the black fluid that resulted wasn't at all like oil. Several students ran to the shelves and produced mineral oil, olive oil, cooking oil, motor oil, and some sewing machine oil. Vic's oil didn't match up! After much discussion, it was decided that Vic had discovered ink.

Although this episode of Vic's exploration toward the discovery of oil indicates the sort of divergence that grows out of students' self-directed inquiry, we have found that teachers can give certain assignments that tend to nurture this same kind of exploration. The Environmental Studies Project has been working in several large cities with students from primarily inner-city situations. There have been four major areas of concern: change, mapping, counting, and judging. There is no specific reason why these four areas are any more or less virtuous than any other four. The reason for the decision to focus on these topics was simply that our level of funding limited what we could do, and these four seemed to be among the most fruitful ones to develop. With each of these topics the teacher's initial step is to provide the students with ambiguous assignments. We have been using instant photography in many of the assignments, primarily because it is such an excellent device to provide the student with a real sense of accomplishment and gratification. The use of inexpensive cameras and the 10 or 15 second film have proved to be highly effective and energizing for ages ranging from very young children all the way up to college professors. In all instances we found that although our observations were qualitative, all of the staff members were deeply impressed with the enhancement of personal accomplishment on the part of all people using these instant feedback documenting materials.

The ambiguous assignments given the students after they have received the instant camera equipment are varied. In order to develop the materials on change the assignment was "Go outside the school building and photograph evidence for change." For mapping, we asked the students to photograph the block on which the school was located from various places in the neighborhood. The second part of this assignment was to have the students display the photographs they had taken in such a fashion as to provide a portrait of the block. Counting did not require the use of instant photography, but the assignment was essentially, "Go outside and count something that allows you to know more about it after you count it." For judging we asked the students, "If the cameras are available, go outside and photograph four things you like and four things you don't like." The results have been consistently remarkable. We are convinced that the ambiguity of the assignments have resulted in the kind of creativity that the students have shown in fulfilling the task as they saw it. In addition to simply fulfilling the task, the ambiguity forced the students to determine what the task was. The lack of specific detailed instructions made it essential that the students make the decisions on their own. Upon making these decisions the students were remarkably impressed with *how difficult it was to be wrong.* With the specter of the clear "rightness" and "wrongness' removed from their experience, the students tended to move from rather trivial sorts of solutions to much more elaborate and sophisticated treatments. For instance, we were often tested by students who were attempting to "psych out" the assignment to photograph evidence for change by simply photographing other students in the class. When confronted by two photographs of two students, the teacher would ask the student how that constituted evidence for change. The student, fully expecting to be chastized for photographing fellow class members said, "There are different students in each picture." Students are usually surprised at the teacher's response which, in truth, has to be "That's right."

The use of ambiguous assignments has been attacked on many fronts by educators. The rationale for such attacks has generally been that students are confused, bewildered, and threatened by ambiguous assignments. In our experience, we have found the opposite to be the case. *Teachers* are confused, bewildered, and threatened by ambiguous assignments *because they always result in divergent behavior on the part of the students.* Many teachers are made quite nervous by children doing their own thing. Robert Karplus, a physicist teaching at the University of California, once talked about the neurotic condition among teachers he called *loosophobia.* He defined this condition as the teacher's fear of leaving loose ends — meaning that teachers are fearful when all of the students are not doing the same thing at the same time and will probably not reach the same conclusions. Rewarding the divergence of conclusions and the different means of reaching these divergent conclusions is an important condition of an intrinsic environment. Ambiguous assignments represent a procedure for gaining divergence of conclusions and means.

Rewarding Divergence
Since convergence is the style of rationality and rationality is highly

valued in our schools, little formal effort has been given to encouraging and rewarding differences in method or conclusion. Nearly all the psychologists engaged in research on creativity (see Sonntag, chapter 10) recognize that divergent thinking tends to result in more creative alternatives to the solution of a problem. Industry, government, and the arts have long rewarded people who can create new and alternative solutions to a single problem. It may well be that this appreciation of new alternatives has been largely responsible for the explosive technological growth of America. However, there is a counter-attitude that tends to prevail as well. It would appear that there are many people who view the production of creative alternatives as being virtuous but who think that once the alternatives have been created a single alternative should be selected and become the focus of attention thereafter. According to this attitude, it is OK to play around and come up with a lot of possible solutions, but sooner or later people need to "get down to business," pick the one solution that appears most effective, and commit themselves to that one. In effect, once a selection is made, it is often considered to be irresponsible to continue searching and trying out other, alternative solutions.

In most cases where divergence has been allowed to prevail in classrooms, it has generally been allowed only to the point at which first order decisions are made. A good example of this level of permissiveness is the science teacher who asks the students to pick a particular area on which they wish to research and report. Once the selection is made it is assumed that the student has been motivated by his own deep interests and that he will pursue the area in a dedicated manner. Once the student makes the selection teachers tend to act as if the student has become married to it and should forget other possibilities. Should the student later decide that he is not quite as interested in the topic "Life on Mars" as he is in the way that lichens grow, he will probably be confronted by a teacher who is upset by his lack of decisiveness and direction. If the teacher is even more upset, she may suggest that it is unscientific not to follow an investigation through to the end and that the student is obligated to do so.

Although this kind of hypocrisy is typical of environments that reward convergent and focused behavior, all one has to do is read some of the accounts of scientific discovery and artistic invention to find that truly creative work occurs in environments where divergence prevails. Thus if students produce eight or ten alternative solutions to a given problem, the odds are that far more mature and sophisticated solutions will be reached than under conditions where a single, convergent answer is sought and achieved.

An important attribute of divergence is that, like the piles of junk heaped on the classroom floor, students are capable of creating their own relationships and categories. In an essay written in the *Colorado Quarterly*, David Hawkins, a philosopher of science at the University of Colorado, once likened a true course of inquiry to the activity of climbing a tree. Hawkins pointed out that whereas most school activities are created in a step-by-step ladderlike fashion, a branching treelike structure is far more interesting and fruitful. When divergence prevails in a classroom, we have actually created a situation where several different branches have emerged and developed from a common trunk. Students who explore each of the branches on their own sense that they are still dealing with the same structure. They can look at each other and realize that the alternatives being explored by the other students somehow relate to what they are doing. Stemming from a common assignment that permits individual exploration, intellectual atmosphere is more apt to create relatedness than separateness. Remember, there is a greal deal of difference between these two assignments: "Write a report," and "Present evidence for change." The specificity of "Write a report," requires adherence in format and mode of presentation and tends to limit the divergence of anything except content. In the assignment, "Present evidence for change," the content is infinitely variable; even more than that, the concept of the presentation is remarkably variable. If all of the students in a class are simultaneously working on the assignment, "Write a report," there is no certainty that what they are doing individually will have any interest or relevance to the activities of other students. If, on the other hand, the students are simultaneously working on determining evidence for change, there will probably be a commonality of interest on how change is treated by others despite the divergent approaches to that topic.

Signposts Along the Intrinsic Path

At the risk of appearing to adopt a format common to most education textbooks, the following one-line expressions are presented as a list of ideas. In a society in which slogans tend to determine a great deal of what we do, a new set of slogans has to be invented to counteract the convergent tendencies of the cliches of the past. Traditional expressions like "the devil finds work for idle hands," "practice makes perfect," and "put your nose to the grindstone," and such admonitions as "be reasonable," "that's a perfectly logical solution," and "don't mix business and pleasure" seem to have created attitudes that each of us has inherited from society. Very often we find that the societal context of education is very different from the human or individual context of education. When society, by its very structure, creates bell-shaped curves of expected performance and behavior, many educators attempt to create instructional situations in which bell-shaped curves will emerge. Teachers often *assume* that because they are creating situations in classrooms that conform to certain conditions of society, e.g., ability, motivation, and competition, that they are in fact serving society. What they are actually serving is a coercive kind of conformity that exists in some societies and in some parts of our society. This does not make conformity desirable nor does it produce effective students. The educational cliche that schools are invented to perpetuate a society has biased a great number of teachers into *thinking in terms of groups instead of individuals*. This attitude has allowed people to think of motivation as an act that teachers can *perform* instead of as a quality that students *possess*. The result has been that we as teachers have asked students in groups to accomplish goals we set up and then have been disheartened by their lack of energy. According to this analogy student lack of motivation is an indication of our poor performance as teacher-motivator, rather than a deficiency of the students. To shift the responsibility from the teacher of groups to the teacher of individual student requires a considerable change in basic assumptions about teaching. I have found the five assumptions that follow provocative and useful. (They were first published in *The Biology Teacher* in the spring of 1970.) A teacher who is willing to look at herself openly and is interested in developing intrinsic motivation in her students should find the students personally and professionally rewarding.

1. The student (at any level) is a reservoir of relevant experience.
2. The student is capable of making decisions about what happens to him.
3. The student knows the difference between relevant things and nonsense.
4. It is more important for the student to sense and know himself than anything else.
5. Once the student trusts the environment to provide a realization of all the previous assumptions, he generally will learn far more capably than he did before.

Now, let us consider and examine these assumptions more closely.

1. *The student is a reservoir of relevant experience.* Students are about six years old when they come to the schools. This is six years of

experience in *LIFE!* The unstructured or self-structured universe of experience they bring to the classroom far outweighs the curriculum for the year. By rewarding the student for drawing upon *his* experience, a teacher provides him with the experience of being an authority. He *is* an authority about what he knows. This is a vital step in establishing a positive and constructive self-image.

2. *The student is capable of making decisions about what happens to him.* In extrinsic coercion situations all decisions are made for the student. A democratic form of extrinsic coercion is realized when the student is given the option to choose between alternatives that the teacher (or curriculum maker) provides. The element of choosing between someone else's alternatives is often confused with intrinsic decision making. Real intrinsic decision making means that the student must make choices between alternatives *he* creates. This requires that the student have some control in determining what he does in school.

3. *The student knows the difference between relevant things and nonsense.* To a black student in Detroit or Watts, the people of his own race who were killed in race riots are highly relevant, and their deaths not merely incidents. To these children the rebellious Bostonians killed at the Boston Massacre are shadowy, irrelevant figures. When teachers attempt to lionize the mythology of the one act with children who have recently experienced the other, they can create an unreal, distorted, and nonsensical environment. Even more significant than the exhibition of irrelevancy and mythology is the cruelty exhibitied by tests that punish the child for refusing to accept the curriculum's message as well as its content. The intrinsic punishment the child feels when he *pretends* to accept these myths is humiliating and likely to result in a lessened credibility of the entire educational system.

4. *It is more important for the student to sense and know himself than anything else.* Life is lived by each of us. The worth of the enterprise is a personal thing. We can be what we want to be with real pride if we know our capacities are in line with our aspirations. In extrinsically coercive environments the student learns to exert himself in the name of someone else's aspirations. As a result, his potential toward goals *he* sets may or may not be realized. Many studies show that students who know themselves do better than students who do not. In a life situation the fondest hope that each of us can realize is to develop a realistic set of aspirations and to move toward them with the degree of progress directly proportional to our capacity to perform.

5. *Once the student trusts the environment to provide a realization*

of all the previous assumptions, he generally will learn far more capably than he did before. This last assumption is by far the most comprehensive because it embodies all the others and extends them into the arena of learning. Trust is the key word in this assumption. If an honest effort born of real involvement in the first four assumptions is attempted, then learning will be realized. This realization is not an empty hope. The Nuffield Infant School (i.e., Open School) approach in England has years of experience to testify to the validity of this idea. Intellectualization and skill development are inevitable when children feel secure with themselves and their environment. The entire human condition is served when institutions exist for the purpose of serving individuals instead of individuals existing to serve institutions.

It may be noted that each of these assumptions is highly ambiguous. If so, they are in direct contrast to the kind of specific objectives, behavioral or content, that generally prescribe the teacher's attitudinal framework in classrooms. This is intentional and in fact necessary.

If an intrinsic environment is to prevail, the specificity of extrinsic objectives cannot exist. For intrinsic motivation to prevail in the classroom, teachers must give up coercive and manipulative techniques. Such techniques can, as indicated earlier, be derived from the teacher's basic personality or from the teacher's response toward extrinsic pressures, such as the biases of teacher training, the biases of the curriculum, and the biased pressure from authority figures within the school. All of these potential influences are quite easy to recognize if the teacher *wants* to recognize them. If the teacher recognizes them and *wants* to get rid of them, it is possible to do. The fundamental responsibility of the teacher who claims to want to establish an environment of intrinsic motivation is to create an environment in which intrinsic motivation can grow and flourish. Only the teacher can create that environment.

WHAT DOES IT ALL MEAN?

Marshall McLuhan said that today's youths want *roles* not *goals*. The very nature of the attitudes toward motivation and stimulation presented in this paper is embodied within the context of his statement. When McLuhan uses the word "role," we have to remember that he is not talking about a pretense or a mimicking of some external quality. He is talking about the invention of a quality of action that is created by a person when he becomes involved in the process of learning or living. When he says today's youths want roles, he means they want to be part of the action, not simply poor actors mimicking a playwright's ideas and attitudes. In education we have not allowed students to be part of the action; instead we have imposed extrinsic goals. We generally have been paying lip service to the quality of human drive that we call motivation. If motivation is an expression of our inner capacities and aspirations, then the creation of environments in which this motivation will flourish requires drastic changes in our educational strategies and tactics. As indicated in the previous pages, I firmly believe that these changes are possible. However, in order to create such motivational environments teachers will have to reexamine and restructure the training that led to their present ideas and procedures. In addition, teachers must create material environments that are compatible with the motivations they say they want. They also will have to assess their *own* personality characteristics in an attempt to remove personal prejudices that might retard the development of intrinsic motivation. Such an analysis and attempt to create a motivational environment requires that the teacher become aware of the obstacles to that environment that exist in them as well as other faults of the educational system. If a teacher has been trained in biology, for example, he must realize that his training has probably biased him and caused him to eliminate certain alternatives and employ certain views as final. If a teacher's preservice training in psychology was primarily in the work of cognitive psychologists, the teacher must realize that cognitive psychology may bias him away from considering the importance of affect, awareness, and involvement. If in his preservice educational training he was exposed to such procedures as modular scheduling and audio-tutorial instruction, the teacher might consider that these ideas may limit and bias him in his posture as to what are effective and desirable methods of increasing student interest.

Creating motivational environments is hard work primarily because it asks the teacher to give up postures that the abundance of training, experience, and instructional management in schools now reward. The safety of stimulation may be more than many can turn away from, but, nonetheless, we cannot appease ourselves and talk about how we *can* motivate. We can only allow and help motivational environments to exist. *To do this the teacher must give up control.* By giving up control the teacher can establish the most appropriate control of all, and this is the kind of "control" that we should be encouraging. This is the kind of control that leaves the classroom within the psyche of each student because the *student has learned how to create within himself a control system that will guide him through life.*

6
Process Education
and the Needs of Young Children

Bonita Burgess and Terry Borton
Philadelphia Board of Education

INTRODUCTION

Today's teacher is bombarded by a mass of innovative changes encouraging her to stand up and be counted for a more open, more humanistic, more relevant kind of education. Often she is made to feel that she must run in a popularity contest or feel something less than human. She faces the school reality too. She has a curriculum to teach and her regular classroom administration work to complete. Of course, she is also required to know what every child is accomplishing and to be able to specify the particular materials and procedures that will be effective for each of her students.

On the other side of the desk, the student faces realities too. What is life in the classroom like for him? Philip Jackson's book *Life in Classrooms*[1] describes it as follows:

> The characteristics of school life to which we now turn our attention are not commonly mentioned by students, at least not directly, nor are they apparent to the casual observer. Yet they are as real, in a sense, as the unfinished portrait of Washington that hangs above the cloakroom door. They comprise three facts of life with which even the youngest student must learn to deal and may be introduced by the key words: *crowds, praise,* and *power.*

1. Philip W. Jackson, *Life in Classrooms* (New York: Holt, Rinehart, & Winston, Inc., 1968), pp. 10-11.

Learning to live in a classroom involves, among other things, learning to live in a crowd. This simple truth has already been mentioned, but it requires greater elaboration. Most of the things that are done in school are done with others, or at least in the presence of others, and this fact has profound implications for determining the quality of a student's life.

Of equal importance is the fact that schools are basically evaluative settings. The very young student may be temporarily fooled by tests that are presented as games, but it doesn't take long before he begins to see through the subterfuge and comes to realize that school, after all, is a serious business. It is not only what you do there but what others think of what you do that is important. Adaptation to school life requires the student to become used to living under the constant condition of having his words and deeds evaluated by others.

School is also a place in which the division between the weak and the powerful is clearly drawn. This may sound like a harsh way to describe the separation between teachers and students, but it serves to emphasize a fact that is often overlooked, or touched upon gingerly at best. Teachers are indeed more powerful than students in the sense of having greater responsibility for giving shape to classroom events, and this sharp difference in authority is another feature of school life with which students must learn how to deal.

In three major ways then — as members of crowds, as potential recipients of praise or reproof, and as pawns of institutional authorities — students are confronted with aspects of reality that at least during their childhood years are relatively confined to the hours spent in classrooms. Admittedly, similar conditions are encountered in other environments. Students, when they are not performing as such, must often find themselves lodged within larger groups, serving as targets of praise or reproof, and being bossed around or guided by persons in positions of higher authority. But these kinds of experiences are particularly frequent while school is in session and it is likely during this time that adaptive strategies having relevance for other contexts and other life periods are developed.

These realities of classroom life — crowds, praise, and power — exert an influence over both teacher and students. If they are never examined explicitly, as they usually are not, they may exert a profound effect upon what is learned in school. If they are examined, and if a method is found for working with them, then the realities of classroom experience can become the stuff through which students learn to become more conscious of themselves, and more in control of their own minds. This bringing together of personal reality and conscious knowledge lies at the heart of the various approaches we will describe here.

The particular effects of "crowds" or "praise" or "power" may change depending on whether the class is "authoritarian" or "open structure," but Jackson's point is that these factors are always operating whenever kids and adults are together in a teaching situation, and that the kids are somehow learning to cope with the concerns that are generated. These concerns cover a wide range. Children are concerned about having order in their lives, about justice and injustice, about their bodies, how they grow and why, why they become ill, why they daydream, whether people like them, whether they can learn like the other children, whether their teacher is mean, and whether they will ever have power over their lives. "I wish I were a teacher; then I could do whatever I want to."

The variety and intensity of student concerns was dramatized for us when a class pretended that they were going to the moon and had to choose five out of eight people to go on the spaceship with them. A series of pictures were put around the room, a nurse, a teacher, a policeman, a father, a mother, a crippled girl, a fat woman, and a nun. Nearly every child chose to leave the nurse, teacher, and fat woman behind. Their reasons were as follows:

The nurse gives needles and that scares them, the teacher would not need to go because the nun could be a teacher and she is kind too, and the fat woman would eat too much and there would not be enough food for everyone else. It was particularly interesting to us that the children felt the need for the nun who would be a teacher and a religious comfort. The crippled girl was taken because "you can't leave somebody like that behind — she can't take care of herself." We would not have predicted that children had this sort of concern. That is the point — our children have lots of concerns — many are obvious and many not so obvious. What we are attempting to do is to locate them and then to find ways to help students handle their own needs.

How can students be taught to deal with their own inner problems as well as those (such as reading and math) that are usually taught in school? The approach we have evolved is one that makes explicit the processes through which people perform their daily interactions. Most of us, most of the time, are not used to examining our own behavior — we simply do what we do, and that is the end of it. The same is true for children. A curriculum that makes them aware of what they are doing gives them control over their own behavior and allows them to generate alternatives for themselves. Thus, as we shall see later, the child who is concerned for justice can learn how to perform a variety of processes that help to produce a just solution, i.e., gathering evidence, using witnesses, providing an impartial judge. When he knows how to perform a series of actions to get what he wants, he has gained a very immediate control over the world which can then be extended to other areas.

To teach processes to young children, our first job was to make them aware that a process was a way of doing something and that using the right process could produce the desired result. We began this process of producing awareness with a brief discussion about other processes they use everyday: walking, eating, going to bed, coming to school, putting things away, and all of the many everyday activities. The children began discussing the processes that would be necessary to make an instant pudding — the ingredients for which were spread before them. They discussed what subprocesses they might have to use to get the job done. While they were making the pudding the class had to "freeze" periodically to identify the process they were performing at that time. The kids liked this activity and, of course, they got to eat the pudding. Afterward the class played a game. "What Is My Process?" The children volunteered to act out a process, and their classmates had to identify it and act it out with them.

Processes that are useful for handling children's concerns are not usually as clear and precise as those in making a pudding. Let us take the concern for justice and injustice. One method or process for handling this concern is to get up a judicial system for the classroom. Children will be taught a process for setting up rules to handle conflict situations. The test of the process is whether the process works. If it does not, whether in the "pudding-making process" or the "establishing-justice process," then the process must be reexamined, and a new one tried. This examination of the intended effect of a process, contrasted with the actual effect, provides the feedback information through which the student can learn more about the processes he is using.

In our discussion so far we have concentrated on those processes that are most directly related to a child's concerns. However, there is wide applicability for the approach of making a child aware of the processes he is using and consciously improving these by examining the feedback he receives on the effectiveness of his actions. Process courses are highly developed in the fields of science and mathematics, where the most advanced curriculum work has been done.

The general advantages of this process approach are the following:

1. *Process learning can bridge the gap between the cognitive (intellectual) areas and the affective (emotional) areas.* There seems to be a gap between the student and subject matter. Yet, subject matter is only the product of other men developing and employing processes that are like those the student has available to him. Process learning is an attempt to connect the private world of the student with the public world of subject matter, to pull out the processes in man's experiences and to use these processes to connect these worlds.

2. *It is obvious that knowledge is no longer a stable thing and that we as educators cannot possibly teach all the content that there is to know.* The typical physical theory goes out of date in about ten years. Ninety percent of the products on the market today were not around ten years ago. On the same day that you teach a certain fact, television often disproves it. Process teaching is appropriate in these times of "knowledge explosion" because it can teach children to be more independent learners. It helps to facilitate the adjustment to change, and it has greater transfer value.

3. *Process learning can be used for self-exploration.* Folk societies were less complicated than those of the city. Their patterns of life were relatively clear. The complexities of our society cause many anxieties, and the process approach allows a way to deal with these anxieties. Children with anxieties can, through a process such as pretending, learn to become an animal or object in order to express a feeling. Use of this process can make the situation less threatening since it can allow the student to safely explore it "in his mind." Such techniques can be helpful to the teacher because they can reach many children at once and give them the tools for their own learning. It relieves the teacher of the impossible burden that many of us carry — to reach every student every day, in a personal way. The process approach allows the students to reach themselves and each other.

TEACHER CONCERNS

The teacher's goal to help her students gain increased awareness and understanding of their feelings applies equally well to the teacher herself. Much as she focuses on how to give her students increasingly sophisticated processes for dealing with *their* concerns about themselves and the outer world, she should also recognize and respect the importance of those processes and concerns within herself. All too often in the press of assuring that classroom activities proceed in an orderly and effective manner, teachers fail to express how deeply they care about their students. The teacher's conviction that she has "made a difference" — even with a few students — reassures her that education is something more complex, fundamental, and human than training students to recite poems or solve problems. Ultimately, what the teacher has to give that cannot be given by any machine, book, or teaching materials is herself — her love for life, her enthusiasm for what she teaches, and her ability to respond to her students. Unhappily, these virtues of teachers are not frequently expressed in schools. All too often, even the well-intentioned teachers are bores and their classes are dull and mechanical. Needless to say, some teachers are not well-intentioned — some are incompetent, some are petty, and some gain pleasure from their tyranny over students, but the vast majority of teachers are good people who want to do a good job. If they do not succeed, it is partly because they are locked in a system that denies them their own humanity and the opportunity to give of themselves.

Within the recent past a barrage of books and studies has documented the devastating effects of such a system. Among these we can note John Holt's *How Children Fail* which describes the immediate fear that children feel in public and even private progressive schools. Peter Schrag's depressing account of big city schools in *Village School Downtown* is dramatized by Jonathan Kozol's attack on schools' racism and brutality in *Death at an Early Age.* Herbert Kohl's descriptions of qualified success in teaching his *36 Children* in New York was matched on the West Coast by James Herndon's year of teaching described in *The Way It Spozed To Be.* All of these books are united in attacking what Mario Fantini and Gerald Weinstein in *The Disadvantaged* call "the phony school" and "the irrelevant curriculum," and all of them wince, roar, and weep at what is happening to kids.

Added to these personal evaluations was the massive government report on "Equality of Education Opportunity" conducted by Dr. James Coleman of John Hopkins University. This study surveyed 600,000 children to determine what factors in the school affected student achievement. When the statistical analysis was completed, Coleman concluded that of all the factors studied "including all measures of family background and all school variables these attitudes [interest in school, self-concept, and sense of control] showed the strongest relation to achievement at all three grade levels." Coleman's findings mean that all the money spent for teaching devices, higher salaries, and fancy buildings are unlikely to result in marked improvements in student learning. What will produce such improvements are apparently the procedures that give students a high self-concept and greater sense of control. To effect such procedures notable changes will be required in our school system. Among such changes is the requirement that the teachers begin to look at the concerns of their students, that they try to find out what the youngsters are feeling and doing when they are not made to do what teachers want them to. This is not an easy thing to do since students rapidly learn that they must be guarded in what they do in the classroom and sensitive to what the teachers want them to do. Teachers who encourage students to express themselves are rare, but they are on the road to gaining involvement and motivation from their students.

Some teachers turned to "freedom classes" where the kids could do whatever they wanted. These efforts seem to reflect a confusion between love and freedom. The teachers wanted to express their love for their students, but not knowing how to teach love, they gave freedom in its place. Some students may have needed such freedom, but more needed help and guidance; they wanted their teachers to teach and not to emancipate them from the underlying structure and concerns of life. Weinstein and Fantini[2] have organized a model for developing courses around the basic concerns of students. In this model they seek ways to direct lessons toward the shared, yet personal, concerns of an entire class. Weinstein and Fantini make two major distinctions on how student feelings can be constructively employed in the classroom. First, they are more interested in exploring the more basic and persistent needs, anxieties and pressures of their students than in temporary interests and fads. Thus, student interests in cars might be properly explored in terms of understanding power rather than a study of new models in "souped up hot rods." Secondly, Weinstein and Fantini do not see the classroom as a place to solve personal problems or a locale for providing group therapy for youth. They focus instead on finding ways of directing lessons towards the common personal concerns of their students. That focus is defined in terms of three broad areas of concerns: "relationship" (connectedness), "self-identity," and "control." By relationship they mean the student's sense of the relation between himself, other people, and the world. By self-identity they mean the student's sense of himself. By control they mean the student's sense of his ability to make himself felt in the world. These broad areas are regarded as legitimate and useful sources of involving students in the educational process and providing teachers with a means of focusing and utilizing their own concerns for their students. This focus on concerns requires that the

---

2. Gerald Weinstein and Mario Fantini, *A Model for Developing Relevant Curriculum*, Ford Foundation Publication (New York: Praeger, 1970).

student become more aware of his own feelings, motives, and actions in the course of fostering his own growth.

PRINCIPLES OF APPLICATION

The basic teaching strategy for utilizing student concerns is a process approach. This approach is used to create an environment in which the student can experience himself using a process, then step back and examine the implications of what he is doing, and then apply the new process knowledge gained from that exchange. Using the kids' colloquial language, we have called this the *What, So What, Now What* sequence. A description of each phase in this sequence follows:[3]

What

An experience causes the student to make a response in a situation where he can be helped to examine its actual and intended effects and the kinds of concerns which it raises. The experience should involve things which are close to the student and raise concerns in a very direct fashion, or the process to be taught will seem an obvious cliché with no importance. If the experience is a 'hot' one which gets kids talking about what is important, then the teacher has an opening onto a deeper level and can show kids how the processes can be used to help work out their concerns. It is vital not to duck concerns about race, sex, power, or anything else that students find important. If the process will not work on the things that concern them, then they will never believe that it is worth learning, and they may well be right.

The What phase of a lesson often produces a good deal of fun and uproar — if the experience is a good one, the kids will be involved in it, and that probably means they will be talking and laughing. But contemplation and analysis cannot be conducted in such a setting. Quiet down the classroom for the So What stage. The transition between the What and So What will be easier for the students to take seriously if the teacher makes it clear ahead of time that the rules for the class are going to change during the hour. There is no reason why a process education need be chaotic. Students should use the freedom of

---

3. Terry Borton, *Reach, Touch, and Teach* (New York: McGraw-Hill Book Company, 1970), pp. 95-98.

the What experience for a purpose, not for horsing around, and they are perfectly capable of understanding this distinction if the teacher means it. The transition to the So What stage will go more effectively if the stepping aside from fun and uproar is dramatic and physical. For instance, the seating pattern can be changed to a tight circle with the teacher taking a prominent position, there can be clear rules for discussion, one at a time, hand raising, etc.

So What

The So What stage is close to what a good teacher might normally do with an English or social studies class, except that the focus of attention is the experience which the students have just had. The So What stage is rational, intellectual, cognitive — a delving into the meaning of what has just happened as that meaning is interpreted through the many different value systems of the students in the class. In the So What stage it is particularly useful to employ two different modes of approaching a problem — analysis and contemplation. Analysis is useful because it clarifies meaning and intention, but it must be used sparingly. An incessant "Well, so what?" can dissect a feeling, a value, or a rational structure to the point of disintegration. Contemplation allows a more relaxed approach to the problem, where values and meanings are allowed to suggest themselves rather than be driven into a corner.

Now What

The Now What phase is the most difficult of all and requires the greatest skill from the teacher. Here the teacher must take the concerns which were raised earlier (slightly different for every class), mesh them with the analysis of those concerns which the students have made (different again), and then show the students how an application of a particular process can help them work through a concern.

The advantage of having a clearly defined process is that it gives the students somewhere to go with their concern — it does not open the kid up and then leave him hanging as do so many attempts to "get at" kids. The disadvantage of a precise process objective is the necessity to make the process explicit and then join that neat little abstraction to a huge messy mass of concern.

The more explicit the process, the more helpful it is. There are a number of ways to specify such processes. One of the simplest is to draw upon personal experience, by thinking back to ways in which you yourself have worked out difficult problems, and then generalize. In the academic fields, Jerome Bruner's idea about "the structure of the disciplines" suggests a number of processes which can be used to understand new material. Similarly, psychologists can catalog a variety of different processes which people find useful in dealing with social or personal changes. Works of literature, particularly auto-biographies such as those of Benjamin Franklin and Malcolm X, contain many examples of men learning by insight and then applying that insight consciously to new situations. Finally, the students themselves are excellent sources of information about the kinds of processes which they need, or already have and can teach others. These various sources might suggest such diverse possibilities as generating negative categories, hypothesizing, reducing to single variables, reducing to first principles, second guessing, backing into a corner, flipping out, and analyzing function.

Once the process is clearly identified and understood by the students in an intellectual form and its meaning for them is analyzed and discussed, they should experiment with using it. Experimentation with a new process should be done first in class, where there is the support of the rest of the group for trying out new behaviors, and then in as many different situations as possible. The more situations that students see a process can be useful in, the more wholeheartedly they are likely to try it themselves. Finally, if the student is going to utilize the process in real life, he will need to practice using it there. "Homework," in a process curriculum, is working on the process at home. Students should be encouraged to specify what applications of a process they want to make to their own lives. The class and the teacher can help to make sure that these applications are reasonable and can act as a support group later to check upon students, help them reassess, etc. Without specific goal setting, support, and follow-up, there is little likelihood of change.

This "What, So What, Now What" format can be adopted to help define a wide range of curricula — newly written materials, other current curricula packages, and lessons that are improvised in the classroom. There are, in this regard, several curricular implications from a process approach to education. When we think of concerns as *ways* of experiencing rather than *what* is experienced we have begun building a "curriculum of concerns." Such a curriculum would teach students new ways of experiencing and obtaining feedback and place lesser importance upon the particular subject matter that is being taught. Another implication is to take the curriculum out of the past and move it into the present, immediate reality. Teachers have little ability to influence the student's past and relatively little influence on the present that exists outside the classroom. The teacher's greatest impact on his students is on those events that occur right in his classroom every day. Another curriculum implication of process education is that which does not rely on the teacher's manipulation of reinforcement categories. Reinforcement is used when appropriate, but the major focus is based on the child's conscious awareness of what is happening and how he considers his options and alternatives. This ability to see himself more fully, objectively, and perspectively is a prime force in helping the child gain a new vision of how he can deal with his life.

The purpose of a curriculum of process concerns is to turn the information processing system in on itself and to thereby increase the student's understanding of how he handles information. The "What?" part of the processing system is geared to sensing; the "So What?" to transforming that information into patterns of meaning; the "Now What?" to deciding on how to act in the best alternative and reapply it in other situations. This sensing, transforming, and acting sequence is designed to make students more aware of how they function as human beings.

DESIGNING YOUR OWN CURRICULUM

The What, So What, Now What model for process education is a means for gaining the self-knowledge that has long been advocated by the great sages of history. The model provides an organized way of increasing awareness (What), evaluating intention (So What), and experimenting with new behavior (Now What).

Although the model suggests how to build lessons that lead to greater control of the sensing, transforming, and acting processes, it is still very general. It means little to teach a student to sense better or act better without specifying the processes that are to be taught. Since our focus is on how the teacher can base a curriculum on *her* student's concerns we have kept the examples in this chapter at a fairly high level of generality. We have sought to give some general rules of methodology and a sense of how processes can be taught rather than a discussion of specific lessons.

In general it is important to recognize that the What, So What,

Now What sequence represents a fluid process rather than a set of discrete, segregated steps. For that reason it is confusing to think of clear, definite "beginnings," "middles" and "ends." Start where the students are and pick up the other parts of the process as they become appropriate. "If the sequence no longer seems helpful in a real situation, then abandon theory and follow intuition. The model, after all, grew out of attempts to systematize intuition; its validity does not rest on empirical or scientific proof but on its usefulness in real strategy. When the model does not prove useful, change it." [4]

Moving to classroom implications and practices, we turn to a specific elementary curriculum relevant to this discussion. We have titled that curriculum *The Living Classroom* for two important reasons. First, it emphasizes the process approach that requires action. Secondly, it suggests the need to connect the student's world with the public world — his home, his playground, his family, and his school. We chose to do this through the study of social/political issues that contain past, present, and future issues. In traditional terms, these issues are usually studied under the subjects of social science, civics, or government. However, we would rather refer to it as relationship. A government, in very simple terms, really implies an understanding among its citizens that includes interaction, rights, and responsibilities. It therefore seems appropriate to use this content area for three reasons:

1. Social/political issues require action, and this is the foundation for process learning and democracy.
2. Social/political issues proved to be a traditional and natural habitat to facilitate the connection between the cognitive and affective areas. Process learning aims to do the same.
3. Social/political issues focus on interactions, rights, and responsibilities. These areas seem to be salient concerns of children.

In *The Living Classroom,* we see each student as a natural problem solver who needs to be sensitive to his thoughts and ideas. He is at first required to sense and question not only others but also himself. The student is to question the what, why, and how of things and to realize that his questions will direct him to his concerns, a problem, or an interest. It is noteworthy that in this sequence the student *locates* the processes and concerns by his questions rather than by his direct experiences. Just as a scientist's way of life is inquiry, the goal for our students is to have a well-informed mind equipped to continuously

---

4. *Ibid.*

renew itself and be able to confront issues. Questioning is the most effective way to do the job. First, the students must learn to question, to formulate questions, and to seek answers to their questions. A more advanced stage would be to learn to order questions. What we are actually claiming is that one important part of sensing is how to ask questions because the questions that we ask limit what we can discover.

No day seems more appropriate than the first day of school to begin the questioning process. On that day you (the teacher) and the children probably have a multitude of questions that are indicative of concerns, fears, or interest for the coming year. The very first day is a time to learn to begin sensing, to utilize the interests and concerns that already exist as a basis for helping children learn how to ask. As we see below, the teacher utilizes the existing interests in a spontaneous unplanned type of exercise.

PROCESS: SENSING

What	*Class Activity*
Children and teacher are given the experience to reveal their concerns in a less threatening way by questioning.	Greet the children on the first day of school. Point out that you and they must have many questions about the new school year.
Teacher breaks the ice by expressing some of her concerns.	Write down one of your questions.
Teacher demonstrates her concerns by using the inquiry term "curious."	Write on the paper after you say something like, "I am very curious about all of you and about what we'll be doing this year."
Plan prepares the children for thinking about the year's activity.	List children's questions on the chart paper.
This running chart of concerns will be kept until the end of the year to evaluate the year's activities and how their concerns, What, were met.	Answer those questions which can be answered now.

So What

Through questioning, children should realize the benefits of the process.

They were not alone in their concerns.

The teacher has concerns.

Questioning brings forth information.

Questioning focuses on concerns.

Class Activity

Use questions that will facilitate a discussion about their questions.

1. Did you think we'd have so many questions?
2. Why do you suppose we had so many?
3. Did anyone have the same questions as you?
4. What do many of the questions want to know about?
5. Do you know a lot more about our class now that we've answered many of our questions?
6. Do you feel any differently about our class and our first day of school now that we've answered some of the questions?

Now What

Children will use this part of the lesson to use the questioning process.
Teacher will need to start off the activity. Then the children will take over to find the wealth of information that can be gotten from asking questions.

Class Activity

Explain to the children, "We've brought up many questions we have about our new class. We've talked about how they can help us learn about each other. We have spent some time answering these questions together. For some of them we'll need time before we can have the answers." (It is important to give an example from the paper, i.e., "Will I do better in reading?" or "Will I like my teacher?") Right now I have an activity which will help us find out something about questions.

Write one sentence on the black board such as:

"The teacher walked in."

Explain to the class that you will tell them anything they want to know about the sentence if they ask you questions. (Do not offer information beyond what each question asks and do not give information if the child has not asked a question.)

When finished, ask the children:

How did you find out so much about the sentence?
Why did you ask more questions?
Why was it helpful to have so many questions?
How were your questions answered?

Use sentences that involve people and social issues. If at first children cannot think of their own sentences help them. Emphasis is on the questioning process. And more importantly, asking questions about that which *concerns* you.

This lesson is followed by a series of lessons using the questioning process. The children play questioning games, they make an analogy with animals that question themselves in order to survive, they question their surroundings, and they question social/political interactions as people-watchers.

Many people have inquired about why we emphasized the questioning process because they see children as natural curiosity seekers.

We believe that questioning is a natural part of us and that we need only to make our children increasingly aware of this process, be aware of its use, and encourage them to use it to their advantage. After using some of these lessons we found that children do become aware of their ability to ask questions and its importance. The harder part of the process is to get them to ask more useful questions and to order them in a more effective sequence. We are not sure about just how to successfully accomplish this.

Another kind of lesson we teach involves the process of pretending. We use this process as a research tool for locating data and feelings. We do not exclude other processes, but we want to make children realize that they possess, in their private worlds, a process that can help them to make connections with the outside world of subject matter.

Pretending takes on the body, mind and feelings; it puts the student right into the action of things. It is part of the easygoing, contemplative way to thinking that allows the student to employ the nonanalytical as well as the analytical levels of the mind. Most importantly, pretending can make things that are strange to children familiar, and things that are familiar can be made strange to them. History, for example, can become real; threatening situations can become less threatening by taking on another role.

Creating a spectrum is another process for locating action possibilities. It involves the charting, or laying out, of alternatives so that a decision can be made.

In summary, *The Living Classroom* challenges its students with the problem of setting up a relationship in the classroom that will be viable for all. The students are taught some necessary processes to accomplish this task, and then they are charged with the responsibility to carry over their plan. A game is established in order to provide a check-and-balance system for the purpose of achievement and progress. A commitment to this plan will help answer these questions of concerns: Who am I? What can I do about things? Who am I connected to? How do I fit into the scheme of things?

For educational purposes, the conscious use of metaphors can make two kinds of contribution to students. They can absorb and apply substantive knowledge, and secondly, they can describe their internal and external world in personal and inventive terms.[5]

A group of lower elementary children were inquiring about how the brain works, how they learn, and how they remember things. The lesson below was used to introduce a process that helped us to learn more about this complicated part of our bodies. As will be noted, the behavior actually occurs before the children discuss it. This sequence,

5. W.J.J. Gordon, T. Poze, and M. Reid, *The Art of the Possible* (Cambridge, Massachusetts: Synectics Education Systems, 1969).

rather than a discussion before the behavior, brings the child's senses, feelings, and meanings into the immediate teaching situation.

PROCESS: TRANSFORMING

Explanation of Sequence

What

Children play a game (Simple Simon) that reveals some of the complexities of the mind. They really want to win the game, but something happens.

Class Activity

Let's play a game called *Simple Simon* to learn something about what happens between our senses and the brain.

What

You needn't use all their questions; use just a few to require them to give thoughts to their actions.

Class Activity

After the game ask the children:

> Could you hear Simon?
> Well, what happened?
> Did your mind go to sleep?
> Did you put the information in?
> Were you too excited?

So What

Always give the little ones an example so that they get the idea.

Class Activity

Today we are going to form some analogies. We are going to look for some things in this room that work like our brains.

Using their ideas can help you to reach the children on their level and then expand their knowledge.

For example the top of this mountain looks like an ice cream cone because it's white on the top and it looks like it's dripping over the cone.

Some of our children had been around computers and used that analogy. Others used a window. I used a door with another class and it went over very well.

We know that our minds let things in and put things out. Look around. See if you can find two things that will work in the same way.

We discuss these concepts and questions:

A door has a lock.
You can use a key to
unlock the door.
What do you see when
you get inside?
How big is the inside?
How big are our
minds?

It's very important to use those analogies that are like our minds, and to throw out those ideas that are not like the mind.

List children's ideas. Choose one and work with it.

Summarize information and inaccuracies by asking what they learned from using the process.

Now What

Open up the use of the process to other areas of concern.

Class Activity

Then use the process to form an analogy, i.e.,

What animal would
you use to tell about
yourself? Why?

This lesson worked out fairly well for two reasons. Children seem to like taking on the "personalities" of animals or other living or nonliving objects. It seems to be less threatening for them. Direct analogies often develop into personal analogies. In this situation, the children not only likened themselves to another object, but also they became the *thing.*

Secondly, the children, through the use of games and forming analogies, realized the complexities of the mind. It takes in and puts out. Sometimes it appears to lock. It is awfully small to have so much in it. Perhaps we need to be very careful about how we put things inside of it. The discussion does not end here because later the children will have more questions about the mind. Then you will need to use other processes or use the same process to do more in-depth research about the mind.

The process of using direct analogies has been successful in explaining many things about ourselves, concepts, and vocabulary words. There is another kind of analogy that provides a more interesting advantage. The use of personal analogies — a form of role playing — has been particularly successful. Children through pretending take on the "personalities" of living and nonliving objects. We have found that the lower elementary children are especially fond of being animals. It is interesting to observe which children choose which animals. They reveal a great deal of themselves through this process possibly because it provides a nonthreatening means of expressing and revealing themselves.

Personal analogies have even been used for disciplinarian reasons. The Synectics Education Systems designed a process for interpersonal disciplinary situations.[6] Illustrated below is a conversation between a seven-year-old and his teacher.

PROCESS: SENSING

What

The boy is experiencing his behavior in an analogue.

Teacher

John, you have really tried my patience today. You don't ever sit down and listen to anything.

Boy

You don't ever say anything to anybody else.

The child is not afraid to express his opinion.

Teacher

John, you remind me of a rabbit.

The child is being asked to examine his behavior in an ego-detached, less threatening analogy.

Boy

A rabbit? The boy laughs. I am no rabbit.

So What

In this part of the lesson he finds out why the analogue was used.

Teacher

You remind me of a rabbit because you're always hopping around.

Boy

I think I'm a fox.

Teacher

Why?

Boy

Because I'm smart.

---

6. W.J.J. Gordon, T. Poze, and M. Reid, *The Creative Disciplinarian* (Cambridge, Massachusetts: Synectics Education Systems, 1969).

Teacher

Yes, you are smart like a fox, but you hop around like a rabbit. Shall I call you "Bugs"?

Boy

No.

Now What

Teacher

This part could have continued but it seemed appropriate to stop at this point so that the student could reflect on this particular analogue. He will have many opportunities to use the process again.

O.K. you may leave. I think tomorrow we should try this again and think about our actions and what it means to you.

Of course, John did not change his behavior immediately, but it did give us another process for discussing the problem. The process also gives a little distance to examine the problem at hand and the student an opportunity to gain some insight into his behavior. Something that we gained from the experience was that we had to begin to study animal behavior more closely.

OTHER PRINTED CURRICULUM MATERIALS

Our program attempted to incorporate *Methods in Human Development*, a curriculum for four- and five-year-olds designed by Harold Bessell and Uvaldo Palomares.[7] The Bessell/Palomares program works on many of the same assumptions that we believe in. Thus these authors believe that every child has a basic need for mastery and approval with the academic challenges of the educational curriculum. They see that education has grown more universal and that there is a gap between the student and the educational system. Motivation is a vital force that is lacking within the students; it is in this gap that we find our social problems. Given this conviction, the Bessell/Palomares program attempts to nurture and tap each child's potential for motivation. They attempt to devise a curriculum through which children should observe how and why each educational challenge carries a personal meaning and benefit. By cultivating an

---

7. Harold Bessell and Uvaldo Palomares, *Methods In Human Development* (San Diego, California: Human Development Training Institute, 1967).

awareness of the self and others as creatures of thoughts, feelings, and actions, Bessell and Palomares feel that they are designing a preventive measure to unhealthy self-concept. The child will have the means to come to recognize, to question, and to experience educational achievement in a very personal way.

Their manual suggests that each teacher is to use the material according to his own style. We did just that. The materials dealt heavily with concerns and teacher behavior, and we attempted to stress the processes emphasized in our What, So What, Now What program. For example, in the lesson below the teacher's task is to elicit self-expression. We, instead, chose to emphasize the process *expressing ourselves,* what it is like and *why it is* important. The content is expressing *pleasant thoughts.* Beside each activity we have incorporated the changes that make it more consistent with our own program.

PROCESS: ACTING

Explanation of Sequence (and Our Changes)

What

Children are immersed into an experience for self-expression about pleasant thoughts.

Class Activity

The teacher brings a medium-sized lump of clay to the group.

Children are assembled in a circle for the group session. The teacher says, "I have a lump of clay here. I am thinking of something nice that I could make with it. I am thinking of my friend. That's my thought. Now I can make him." The teacher makes the friend's face so that the children can easily see what she is doing. *"Who has a nice thought of some other thing or person I could make?"* The teacher gave as many children as possible the opportunity to express a *pleasant thought* which she repeats back to the group as being this particular child's pleasant thought. Then she makes a symbol of the pleasant thought out of the lump of clay.

Bonita Burgess and Terry Borton   183

So What

Emphasis is given to what was done. Our preference is to ask a few questions to emphasize what children have done and why it is important.

For example,
> Did you find out
> something about me or
> your classmates?
> Do you think we could
> do it again?
> How would we do it?

This would get more specific about the process for self-expression.

Now What

This runs throughout the week. Each day following gives the children a chance for using the process as well as learning the associated concepts such as:

> *"I am the same as*
> *other people."*
> *"People are different*
> *in some ways."*

Since our major objective was to stress the process of self-expression, then we used other ways to express the self. For example, the children used the clay to express a pleasant thought. They colored a picture of pleasant thought. This in some way helped us to incorporate more action into the lesson as well as to teach alternatives for self-expression. This sequence in which children express, examine, and act on their pleasant thoughts provides an opportunity to gain

Teacher should use the last few minutes of the session to restate each child's pleasant thought in almost verbatim form as they themselves expressed it.

Avoid any type of unfavorable comparison.

Follow-Ups: There are further opportunities to do more of the same thing for that week.

a new behavior that has depth
as well as positive feelings. By
bringing in a variety of
processes and media, the child
can gain an action pattern that
has been examined and ac-
cepted.

We are especially impressed with the Human Development Program because it provides well thought-out and detailed lesson plans. Those of us who have used the program have observed three specific advantages. The program enables us to learn more about our children in a shorter amount of time. In a relaxed atmosphere the children are apt to reveal personal things about themselves such as liking to sit in their mother's lap or riding a bus or holding their teacher's hand. In return, they seem amazed about the things that teachers reveal to them. One teacher revealed that thinking about her boyfriend was a pleasant thought. The children were shocked but overjoyed with such information. I don't think they ever forgot that particular piece of information.

The children learned a process for sharing information about themselves and used this information in their social interactions with each other. In the classroom you might hear one child say to another, "Remember when you said that you like chocolate cake?"

The program provides a rating scale that provides an interesting picture of each child. There was a child who was particularly perceptive in interpersonal comprehension — he understood how a person's behavior causes approval or disapproval of that behavior in another person. He scored very low, however, on considerateness because he rarely adjusted his behavior in ways that were thoughtful and beneficial to others. Thus the scale picked up this fine but important distinction.

The greatest problem we had with this Human Development Program was in finding the best way to use it with our children. Just putting our kids in a circle did not work in the beginning; so, a low round table was used. This seemed to give the children some structure, and their little legs partially touched under the table. The program suggested using no more than fifteen children at a time for no more than twenty minutes. We used nine children as a part of each session. The librarian had the other children during the session. Originally we held the session for twenty minutes, but we soon decreased the time to approximately ten minutes. This was done for two reasons. There is a whole year for the program, and each unit is repeated during the year. Additional time can be used to provide more activity for the children. Some of the lessons require the children to be relatively inactive with their bodies.

As we continue to use and evaluate the program, we will put emphasis on requiring the children to question the process as well as becoming aware of the self. We will also extend the program to children who are six and seven years old.

A FRAMEWORK OF CONCERN

Some people who take a quick glance at the "What? So What? Now What? Program" get the impression that we favor student freedom in large and unlimited doses. In so doing, they are confusing the processes of making teaching relevant to student lives with greater liberty for students. Although we believe that children should have more freedom than they generally have in American schools, we also believe that the processes of learning are more likely to occur under conditions of disciplined concern. In the public mind relevance is equated often with freedom, and discipline is associated often with punishment. In our minds the relevant curriculum is associated with discipline — a nonpunitive discipline that stakes out limits and treats students with trust and respect. At the heart of our belief in discipline is the view that a certain minimum level of order is necessary for effective teaching. If teachers believe that they have something important to teach and if they are going to try to teach it within the framework of compulsory education, then they owe it to themselves and the students to maintain the kind of order in which they can function.

The major point in maintaining an order that is consonant with a curriculum of concerns is not the particular limits set on behavior — whether kids sit with hands folded or whether they play thumb games. The essential point is *how* those limits are set and the *process* that is employed. Limits work where the teachers are warm and concerned about their students, are convinced that they have something worthwhile to teach, and are using the limits to establish an environment in which students can learn. The limits and the authority they represent are not important, but what is important is setting and using them in such a way that students can connect with greater ability to learn. In setting up limits teachers can follow some procedures we have found used by very effective teachers. Specify the behaviors you do not want — yelling; specify the behaviors that you do want — raising hands before speaking. Reward the behaviors you do want with clear, obvious rewards — praise, thanks; punish the behaviors you do not want with clearly defined punishments — staying after school, ignoring. "Shape" behavior a little bit at a time, and do not expect total or extreme changes in a single episode or short time. Above all maintain a tough-minded consistency — mean what you say and do not avoid directness and expression of your views. Teachers who are convinced that they have something of value to teach have come to recognize that they can give their students more when they teach in an environment of disciplined concern.

SUMMARY

In summary, our program attempts to accomplish three major objectives. First, we attempt to bridge the gap between the student's private emotional world and the world of subject matter. Secondly, we attempt to facilitate the kind of learning necessary in a rapidly changing society. Finally, we search to provide the student with a way for exploring and expanding his inner self and the resources he has there for coping with the world. Our approach begins by locating children's concerns. We then find processes that help them to handle and understand them and train them to apply these processes in real life situations.

The applications of our model can be found in the What, So What, and Now What sequence of every lesson. This sequence has been applied in several ways: (1) Newly designed materials; (2) The creation of new books and stories; (3) Revamping other curriculum materials, books, and lessons to emphasize our approach.

RESOURCES [8]

Alschuler, Alfred, James McIntyre, and Diane Tabor, *How to Develop Achievement Motivation: A Course Manual for Teachers.* Education Ventures, Inc., Middletown, Connecticut, 1969. A self-instructional course for teachers who want to help students set goals for their own achievement and develop a "motive pattern" which will help them get there.

American Association for the Advancement of Science, "Science: A Process Approach," *AAAS Misc. Publication* 65-67, 1965. This extensive K-6 course teaches such scientific processes as hypothesizing, predicting, and controlling variables, using whatever scientific content best illustrates the

---

8. Adapted from the "Resources" section of *Reach, Touch and Teach* (McGraw-Hill, 1970).

process. By using some of the methods suggested in this book, the teacher can broaden this process approach so that it applies to personal growth as well as scientific content.

Barth, Roland, and Charles Rathbone, "Informal Education," *The Center Forum*, July 1969, published by the Center for Urban Education, 105 Madison Avenue, New York. An extensive annotated bibliography on the "Leicestershire movement," or "integrated curriculum," an educational program which provides a wide variety of materials and problem exercises so that children have the freedom to choose much of the direction and pace of their own learning. Most material is elementary level, but the principles are applicable at all levels.

Bessell, Harold, and Uvaldo Palomares, *Methods in Human Development*, Human Development Training Institute, 4455 Twain Avenue, San Diego, California, 1967. A program for primary and early elementary school, providing structured group experiences that give students self-confidence, a sense of mastery, and the skills to help each other.

Big Rock Candy Mountain, 1115 Merrill Street, Menlo Park, California, available Fall, 1970. Extensive catalog containing sources, reviews, and graphics describing educational materials, ideas, and environments related to personal growth and process education.

Borton, Terry; Lynn Borton, and Mark Borton, *My Books*. For information, write Office of Affective Development, Board of Public Education, 21st and the Parkway, Philadelphia, Pennsylvania. A series of twenty supplementary readers that speak directly to a student's basic concerns. Physical activity, drawing, role plays, and programmed open questions involve the student in making his reading books his own.

Brown, George, *Now: The Human Dimension*, Esalen Publications, Big Sur, California, 1968. A report on a training program for teachers which combined cognitive and affective learning to create a "humanistic education."

Burgess, Bonita, *A Bibliography for a Human Development Curriculum*, Intensive Learning Center and Office of Affective Development, Philadelphia Public Schools, Intensive Learning Center, 5th and Luzerne Streets, Philadelphia, Pennsylvania. Extensive information on both adult and children's materials (books, films, stories, records) appropriate for developing the human potential of elementary children. Sources for instructional materials are listed. Emphasis on intergroup relations.

Burgess, Bonita, *A Working Bibliography on Games*, Intensive Learning Center and Office of Affective Development, Philadelphia Public Schools, Intensive Learning Center, 5th and Luzerne Streets, Philadelphia, Pennsylvania. Describes games, sources of games, and background discussions on how games may be used to teach thinking processes. A curriculum outline is being developed.

DeMille, Richard, *Put Your Mother on the Ceiling*, Walker, New York, 1967. A series of exercises in creative thinking with, as the title suggests, a droll and fanciful bent. Useful for encouraging the use of fantasy at almost any level.

Gibson, John, *The Intergroup Relations Curriculum: A Program for Elementary School Education, vols. 1 and 2*, Tufts University Press, Medford., Massachusetts, 1969. Contains specific lesson plans covering overall program, ways of dealing with different cultures, decision making, group processing, racial differences, etc. Research results and general discussion are extensive.

Jaynes, Ruth, and Barbara Woodbridge, *Bowman Early Childhood Series*, Bowman Publishing Co., Glendale, California, 1969. A series of picture stories, story books, and recordings designed to develop positive self-identity, awareness of self as a person, motor-perceptual skills, and ability to relate to others.

Lederman, Janet, *Anger and the Rocking Chair*, McGraw-Hill, New York, 1969. Describes in a prose poem how one of the program's teachers used gestalt awareness with children. All levels.

Moffet, James, *A Student-Centered Language Arts Curriculum*, vol. 1 (grades K-6) and vol. 2 (grades K-13), and *Teaching the Universe of Discourse*, Houghton Mifflin, Boston, 1968. A comprehensive English program centered around the students themselves and the kind of discourse — drama and speech — with which they are most familiar. Specific lesson plans and exercises are given.

Muessig, Robert, *Discussion Pictures for Beginning Social Studies*, Harper and Row, New York, 1967. Ninety large pictures on such basic human themes as the unity and diversity of man and man's search for security. Primary level, but useful in many contexts.

Myers, R.E., and Paul E. Torrance, *A Complete Program in Creative Development*. Ginn and Company, New York, 1966. A series of idea books that provide children in the lower and upper elementary grades with experiences in sensing difficulties, problems, gaps in information, nursing elements; making guesses or formulating hypotheses about these deficiencies; testing guesses and revising and retesting them; and finally communicating the results.

Randolph, Norma and William Howe, *Self-Enhancing Education: A Program to Motivate Learners*, Stanford, California. A book of specific procedures for teaching kids to learn more about how to control themselves, direct their own learning, and create their own selves. Directed toward teachers dealing with elementary students. Based on programs developed in Cupertino, California.

Shaftel, Fannie, and George Shaftel, *Words and Actions: Roleplaying Photoproblems for Young Children*, Holt, New York, 1967. Uses roleplays centered around such problems as spilled groceries, disagreement with parent on shoe styles, fight over blocks, etc., to teach young children to recognize and deal with their feelings. One set of pictures raises problems common in entering a new school situation. Urban emphasis.

Spolin, Viola, *Improvisation for the Theater,* Northwestern University Press, Evanston, Illinois, 1963. A sequential program for teaching improvisation, containing exercises which can be easily adapted for many classroom activities.

Squirms, Contemporary Drama Service, Downers Grove, Illinois, 1970. A can of squirmy situations for lower and upper elementary children which require insight and imagination. The children roleplay a variety of life situations as animals.

Synectics, Inc., *Making It Strange*, Harper & Row, New York, 1968. A four-book series designed to teach children to be more creative. The books also lend themselves well to an exploration of the inner life out of which creativity springs.

Tannen, Robert, *I Know a Place*, City Schools Curriculum Service, Inc., 60 Commercial Wharf, Boston. A series of booklets provide open questions and the opportunity for children to help write their own book as they explore their relations to their environment. Elementary level.

7
Personality Profiles
of Disadvantaged Youth

Arthur Pearl
University of California, Santa Cruz

People are confused about disadvantaged youth and their capacities, aspirations, life-styles, and relationships with authority figures. Is it really true, as many people believe, that disadvantaged youth lack intellectuality, are impulsive, have a paucity of language, are preoccupied with physical violence, rely on fate, and have a propensity for totalitarian leadership? These conceptions have considerable bearing on social policy. Manpower planning, educational programs, police activity, and correctional practices are shaped by them. If there are serious misconceptions, (which I believe there are) the results can be disastrous.

People tend to look at disadvantaged youth "clinically," to look at them as maladaptive, and to view their deficiencies as an inevitable part of their psychological makeup. Disadvantaged youth are believed to resist change and to continue to maladapt when opportunities to behave differently are offered, even when professional assistance is extended. I do not agree with these views. I believe that all youth learn to negotiate their environments and that their "personality" is a function of the options available to them. Disadvantaged youth generate a life-style based on their continued struggle to gain a sense of competence, belonging, and usefulness. They are believed to be maladjusted because, as a society, we fail disadvantaged youth and frustrate their efforts to achieve gratification. We deny them competence, belonging, and usefulness. We further humiliate and degrade them when we disparage their efforts to succeed in their own terms.

In this chapter we will examine three sources that limit the options for competence, belonging, and usefulness of disadvantaged youth.

These sources are the schools, the street, and parent-child differences. Individually these sources have unhappy, limiting affects upon the development of a disadvantaged youth; together they sharply reduce his alternatives for a productive and useful life.

THE SCHOOLS

Many misconceptions about disadvantaged youth stem from their behavior in school. From school performance, disadvantaged youth are described as lacking intellectual potential and possessing deficiencies in character. There is a more concise explanation — disadvantaged youth are denied any other adaptation.

The Denial of Competence

Student competence (and lack of it) is reported periodically in the schools. Children, parents, school authorities, potential employers, and sometimes correctional authorities receive the reports. Competence is measured by standardized tests or teachers' subjective opinions. Only a few disadvantaged youths are judged to be competent in school on the basis of these tests. Some critics of education object to the tests used; they argue that the criteria used are neither "culture free" (i.e., they favor features of the dominant culture) nor "culture fair" (i.e., they are unable to give equivalent treatment to all cultures). I think it would make little difference what criteria were used. Very early in their school career, the disadvantaged would still be shunted aside. Currently, many techniques are used to deny the competence of disadvantaged youth. The disadvantaged are concentrated into low ability groups. They are diagnosed as intellectually inferior by teachers and other school personnel. They are not *allowed* to exhibit intelligence. If they aspire to an intellectually challenging future, e.g., a medical doctor, they are informed that such a choice is "unrealistic." The *fact* that they wish to be a doctor is further "evidence" of intellectual and emotional incompetence.

The disadvantaged youths' response to these insults is one of withdrawal broken by sporadic outbursts of anger. To avoid accepting the notion that indeed they are stupid, disadvantaged youth disparage the importance of school activity. The more they are characterized as inferior and the more they lose interest in school work, the more they are driven to resenting those designated as intelligent.

Teachers unwittingly irritate the situation through the strange reward system used in schools that forces children to compete against each other. The contests are held in "foreign" areas with frightened contestants who are terrified to lose but are not anxious to win either. The more disadvantaged children are unable to feel competent in school, the more they search for competence outside of school, and the more they align themselves against those who do "good." As the gulf between the "goods" and the "hoods" widens over the years, each group develops distinctive patterns of behavior.

The disadvantaged "hoods" appear sullen, slow, inattentive, and hostile to the external observer. They are either silent or monosyllabic when they do speak, particularly with teachers. They do not want to read. They try to manipulate school activities away from anything that will defeat them. They disrupt, sometimes with an ingenuity that shows enormous intellectual competence, but they never receive credit for that creative thinking. Such efforts only reinforce the image already held by their teachers.

The disadvantaged hate those youth who are making it. They hate those who are eager, polite, and straining to show off. They try to ignore them; although, some spend hours in plotting revenge. If the disadvantaged are black and those who excel in school are white, racial tensions result. If the competent school person is black (an unusual occurrence), he is derided as a "Tom."

The Denial of Belonging

The school not only denies the vast majority of the disadvantaged an opportunity to be intellectually or socially competent, but also it precludes belonging. The school is an alien place. Nothing about the school attracts youth. The atmosphere appears hostile and the architecture is often cold and foreboding. Buildings and classrooms are locked most of the evenings and weekends when many disadvantaged students desperately need a friend, advisor, or counselor, and it is during those hours that disadvantaged youths are most likely to need a sanctuary. The school has nothing to offer to meet these needs. On the contrary, the staff is viewed as the enemy. The social organization of the school does not permit interpersonal relationships beyond the most superficial encounters. The latitudes of behavior are restrictive and inconsistent. School values are not remotely applicable to street or home conditions, with little regard for local community opinions. Perhaps the most damaging effect of the school is the primitiveness of its social constellations.

The disadvantaged child cannot gain a sense of belonging because there is so little to belong to. He is virtually alone. He is not *permitted* to relate to others. His efforts to relate, in the only ways he knows, are frustrated. When he is not being shushed for noisiness he is being chastised for bullying or cheating. The only social role he is allowed to play is that of nuisance or flunky. He can elevate the former into troublemaker and that role becomes habitual and accepted as time goes on. The school is nonredemptive. Once a student establishes a reputation, the reputation follows him. He becomes a stimulus figure that provokes responses. He comes to believe that no matter what he does he will still be accused of wrongdoing.

The school drives away many students. The *classroom* attracts only a small number of students. They are comfortable. They radiate ease and enjoyment and feel that they belong. A very small percentage of these students are disadvantaged. *Sports* attract other students. They become so occupied in their athletics that everything else about them reduces to insignificance. They not only *belong* to but they are consumed by these activities. Disadvantaged boys and girls generally do not get involved in organized athletics. School *clubs* and *social activities* offer students an opportunity to belong. Often the disadvantaged youth feel their exclusion most intensely in these areas. They are not extended invitations to science or chess clubs. In social activities, their poverty really hurts. School sponsored affairs are often beyond their means.

In many ways, the school is like an exclusive club. It develops a distinct culture, a language, a style, rituals, norms of acceptable and unacceptable behavior, and distinctive values. Disadvantaged youth are denied admission to the "club" and respond by generating counter-cultures. Some counter-cultures derive from and are diametrically opposed to the school culture. The members of this group are at war with the "Dudley-Do-Rights" who belong in school. Their behaviors, language, and style are dictated by the school activity they are out to crush.

Most counter-cultural activities, however, are not specifically directed against the school. They are desperate efforts to generate social support for the isolated and the lonely. To generate a sense of belonging disadvantaged youth develop a style of expression, a unique approach to dress, an orientation to music and other art forms, a language that at the very least has its own argot, and sometimes a syntax and vocabulary bank. The norms of acceptable behavior are not set up to insult school norms, but they represent accommodations to one another. Members of the counter-culture tolerate certain behaviors that school personnel find unruly or graceless, but they do not tolerate the smart-alecky show-off that school personnel so often prize. They feel a tenderness toward others that is seen as a weakness by school authorities. Conversely, they are apparently insensitive to some acts that cause a school-bred observer to wince.

School authorities often trample the disadvantaged youths' efforts to establish their own identities. Symbols of social group membership — language, style, tone, tempo, or volume (e.g., boots, long hair, sideburns, "naturals," leather jackets, mini-minis, or "undelicate" use of makeup) are sometimes outlawed. In other instances less direct pressure to conform to the club rules is applied. If the school authorities succeed, the youths' efforts to derive some feeling of belonging while at school are crushed, and this action has considerable long-term impact on their behavior. If the school authorities fail to destroy the youths' social group, they are locked into a continued warring relationship with the "establishment," and this relationship affects dramatically their perceptions, contacts, and perspectives.

The behavior of a disadvantaged youth is determined considerably by the groups to which he belongs and the roles he is allowed to play in these groups. Some youths profit from belonging to many groups and develop from these relationships an extensive repertoire of behavior. The athlete who is also a scholar and lover in school (and part-time clerk in a clothing store and a pool hall hustler outside of school) has much more going for him in his choice of behaviors than a person who cannot make it in any of these social arenas. Membership in groups that are incompatible can be a source of considerable embarrassment. An athlete who is discovered by his buddies in the incomprehensible, serious intellectual activity of "booking" may go through considerable "changes" (become physically or vocally aggressive) that are inexplicable to the teacher who has at all other times found him so well-behaved.

The variety of group memberships or lack of them and the roles a youth plays in the groups to which he can belong shape the personality of the disadvantaged youth. There is quite obviously a differential sense of belonging if one is a leader than if one is a follower or hanger-on. Depending on the nature of the group, the role played can have a variety of consequences. The hanger-on in a deviant subculture is much more likely to escape than a person who is totally engrossed in the group's activity. There is great personal tragedy when a person who exercises leadership in a deviant subgroup wants out. He has two major obstacles to overcome — he has to escape from where he is, *and* he has to go somewhere else to belong. This may explain why people of obvious intelligence continue to defend what appears to be the indefensible to everyone else. The more the school and its authorities attack the social group to which the deviant belongs, the more he is driven to defend himself and his group, and the more he is locked into that group. He generates a code of ethics that has a hold on his conscience as do codes of ethics for "establishment groups." To knuckle under is to betray comrades. To knuckle under is to humiliate, demean, and humble oneself.

Teacher understanding of the dynamics of belonging and action based on this understanding could do much to prevent the disadvantaged child from walling himself into corners that lead to rigidification of behavior.

The Denial of Usefulness

Perhaps the boundaries of personality development of a disadvantaged youth are most limited by his sense of uselessness. In this attribute, the disadvantaged youngster is different than his predecessors. For example, despite the brutality, the indignity of slavery, and the indenture that followed, the black was an economic asset. He was brought to this country because of his economic value, and he could find some self-worth because of this desired capacity. He generated folklore and songs and styled his life around his ability to produce. He could remember his mother rocking him in his cradle in those "old cotton fields at home"; he could "feel for those who had to jump down, turn around, pick a bale of cotton"; he could revile a little bug who "could eat half the cotton while the merchant got the rest." He could identify with a John Henry who could drive steel faster than a machine and John's wife, Polly Ann, who could drive steel like a man. Work and the utility of the man as a worker made possible an otherwise impossible existence. There is no need to romanticize the arduous nature of the life or to ignore the degrading exploitation of humans by humans. Slavery reduced man to unspeakable ugliness, and its aftermath has plagued its descendants for generations. With all of the unpleasantness, there was a utility to an existence that gave a meaning to life and filled what would otherwise have been a tortuous void.

The disadvantaged youth of today is unable to derive even that little gratification. He is a superfluous person. He has been driven out of rural America because he no longer is needed. The means used to drive him from his home degraded him. His family has been denied adequate welfare. He has been given none of the skills required for participation in a technologically advanced world. He has been forced into the most dilapidated and crowded areas in the big cities. These are ghettos in the classic sense. Once in them, there is little likelihood of escape. The ghetto grows like a cancer, involving more and more people in an ever increasing entrapment. These same areas were once occupied by European immigrants who came to America eagerly, bursting with hope and wild dreams. They were sobered by the reality they met, but they knew that their sojourn into the depths was not to be long-lived. To a large extent, they were right. They moved on and were replaced by a new underclass who soon made way for the next move. This was not so with the "black ghetto" or the "brown barrio." To escape the ghetto, one needs to be an economic asset. It was never an easy trip for even the short-term residents. The Jews, Italians, Irish, and Poles were willing to venture out only when the economic inducement outweighed the loneliness and the insults. The first few pioneered the way for the others. The black is physically and psychologically imprisoned in the ghetto, and the school adds to that feeling and is affected by it.

In at least three ways, the school contributes to the disadvantaged youth's feeling that he is useless: (1) he is useless in school, (2) he is useless out of school because of lack of school preparation, and (3) he is made to feel responsible for both (1) and (2). Let us analyze how each of these aspects help shape the personality of the disadvantaged.

Many of the schools, as currently constructed, do not allow the majority of students to contribute to the educational process. The only contributors are the "brains" and, as has been previously indicated, the poor are rarely categorized as "brains." The brains help with the instruction. They assist in demonstrations. They help prepare curriculum. They tutor. They engage in public relations. They are valuable adjuncts to the instructional activity, and they derive satisfaction from their utility and are in turn rewarded by the attention they receive. The disadvantaged child often has a much less useful function in the school. He is reminded how much better off the class would be if he would not come. (However, if he decides to take up the implicit invitation to remove himself from the premises, he is searched out and punished for his truancy.) The disadvantaged youngster is seldom trusted with any important instructional assignment. Sometimes he is co-opted to collect papers, erase blackboards, or distribute pencils. He sees through such subterfuge and is embittered by its obvious attempt at manipulation. He is seldom credited with knowledge that is worth sharing with his classmates. The education he has acquired about interpersonal relationships, crime, drugs, dietary habits, and language is not allowed expression in school. If he tries to bring into schools some of his out-of-school education, he is worse than useless — he is a trouble-making hood. Recently educators have been using older students to assist in the education of children younger than themselves. This procedure is not new to education. It has always been with us, but, in the past, the efforts were from necessity and not design. Such procedures if carefully planned can alleviate the disadvantaged youth's feeling of uselessness in the school. Ron and Peggy Lippitt have demonstrated that students with limited educational achievement can be of value in the education of others.[1] Frank Riessman has labeled this the "helper principle." He suggests that self-help organizations (e.g., Alcoholics Anonymous or Synanon) gain their effectiveness because of the sense of usefulness that the formerly afflicted gain from the help they offer to others. The opportunity to play truly useful roles in school can alter the student's self-image and start a chain that can affect his entire life adjustment.[2]

Secondly, the school causes disadvantaged youth to feel and be treated as useless when he is out of school. Our society can be termed a "credential society." The school affects all subsequent life adjustment because school performance becomes a prerequisite for work eligibility. Perhaps the emergence of school as the single most important determinant of work activity explains the changes in permanency of ghetto residence. Prior residents of the ghettos came not as ambitious professionals; they were old country craftsmen or blue collar laborers. They had a calling. Their nationality or religion was an economic asset because there was work to do and those who preceded them could sponsor them into jobs. The city was the cultural center and far surpassed in educational opportunities that which rural America offered. For example, the eastern European Jew was especially advantaged. He immigrated to New York when it was America's center of culture. Education was tailored to his aspirations and his style. He faced up to prejudice and suffered discrimination, but he was not denied admittance to privileged work situations. It was not unrealistic for him to aspire to be a doctor or a lawyer. (He would be challenged if he did not.) The denial of competence and belonging, previously mentioned in this chapter, leads to lifelong uselessness. The disadvantaged student can sense this. He often feels that he is shortchanged. Yet, he has neither the skills to put together a case for himself or the access to power to make a difference.

Thirdly, the school and society try to make the disadvantaged youth feel guilty for his failure to contribute. Guilt in our society is a feeling that one often rids by continually passing it off to someone else. No person in the school system wants to assume responsibility for the now and future uselessness of disadvantaged youth. The guilt for that

---

1. Ron and Peggy Lippitt, *Cross-Age Peer Help* (Institute for Social Research, University of Michigan, 1969).
2. Frank Riessman, *New Careers for the Poor* (New York: Free Press, 1965).

crime *has* to be displaced and who are the most available but the disadvantaged themselves.

Over and over again disadvantaged youth are belabored because of their "uselessness." Sometimes a teacher can be cold and brutal — "I just don't know why we waste our time on such a useless thing like you." Sometimes the teacher is arrogant — "How can you be so worthless after all we have done for you?" Sometimes the teacher is only insensitive — "Johnny, you just try to keep the brush between the lines and you will have done just fine. Meanwhile, the rest of us will continue with our lesson" — ignoring completely that such activities generate no skills or knowledge. The teacher is not empathetic to the student's feelings of emptiness, anxiety, and guilt for activities over which he has no control.

Sometimes the teacher generates guilt because of the way he sets priorities and activities. When the other students are allowed to tutor children younger than themselves, the disadvantaged youth is told, "You must first complete your homework, and then you can help the others." This response is a simultaneous blow to the head and stomach. The disadvantaged student already feels that he is dumb, he is aware he doesn't belong, and now he is told that he cannot help anyone else. How much more logical it would be if the teacher had suggested that after helping those youngsters, it might be a good idea to try some homework. The guilt that is placed on the disadvantaged youth in school is augmented by similar action at home. Mothers are asked to get after their children. The child is blamed for the tears shed and for the squabbles between parents. The child has no possible course to steer because he cannot conceivably meet that which is demanded of him. He is asked to behave, be good, and act nice, but no response would be acceptable except a willingness to acknowledge that he is stupid and to dutifully be dumb. Such a response not only would be personally destructive, but also it would mean that he could not live with his "buddies."

If parents attempt to defend their child, the situation may get even worse. The child may be perceived to be part of a subversive conspiracy that is undermining the entire educational structure. He is driven to defend his parents, but the debate is unequal from the beginning. It is carried on in a style, a language, and a set of ground rules that gives every advantage to the established authority. When the disadvantaged boy reaches the age of ten, he usually has made the only accommodation available to him. He has made the decision that school is not for him. He refuses to invest further in school activities (with the exception of athletics and then he generally shuns some, if not most, of the training regulations). His presence may still be detected in the building because he simply has no other place to go.

Some Documentation for the Charges Against the School

The school, as an institution, has been charged with undermining the personality structure of the disadvantaged child. The school has been accused of thwarting the growth of disadvantaged youth by systematically denying youth opportunities to gain gratification from a sense of belonging, usefulness, and competence. Up until this point, there has been no documentation for the indictments. Documentation, however, is readily available from a variety of studies and observations on the education of disadvantaged youth. Teachers have given their accounts of the school and its activities. Sociologists and psychologists have offered their insights. Some few disadvantaged youths have mastered communication skills sufficiently to tell their own story. Aggregate statistics are also available to reinforce the case against the schools. All analysts do not come to the same conclusion about the cause or the nature of the devastation, but there is little disagreement that such devastation is taking place.

Herbert Kohl's *36 Children*[3] is drawn from his teaching experience in Manhattan. His is a powerful account of the destruction of children. He vividly cites how children are made to feel alien in the school and how their efforts to bring into school scenes of their life experiences are frustrated by insensitive school officials. Kohl's recital is all the more tragic because he attempts to do something about it and *he succeeds*. His students are able to gain a sense of competence. They learn to read and write and are exhilarated by the experience. They feel comfortable. They launch into extremely ambitious projects. Unfortunately, all is dashed when they move on to other grades and other schools. A student, who returns to visit Kohl, articulates the sentiment that just cannot penetrate school officials — one good year is not enough.

Death at an Early Age[4] describes Jonathan Kozol's career as a teacher in the Boston schools. He lashes out at the brutality that comes in the form of education. He describes how the children are shortchanged by the unwholesomeness of the physical plant and the lack of supplies. He is particularly vindictive of the "racists" who declare themselves to be "liberals."

---

3. New York: New American Library, 1967.
4. Boston: Houghton Mifflin, Co., 1967.

James Herndon is yet another who has taken the trouble to describe his ordeal as a teacher. His battleground is the Oakland ghetto. His book is *The Way It Spozed To Be.*[5] There are some differences between Kozol's Boston and Herndon's Oakland, but I suspect the major difference is between Kozol and Herndon as people. Kozol is horror stricken whereas Herndon, while embittered and discouraged, is bemused. Herndon presents a travelogue — whereas, Kozol's work is reminiscent of Kafka's *Trial*. Both conclude the children do not have a chance. They are angry about different things. Kozol rages because low ability students are lumped together with the few bright children he has uncovered. Herndon is furious because his ninth grade is separated out into a low ability group. Both are pessimistic, and Herndon, in an epilogue, after eight years of teaching in less strenuous circumstances, concludes that because neither teachers nor administrators are truly concerned the situation is hopeless.

The disadvantaged are not unique in the inability to derive gratification from school activities. The more affluent suffer similar (although not nearly as complete) affronts. John Holt extracts from his experience as teacher in an exclusive private school in *How Children Fail.*[6] He concludes that fear of failure is the major factor. He lambastes the schools for failing a sizable proportion of students (which is but another way of registering incompetence) and for the even worse crime of threatening every student with the prospect of failure. ("I'm continually reawakened to the trauma of impending doom that threatens even the most successful student. I see them fretting before and after an examination or frenzied to a point of mindlessness trying to complete a term paper.")

Nat Hentoff's description is biographical. In his book *Our Children Are Dying*[7] he applauds the efforts of Elliot Shapiro, principal of P.S. 19 in Manhattan, to obtain for his black and Puerto Rican students the physical plant, the books, and the respecting teachers that they so desperately needed. There is no questioning of Shapiro's sincerity. He recognizes the brutality and blunted sensitivities of his own staff. Shapiro (unlike the previous writers) has a measure of power, and he makes waves and fights city hall.

5. New York: Simon & Schuster, 1965.
6. New York: Pitman, 1965.
7. New York: The Viking Press, Inc., 1966.

In *Manchild in the Promised Land*[8] Claude Brown describes his life in the ghetto and his efforts to pull himself out of a sink of squalor, multiple involvements with juvenile authorities, reformatories, and drugs. What is striking in Brown's account is the minimal importance of school. His satisfactions as a person came from his ability to fight, steal, evade police, and obtain and sell marijuana and cocaine. In those activities, he gained the sense of his person and his importance to other human beings. Only when it appeared that drugs and a life of drug addiction were the only alternatives to school did school become important and then only as a lesser of evils.

Jacobsen and Rosenthal compile a list of the research involving the influence that teacher expectations have on student performance. In their book *Pygmalion in the Classroom*[9] they cite their own study indicating that teacher attitudes do affect student's feelings of comfort, ability, and expectations of success. Although their research efforts have been severely criticized, the wealth of evidence they have accumulated cannot be discounted.

The study of the group as it influences children and youth behavior has occupied the attention of Muzafer and Carolyn Sherif for a number of years. They and their colleagues studied the impact of the group on individual behavior in contrived groups and reported their findings in *Intergroup Conflict and Cooperation: The Robbers Cave Experiment*.[10] Later, they studied groups in natural settings and presented the results of their research in *Reference Groups: Exploration into Conformity and Deviation of Adolescents*[11] and in *Group in its Setting*.[12] They present a compelling argument for the notion that the social group to which a person belongs greatly affects his behavior, values, and attitudes. They found that adolescents from a wide variety of backgrounds were similar in many attitudes and behaviors. They were generally interested in personal success as defined by wealth, power, and status. The school had importance for most of them only because it was a place where interaction with other youth was possible. The Sherifs found that the structure of all social groups and the manner in which

8. New York: The Macmillan Co., 1965.
9. New York: Holt, Rinehart & Winston, Inc., 1968.
10. Norman, Oklahoma: The University Book Exchange, 1961.
11. New York: Harper & Row, Publishers, 1964.
12. *Problems of Youth*, ed., M. and C.W. Sherif (Chicago: Aldine Publishing Co., 1965).

they distributed power and status shaped individual behavior. They discovered that different kinds of behavior met with different kinds of tolerance. Groups that emphasized consuming alcoholic beverages could accept into their ranks teetotalers with no difficulty. However, people who collaborated with the enemy (police and school authorities) were not tolerated. In this context, the Sherifs point out that behaviors prized by social leaders are also considered to be virtues by youth groups. They all esteem loyalty, responsibility, and consistency, but because of the estrangement of many of the youth groups those valued attributes are condemned as manifestations of antisocial behavior.

Allegations of Inferiority and Deficiency

A wide number of sources provide support for the allegation that disadvantaged youth are considered intellectually incompetent in school.

Project Talent, an extensive survey of high school achievement, revealed that the twelfth grade low income youths were judged to be less competent than relatively affluent youths on every area that was tested in school.[13] The relationship between social background and assessed competence is even more accentuated when one considers that by the twelfth grade considerable culling out of students has taken place. By that time disadvantaged youth to a far greater extent than advantaged youth have dropped out of school.

Among the minorities, the black has been the most studied and the evidence is most complete on the school's failure to provide psychological support:

Elias Blake showed that there was almost no overlap in assessed academic potential when poor blacks were compared with affluent whites in Washington, D.C. in 1965. Nearly nine out of ten poor blacks were not considered college material whereas over nine out of ten affluent whites were in college preparatory tracks.[14]

---

13. John C. Flanagan et al, *The American High School Student* (Pittsburgh, Pa.: Project Talent, University of Pittsburgh, Matrix 1A).
14. "The Tract System in Washington, D.C.," *Integrated Education*, April-May, 1965, p. 30.

The language that poor blacks bring to school is disparaged and ridiculed. [15]

The opportunities for poor blacks to feel at home in school is frustrated by the underrepresentation of blacks in positions of school leadership. Even at this late date, most schools with a heavy concentration of black students have white principals and every large city has a white superintendent. The situation for poor blacks is even more difficult. Although increasing the numbers of dark-skinned administrators is absolutely necessary, it is not sufficient. Many poor black youths find it difficult to relate to educated blacks. Kohl and Herndon depict black teachers who are antagonistic to the disadvantaged students.

The curriculum reinforces racist attitudes. Jules Henry after perusing high school text books concludes that schools educate for stupidity in several critical areas. Four of which — Negroes, poverty, economics and labor — critically affect the lives of blacks in America.[16]

The flagrant insults that are committed and the necessary insights that are omitted prevent black students from obtaining a feeling of inclusion in classroom activities.

Mexican-American (Chicano) youth suffer many of the same indignities as blacks:

Mexican youth are far more likely than Anglos to be adjudged academically retarded. Those who speak no English are assessed more negatively than Mexican-Americans who speak English. [17]

Mexican-Americans are made to feel unwelcome in school from their very first experience because their native tongue has long been forbidden expression. Teachers have even visited homes to encourage parents to speak English at home.[18]

Mexicans even more than blacks are underrepresented in teaching and administrative areas. In California in 1966 people

15. W.A. Stewart, "Socio-Linguistic Factors in the History of American Negro Dialects," *The Florida Language Reporter*, 1967.
16. *Reason & Change in Elementary Education*, 2nd National Conference U.S., Office of Education, Tri-University Project Elementary Education, February 13, 1968.
17. George W. Mayecke, "Educational Achievement among Mexican-Americans," a special report from the Educational Opportunities Survey, *Integrated Education*, January-February, 1968.
18. William Madsen, *The Mexican-American of South Texas* (New York: Holt, Rinehart & Winston, 1964).

with Spanish surnames contributed 13 percent of the student population and at the same time people with Spanish surnames amounted to less than 2 percent of the certified school personnel.[19]

Mexican history and culture has been denigrated. Their heroes have been slandered as cowards, fools, illiterates, and thieves. Presentations of military encounters have been grossly distorted. In literature lauded by school authorities, the Mexican-American is promulgated as unintellectual, impulsive, and irresponsible.[20]

Some schools reserve their most savage treatment for the native Americans (we call them Indians).

They achieve less and are induced to prematurely leave school earlier than any other minority. Less than half of the native Americans complete the twelfth grade.[21]

In 1966, the Cherokees of Oklahoma measured 2.2 years lower in educational attainment than the blacks in Oklahoma.[22]

The native languages of native Americans are not spoken in schools. Very few native Americans can still speak them because the schools do not honor the native American languages. The languages may even disappear because many of those who do speak them are old.[23]

The destruction of a native tongue has not facilitated a fluency in English. One third of the Navajos are unable to read or write in English.[24]

The inability of "Indians" to achieve in schools leads inevitably to an underrepresentation in the ranks of teachers, and those who do succeed are alien from the language and the customs of their people.

American history textbooks have mistreated the "Indian."

---

19. Frederic R. Gunsky, "Racial & Ethnic Survey of California Public Schools," *Integrated Schools*, June-July, 1967.

20. See *El Grito*, Berkeley, California, Quarterly on Mexican-American thought.

21. President Lyndon Johnson, Message to Congress, March 6, 1968.

22. Edgar S. Cahn, *Our Brother's Keeper: The Indian in White America* (Washington, D.C.: A New Community Press Book, 1969).

23. Ibid.

24. Ibid.

Their contributions have been neglected. In an effort to glorify the United States presidents, flagrant violation of treaties were omitted entirely from texts and the fraudulent nature of the "treaties" glossed over. In textbooks, Indians are treated as less than human, their alleged faults are exaggerated, and virtues are ignored. The textbooks disparage Indian cultural attainment and thereby lend credence to the notion that the native American is culturally deprived.[25]

Some "Explanations" of Alleged "Deficiencies"

There can be no serious argument with the contention that the personality of disadvantaged youth is gauged and to some extent shaped by the mental set of adult authorities in and around the school. The behavior of teachers and other significant adults determine whether disadvantaged are to be *allowed* to gain a sense of competence, belonging, or usefulness in school. Teachers (and other adult authorities) are indoctrinated to believe that disadvantaged youth are seriously flawed and that these handicaps disqualify the disadvantaged from activities that lead to personal satisfaction. Throughout professional training, the teacher may be presented with at least four different theses that "explain" the deficiencies associated with poverty and minority membership. These deficits are said to be: (a) *constitutional* — the disadvantaged is genetically inferior to the advantaged; (b) *accumulated environmental* — the disadvantaged suffers from early life lack of intellectual stimulation, particularly in the area of language. This early deprivation is theorized to be accumulative and extremely resistant to later remediation; (c) *inadequate socialization* — the disadvantaged child's formative years are perceived to be enmeshed in chaos. This leads to an unintegrated and debilitated personality; (d) *cultural* — the disadvantaged child is locked into an autonomous culture that is technologically ill-equipped for the modern world and that depreciates intellectual activity.

An analysis of six reference works reveals the orientation that teachers may receive prior to and during their involvement with disadvantaged children. These works are representative of some of the works prospective teachers may read in their education courses. The analysis of these works is only intended to be an example of some of the theories and ideas a prospective teacher may confront. The works stress the deficits of disadvantaged youths almost to the total ex-

25. Virgil J. Vogel, "The Indian in American History Textbooks," *Integrated Education*, May-June, 1968.

clusion of any analysis of other factors that might arise from social inequities and inadequate school structures.[26]

In every one of the resource works, the accumulated environmental deficit was stressed. J.McV. Hunt's view of limited early childhood intellectual stimulation was found in three of the works (A, B, and D). Martin Deutsch who is one of the primary developers of the notion is also adequately represented (B, C, and D). Only in Hellmuth's collection (A) was the case for genetic inferiority presented full-blown. Arthur Jensen attempts to document the case for both race and class inferiority with the aid of statistical tables and scholarly citations. Arthur Hughnon makes a case for IQ testing as a valid measure of innate ability which implies constitutional inferiority of race, ethnicity, and class (D). There is reference to inadequate socialization in every work; although, the emphasis is far less than the theme of intellectual deprivation. The cultural thesis is also prevalent, although it is sometimes co-mingled with the inadequate socialization argument — i.e., that a looseness in family structure (cultural) leads to a lack of well-defined ego and super-ego (socialization) and vice versa.

Given the weight of argument and given the nature of arguments (many writers deride the importance of poverty itself as a factor which affects adaptation to society, and some assert beyond argumentation one or more of the deficiency theories), it is difficult for teachers not to be influenced by them. Yet, the case is not as convincing as many would have you believe. Not one theory is based on critical experiments, nor is it possible for a critical experiment to have been conducted. A critical test would have required structural changes, and no researcher has the power to produce such change. To determine whether there is accumulated deficit that resists change (either because it is genetic or deeply ingrained) would require that poor people be removed from poverty and given all rights, privileges, and prerequisities associated with affluence. Since that has not happened, there are problems with evaluating the research upon which many conclusions are based.

One problem is determination of what is cause and what is effect. Most research has not been able to isolate cause or effect. Is it the

---

26. The works include:
(A) Jerome Hellmuth, *Disadvantaged Child* (Vol. 1, Seattle, Wash.: Special Child Publications, 1967; Vol. 2, New York: Brunner/Mazel, Inc., 1968).
(B) A. Harry Pascow et al, eds., *Education of the Disadvantaged* (New York: Holt, Rinehart & Winston, Inc., 1967).
(C) Allan C. Ornstein, ed., *Educating the Disadvantaged* (New York: AMS Press, 1970).
(D) Jack Frost and Glenn R. Hawkes, eds., (Boston: Houghton Mifflin Co., 1966).
(E) Staten W. Webster, ed., *The Disadvantaged Learner: Knowing, Understanding and Educating* (San Francisco: Chandler Publishing Co., 1966).

four theses — constitution, cultural, socialization, and intellectual stimulation inferiorities — that lead to the personality attributes of the poor, or is it the current denial of competence, belonging, or usefulness that leads to these attributes? Obviously, the answers to these questions would produce very different intervention strategies. If one answers "yes" to the first question, then one would support interventions like "Head Start"; specific job training for those who lack the capacity to go to college; compensatory education for those who are educationally retarded; training in social amenities for the inadequately socialized; and extermination of cultural norms that are out of phase with dominant society.

If one answers "yes" to the second question, the active consequences are strikingly different. He would demand large numbers of additional jobs with opportunities for people to choose the nature of their work and to advance to higher stations. He would opt for changes in school staffing, curriculum, and approaches to discipline. He would push for rearrangement of power relationships in the city and local control over police, education, housing, and health services. He would propose redistribution of wealth (the most moderate demand would be tax reforms).

It is not as arrogant as it may appear to suggest that the majority of social scientists may well be wrong. There are many reasons to doubt their findings. Look to the most popular belief — accumulated environment deficit and the impoverished language that is the alleged consequence. The argument makes little sense when one considers that a few generations ago almost everyone was deprived by current standards. They were isolated, rural, and deprived of the stimulation that comes from electronic devices, and yet there is no evidence that we have developed, even the past half century, people who are discernably more creative, more facile in fantasy or imagery, or more competent in language arts.

The research cited to show deficits has in many instances been very well-conceived and of high quality (by social science standards). Yet, the studies could be severely defective. Take the study of the language of the poor as an example. Such research is conducted by people who are not very conversant with the language of the poor. Their conclusion that the poor have inadequate language might only be an indication of their own lack of appreciation and knowledge of the language that does exist and not a measure of the people studied at all. Almost all of the research is conducted in situations that are not only uncomfortable but also unnatural for the subject. Under those conditions it is not reasonable to expect the subjects to perform at their very best. The research assumes that the measures used provide a representative index of all languages used in the United States and that the subjects' performances are representative of their communication skills in all settings. The validity of both assumptions is subject to challenge, and inasmuch as similar assumptions underlie other deficit theories, they are all open to serious question.

The central problem of all research into the personality of the poor is that the poor are not allowed to participate in any significant way because of their lack of academic credentials. They are not included in the formulation of the design, in the development of measuring instruments, and in the analysis of the results. We have generated a group of experts who talk primarily *about* the poor but very few who have any conversations *with* the poor (except professionally as teacher, researcher, parole officer, or lawyer). The net result of such selective involvement could conceivably lead to a reinforcement of each other's biases and the removal from the discussion of those people who are in a position to prove the theories wrong.

Suggestions for Changes in School Structure and Instruction

Schools must undergo massive reformation if disadvantaged youth are to attain a sense of belonging, usefulness, and competence. At the very least, the following five courses of actions should be considered.

First, the school must respond affirmatively to the student's cry for relevance. Relevance, very simply, is a call for goals that are consonant with a disadvantaged youth's desperate struggle for survival and his unextinguished hope for a good life. Teachers must connect classroom activity to one or more of the student's salient concerns about economic security, political power, cultural growth, and personal well-being. Students must be convinced that their participation truly leads to more command over their environment and greater choices in life's activities. With regard to economic security, students must be given the knowledge, skill, and experience to keep them eligible for those working activities for which significant growth is predicted. Every student must be kept eligible for the "credential society." Vocational educational offerings must not discourage participants from considering college. Students must be given a realistic account of the shape and geography of the work world very early in their school career. They must be told, for example, what doctors, lawyers, schoolteachers, truck drivers, and marine biologists actually do, how they become eligible for their work, and what knowledge and skills are required for the specific tasks of an occupation. Students must be allowed to engage in a wide range of simulated work activities. By the time a student enters high school he should be assigned for a portion of each day to learning stations in the community. While he is there he should sample work of a wide variety to preclude occupational choice based on either ignorance or premature commitment to a specific career.[27]

Students will gain a sense of political potency and a commitment to democratic ideals when the schools are consistent with democratic principles and provide students with the knowledge required for effective citizenship. Schools must guarantee students' rights to create a setting that permits feelings of competence, belonging, and usefulness in schools and to generate a commitment to such ideals when they later function in adult society. Only to the extent that the dominant society is educated to understand and believe in a bill of rights can the minorities and other disadvantaged peacefully gain a sense of dignity and self-worth. The rights guaranteed students must include freedom of expression, privacy, presumption of innocence and due process in judicial proceedings, and protection against cruel and unusual punishments. Those rights should be guaranteed at least to the extent that adult citizens are covered by the first ten amendments to the Constitution. Students must also become involved in significant exercise in executive, legislative, and judicial decision making. Developmentally students should have an increasingly important voice in determining the rules that govern their behavior, the actions to be taken against people who do not obey those rules, and in the selection of teachers and the subject materials to be taught. The students through these experiences must learn how to share power and to deal with the frustrations that come with less than total control.

The goal of cultural competence can be attained only if every student is regarded as an intellectual being. School activities must challenge him to think, conceptualize, abstract, and defend his inferences and assumptions. In that process, the differences in orientation, style, and aspiration that students exhibit must be honored and encouraged. The curriculum must include the contributions of diverse cultures; in particular, those groups subjected to intense oppression must be given special emphasis.

A student will learn to live harmoniously with himself and with his neighbors when he is given maximum opportunity to explore, discuss, and analyze the nature of his relationships. The school must be so structured that he can experiment with different roles and different settings. The matters that most disturb him must be discussed in an open and scholarly manner. The growing conflict of man with nature

27. Arthur Pearl and Frank Riessman, *New Careers for the Poor* (New York: Free Press, 1965).

must not only be explained, but also models of behavior designed to overcome alienation must be developed and tested in classrooms.

The school must be redemptive. Every action of the teacher, every subject taught, and every student's social arrangement must be projected in such a way that students can feel that they can start anew. To be redemptive, the school must:

1. eliminate all negative grading;
2. strike from the record any item that can lead to special treatment of the child;
3. refrain from any effort at special or homogenous grouping whether this be advertised as reading groups, compensatory education, vocational training, or special help for the socially and emotionally disturbed.

The school activities must have a logic and a rhythm to them. This is especially important for disadvantaged youth because of the foreign nature of the school.

Schools must recognize the importance of Whitehead's notion of a natural order to education. Whitehead makes the case that education starts with "romance" — the titillation of students' interest — goes on to "precision" — the exercise necessary for skill development — and concludes with "generalization" — the ability to put the knowledge to work outside the school.[28] Every school must build into their program romance and generalization. At the present time, there is almost exclusive emphasis on precision. Schools must evaluate class activities according to the criteria suggested by Fantini and Weinstein's "contact curriculum."[29] They argue that all education must make contact with people where they *are* psychologically, that the activity must be coherent and hang together, and that the students must obtain power from their investment of time and energy.

Teachers must function as responsible leaders. The teacher must justify his right to be a leader of disadvantaged youth. A major contributor to the alienation of poor and minority youth from school is the hostility that stems from a lack of mutual acceptance. The school develops negative attitudes in students when teachers are seen as acting as agents of a value system rather than instructors. The inevitable consequence of such antagonism is a continual and constant battleground from which there is no rest, victory, or hope of peace.

---

28. Alfred North Whitehead, *The Aims of Education and Other Essays* (New York: Free Press, 1929).
29. Mario D. Fantini and Gerald Weinstein, *The Disadvantaged Challenge to Education* (New York: Harper & Row, Publishers, 1968).

To become a responsible leader, teachers must be trained to be appreciative of pluralism, accountable, negotiable, stable in conflict situations, and able to view rules and regulations as means but never ends. Promotions and tenure must be based on demonstrations of these attributes of responsible authority. Appreciation of pluralism goes far beyond a single teacher's capability. Each teacher can be helped to resonate better with the style, language, values and social identification of disadvantaged youth. Whatever an individual does as an individual is not enough. The teacher must demonstrate a respect for pluralism by insisting that staff reflect those groups who are now underrepresented in positions of authority (i.e., blacks, native Americans, isolated whites, and Chicanos). To be accountable the teacher must be prepared to defend everything he does (or does not do) with logic and evidence. He must encourage the student to inquire "Why do I have to learn that?", and he must struggle to answer that question to the *student's* satisfaction. (Accountability extends to all relevant questioning publics, i.e., other teachers, administrators, parents, or taxpayers.)

Negotiable teachers are willing to entertain counter proposals for school activity. To be truly negotiable a teacher would welcome the interventions of outsiders to conciliate differences. The teacher must be willing to submit a dispute to some independent body for binding arbitration. There must be equity of power among those who are bargaining. If there is no power on the student's side, the entire process becomes a sham.

Conflicts cannot be avoided in schools. Too much of current education is geared to attainment of consensus. The responsible teacher will not demand consensus because he is aware that such consensus will come at the expense of pluralism. The responsible teacher will struggle to develop ground rules to keep conflicts from degenerating into violence or chaos. The responsible teacher will not become unraveled when confronted by angry students. The teacher's response to rules and regulations has considerable bearing on the opportunity for disadvantaged youth to grow as people. Disadvantaged youth become shaped by their responses to rules and regulations. The nature of these rules and how they are interpreted by school authorities can have a considerable influence on the behavior of these youth. The responsible authority recognizes the race, class, sex, and ethnic bias in most school rules. He also recognizes that there is differential rule enforcement — the very same behavior that leads to severe punishment for the poor goes unheeded when perpetrated by the affluent. Most importantly, the responsible authority interprets rules in the context of ends and acts accordingly. He uses discretion and justifies both enforcement or relaxation or regulations.

My final suggestion deals with training the responsible authority. The problems disadvantaged youths face are largely the result of the training teachers receive. The demand that teachers receive a college education *prior* to their job assignment insures a gulf between teacher and disadvantaged youth. Recall that disadvantaged youth *are* disadvantaged largely because they are denied entrance to higher education. Thus a situation is contrived to place in positions of authority people who have almost no basis for establishing rapport with the youth they are hired to serve. The situation is worsened because the prospective teacher in the course of his education receives the previously described, often distorted pictures of the aspirations and potentials of disadvantaged youths. When they receive a teaching assignment, they come in cold. The contrast of hard reality with the knowledge they received in college can lead to the shattering experiences that Herndon, Kohl, and Kozol so poignantly describe.[30]

Two Directions: Behaviorism and Humanism

Schools of education are criticized from many quarters and a flood of programs have been generated to remedy the situation. High on the list of priorities of the Educational Professional Development Act is preparation of teachers to teach the disadvantaged. Although the legislation is new and evaluation of its effects would be premature, it seems improbable that much good will come from it. There is not much clamor for change within the schools of education — faculties and administrations are often mired down in their inertia. Even more discouraging is the proposed direction for change that is sought. Almost all the changes can be placed in one of two categories. One category emphasizes efficiency in learning specific skills and is based on the operant learning concepts of B.F. Skinner.[31] The other stresses emotional adaptation and is based on humanistic psychology.[32] Advocates of both approaches insist that they have something

---

30. Betty Levy particularizes the lack of relationship between her teacher training and her ghetto school assignment in an article "An Urban Teacher Speaks Out" written as a letter in *The Harvard School of Education Association Bulletin*, Vol. 10, Summer 1965 and reprinted in Staten Webster's *The Disadvantaged Learner*, mentioned earlier.

31. There are many exponents of this highly structural approach to learning — programmed learning, computer assisted instruction, performance based competence, teaching machines — all drawn upon this ideology. A specific manual for training teachers according to the approach has been developed by Wesley C. Berker, Siegfried Englemann, and Donald R. Thomas *Teaching: A Basic Course in Applied Psychology* (Palo Alto, Calif.: Science Research Associates, 1970).

32. George Dennison, *Lives of Children* (New York: Random House, Inc., 1969), and Neil Postman and Charles Weingartner, *Teaching as a Subversive Activity* (New York: Delacorte Press, 1969) represent innovations based on this kind of thinking.

especially valuable to offer the disadvantaged. I am afraid both are wrong, but before that is offically recognized, much more harm will be inflicted on the poor.

The behaviorists claim that they can develop materials and train teachers to enable the disadvantaged to become proficient in basic literacy and arithmetic skills. They emphasize breaking down the learning tasks to simple units and establishing a regimen in which successful performance receives quick consistent rewards and unsuccessful performance is ignored. The logic according to the theory is that reinforced behaviors are learned and nonreinforced behaviors are extinguished. On initial glance such an approach to education should be welcomed. It appears to generate competence, an absolute essential for personality development. It develops in the child those basic skills upon which more complex learning is necessarily based. There are research findings that support the approach, and yet, there are reasons to doubt the desirability of operant techniques, especially in the case of disadvantaged youth.

Operant conditioning techniques are based on the assumption that the *teacher* knows the appropriate response. When it comes to reading, the appropriate mutual response must be in the native tongue of the student. If the teacher does not know the language or if the program is not designed for that language, then the only reading program possible is in the language of the teacher. Such a reading program places the student in an untenable situation. He is unable to draw upon what he already knows; he is not able to put the knowledge to work; and he cannot feel at home in the school. Operant conditioning is based on the assumption that the same response is correct for all children in the class and that the same problem is equally relevant to all. The approach is basically set up for teacher control of the subject matter that is not open to discussion and examination.

Preparing teachers to modify student behavior through operant principles has another failing. The approach focuses the teacher on small learning units to the complete exclusion of analysis of the school and the society. When the procedures used to teach reading by behavioristic principles are viewed, some of the dangers in the approach — particularly the danger of oversell — become more apparent. Behaviorists believe that it is extremely important that children be grounded in the fundamentals of reading. They argue that the lack of such early training leads to the later educational problems of disadvantaged youth. They assert that if the child is rewarded (given praise, blue stars, token, or candy) every time he correctly associates a visual stimulus with a sound, he will learn the relationship and build the base for further success.

Many claims are made for the effectiveness of this approach. These claims are established primarily by citing the progress made by disadvantaged youth when they are taught by teachers trained in operant techniques. Their evidence and their argument appears convincing, but is it? There are problem areas with the research that tend to be glossed over. There are problems with the selection of evaluation criteria; the selection of alternative teacher training approaches for comparison; the assessment of the long-range consequences of the training; the downgrading of educational efforts that do not lend themselves to behavioristic principles, and the approach toward students that is implicit in the strategy.

The criteria selected for measuring success has much to do with the interpretation of the effectiveness of the program. The criteria chosen by those who see the teacher as a reinforcer of externally definable behaviors are generally performances on standardized achievement tests. If the disadvantaged youth taught by their teachers following behavioristic principles score significantly higher on such tests than a comparable group not taught in the same way, the results are interpreted as proof of effectiveness of the method. In contrast, I believe that there are behavioral indices of reading. I believe reading occurs when a person on his own opts to devote his time and energy to peruse written materials and is able to decipher, understand, and utilize the products of his investment. Using such a definition, people can be gauged in a variety of ways; they can be assessed on the quality and the quantity of their efforts. They can be judged on the ways they put the activity to work. They can be assessed on the priority that reading has in relation to competing activities. No research has as yet been conducted that relates reading, as I define it, to any instructional techniques that place a heavy emphasis upon repetitive exercises (which is a critical part of operant techniques). Such exercises can have a short-term positive effect and, at the same time, a long-term negative impact. The six-year-old, if consistently reinforced, does learn to associate a picture with a sound and learns the lawfulness of the arrangments (i.e., that certain elements of a picture almost always are linked to the same sound). At the same time he may acquire some devastating, lingering side effects. Ten years later he may recall only that the proceedings were dreary, and thus he may be reluctant to engage in the activity. The advocates of mechanistic behavioristic principles applied to teaching do not always concern themselves with such issues.

Behaviorist-oriented classes do have some good points. The ordinary student is in a classroom that no responsible critic defends. The regular teacher is often ill-prepared and defeated. The regular teacher may have become convinced that little is possible. The operant trained teacher is optimistic; he believes in the program, and such optimism alone could account for the gains attributed to behaviorism. Teacher attitudes may confound research and student performance in other ways. The teacher in the experimental group (behaviorist trained) often is young, enthusiastic, and dedicated, whereas the teacher of the control group (regular) often possesses none of these desired characteristics (see Kohl, Kozol, and Herndon for substantiation). Teachers who do not follow behaviorist principles also claim success in improved reading and performance. Herb Kohl's *36 Children* made gains in test score achievement as large as any claimed by advocates of behavioristic methods, and he was not only untrained in the technique but violated virtually every principle of teaching reading. More importantly, Kohl was able to arouse a desire to read and utilize reading that has never been demonstrated by behaviorists. If it is true that most classroom activity discourages reading,[33] then perhaps the behaviorists can only rightfully claim that they discourage reading less than regularly trained teachers.

Because behaviorists tend to ignore the structure of inequality they cannot see any possible negative consequence of success. There is a naive assumption among many educators that good responses lead inevitably to other good responses. Assume now that behaviorists really teach disadvantaged youth to read. Suppose once taught these youth read avariciously about their oppression. Suppose that they act upon what they read. I believe that the disadvantaged must be taught to read, but I realize that there is riskiness in the venture. Therefore, I believe we should try to keep the system open and give the student some tools to manipulate it. Behaviorists increase the probability of disaster when they remain oblivious to the risk. I believe one reason that some disadvantaged youth resist reading is that they are aware of the dangers involved.

The humanistic thrust, the open, unstructured approach to education, may also be a cul-de-sac. Although it does not get the favored treatment from the federal government, many "free" schools are run according to its principles. This approach tends to solve problems by ignoring them. Whereas behaviorism carefully schedules student activity — the humanists believe that the student knows what is best for him. The absence of defined goals may be a possible education for youths who have family connections and other leverages that can be translated into decent employment, political power, cultural activity, and personal concerns, but disadvantaged youths

---

33. See Jane Tarrey, *Elementary English*, May 1965.

have none of those advantages and only an education can provide them. The teacher of the open system is essentially a friend and his training is prematurely clinical. In behaviorism, the teacher is trained to perform certain acts. In the open classroom, the teacher is given an education, and then he and his students are let go. Dennison argues that for an elementary school any mature adult with some understanding of group dynamics and personality theory could make it as a teacher.[34] Schools of education for the behaviorists are modeled after any mechanical skill (e.g., typing or welding), whereas training for the humanistic teacher would eliminate much of the schools' education courses.

Music, the Street Life, and the Disadvantaged

Cultural activities — music in particular — play an important part in the adjustment patterns of the disadvantaged. Through music the disadvantaged talk and listen. The music reflects their style and tempo, priorities, and aspirations. Music offers continuity with the past. LeRoi Jones[35] traces the movement of the blacks from slavery through reconstruction to present day urban life with changes in the tempo, style, and mood of the music.

Through music disadvantaged youth bind their groups and gain a sense of belonging and usefulness and competency. In a credential society, music provides one of the few remaining outlets for the disadvantaged to escape poverty, and some outstanding talents have taken advantage of that opportunity. Music has always been an activity for youth. Youth belonging is reflected in singing, dancing, and performing. A very high percentage of the most successful performers are young and most recently a large percentage is coming from impoverished backgrounds. Again as with humor, the music rails out against the oppressiveness of society. The music mirrors responses to life conditions that lock out the poor from the opportunities of the economic and political structures. The music tends to attribute magical properties to drugs and alcohol. Through music youth are told that they can be ten feet tall (i.e., feel competent). The music of the poor deals with racial identities and relationships with dominant society. For example, Nina Simone and Roberta Flack hit very heavily on racism and responses to racism. A native American, Buffy Saint Marie, has charged her country as the primary cause for her people dying. The Chicano's music, distinctive because of its language and

---

34. Dennison, *Lives of Children.*
35. Le Roi Jones, *Blues People: The Negro Experience in White America and the Music that Developed from It* (New York: William Morrow and Company, 1963).

tempo, stresses ethnic pride. The poor white resonates to the Nashville Sound and sympathizes with Johnny Cash's concern about jail and prison life. Each theme gains popularity because it communicates to disadvantaged youth. Through music and humor youth communicate to adults, if only adults are willing to listen. If our programs *for* youth are not to end in frustrating failure, it may heed us to attentively listen to what is being sung and played — and act accordingly.

It seems that whenever drugs, humor, and music combine there is a party. Parties provide ever so transiently all the gratifications that are denied everywhere else. At parties there is potency, belonging, and usefulness. Parties have an appeal that outrides any activity sponsored by adult establishments. Parties are constricted by space and time. Youth must make do with very limited resources. Public facilities are often not considered (a) because disadvantaged youth groups lack a sufficient official status to qualify for their use; (b) because the illegality of drug possession demands secrecy; and (c) because the groups desire privacy.

Partying tends to fractionate disadvantaged youth into cliques. The partygoers set high priority to such frivolity. They like to recuperate only to party again. That style of life runs counter to those who try to make it within the system (students and responsible workers) and to those devoted to reform or overthrow it.

Violence and the Street Life

The violence attributed to the disadvantaged gives to them an unwarranted exotic quality of existence. It is true there is more violent confrontation among the poor than with any other segment of the population. This aspect of adaptation is far more situational than it is engrained as a personality characteristic. The ever present physical contact sparks violence. The stored-up resentment against unrelieved inequality periodically erupts into rampages. The prodding of insensitive governmental authorities is reciprocated (almost every urban "riot" was preceded by a police killing or injury to a ghetto resident). There is violence in every aspect of underclass life. The fighting for a place in a crowded bed is a violent act. The killing of a rat before it bites a baby is a violent act. The physical manhandling of an eight-year-old to get to the principal's office is a violent act. The vain effort to keep warm in the winter and keep cool in the summer is a violent act. Trying to make it home through debris and crowds and suspicious storekeepers is a violent act. A social worker denying welfare, an employment counselor denying work, a judge denying bail, and a parole board denying parole are violent acts. A hospital that denies admission is a violent act. A hospital ward without privacy is a violent act. An ambulance that does not come is a violent act. A telephone company, electric company, water company, or gas company turning off service because of a client's inability to pay is a violent act. An eviction is a violent act. Refusing to give credit is a violent act. Charging exorbitant rates is a violent act. Urging people to buy on credit more than they can possibly afford is a violent act. Telling youth that they must be patient because things are being worked out is a violent act (particularly if things are not being worked out). Going with a problem to a federal, state, city, and county building and being referred endlessly from one office to another without ever receiving the help needed is a violent act. Being faced with so much everyday violence of a more guarded sort leads to violent response in the styles comfortable to disadvantaged youth.

But violence goes beyond that — it becomes a part of the ideology of frustrated youth. More and more disadvantaged youth really believe that the *only* thing the establishment understands is violence. They are moving to the conviction that only fear moves those in power. They cite as proof the Watts conflagration that provoked (in their view) more positive response to intolerable conditions than years and years of peaceful pleading had produced. Violence is also a means whereby the disadvantaged gain feelings of competence, belonging, and usefulness. Claude Brown[36] describes the importance of "bebopping" for group cohesion and for individual status and power. Since that time there appears to have been a reduction in the number of "fighting gangs" in the ghettos. Fighting for the sheer joy of fighting has diminished, but in its stead has come a politicalization of alienated youth (and this has not necessarily led to a decline in violence). The youngster now serves as leader in the Black Panthers or Brown Berets. This evolution provides youth with an opportunity to gain a sense of personal potency and group usefulness. The change to a political form of protest gives legitimacy to activities that no ghetto gang ever had. There are many influential people who regard these youth groups as serious political entities allowing youth groups to radiate in the glow of newfound usefulness, belonging, and competence. For the poor, violence has always had a special value. It offers escape from poverty, perhaps either legally as a professional prize fighter or football player or illegally as a hood or thug.

Violence is an overplayed aspect of the life of the disadvantaged. The poor are not preoccupied in violent activities. Those highly publicized urban outbreaks are rare. Most of the ghetto residents

---

36. Brown, *Manchild.*

avoid physical confrontations; the sensationalizing of sporadic violent acts gives a false impression of low income life. On the whole, disadvantaged youth, despite provocations, are as warm, tender, and personally concerned with one another as any other segment of our society.

The Need for Improved Conditions in the Cities

My own ideas on how the cities could be improved revolve around factors that would bring feelings of belonging, usefulness, and competence. Among conditions that might be important to disadvantaged youth, I would urge that:

1. The distinction between the school and community life must be eliminated by dispersing learning centers throughout the community. We must establish a system for evaluating knowledge and skills obtained through nonschool experiences and give appropriate credit for such learning.
2. Youth be employed *significantly* in community development projects. Whenever possible, youth involved in such projects should be paid for their efforts. These youth should share responsibility for developing the rules that govern their involvement and be involved in the planning of activities. The projects should be designed to provide youth opportunities for belonging, usefulness, and competence.
3. Youth be subsidized to work in conflict resolution centers in which they would try to bridge the gap between races, generations, and the "establishment." These centers should be run by youth and adults should serve only as technical advisors and assistants.
4. Every neighborhood have continually supervised cultural, educational, and health facilities. The programs generated in these centers should be consistent with life-styles of the poor and provide alternatives to drug abuse and other destructive pursuits.

PARENTS AND CHILDREN: THE GENERATION GAP AMONG THE DISADVANTAGED

All of the factors that act on disadvantaged youth in the school and in the street to deny competence, belonging, and usefulness strain parent-child relationships. By and large, parents are unable to understand their children's posture toward school. The parents believe that education offers a way out of poverty. They feel that their children are throwing away a golden opportunity and are dooming themselves to lifelong misery.

Parents are unable to fathom the schools' language, goals, and processes, but they find it hard to fault the school or its staff for their children's problems. They are persuaded to accept an educational responsibility for children that they cannot possibly fulfill, and their inability to help with homework or guarantee classroom attendance leads to increased hostility at home.

Parents do not understand their children's attitude toward work. They are hurt when children are unwilling to follow in their footsteps and become hardworking members of society. They consider this lack of involvement with work a rebuff and a manifestation of laziness. Parents cannot acept or adjust to the tempo of their children's lives and activities. The music, the humor, and the informal nature of personal relationships mystify and then anger the family elders. The difference in attitudes toward religion and the sometime cavalier treatment of a minister by children leads to family conflicts. Widespread drug use is one of the most difficult problems for parents. Parents not only cannot understand what has happened, but also they are terrified that one child's involvement will lead to other children's involvement. To protect those not as yet using drugs, the parents often are forced to reject the child most in need of their love and support.

The child reared and traveling in a world far different from that understood by his rural bred and rural oriented parent tries to keep many of his activities from his parents. His motives are complex — he wants to protect himself from his parents' wrath, and yet he does not want to further trouble his already frazzled mother and/or father. The net impact of all of this is a child who is unable to communicate with his parents, continuous squabbling between the generations, and guilt that neither parent nor child can handle. The efforts to resolve guilt often weaken the family structure even more, such as further involvement in drugs or alcohol or flight from home.

Disadvantaged youth see family problems from an entirely different perspective. They feel parents align themselves too readily with the police, teachers, and social workers. They are ashamed when parents beg for mercy and otherwise demean themselves before the "enemy." Disadvantaged youth are unable to understand the submissiveness of their parents and hold them partially accountable for the intolerable condition of inequality handed down to them. They find it incomprehensible that their parents have been and still are willing to work and slave while others get rich from their efforts.

The children are unable to appreciate the nostalgia about the good old days. They are not sympathetic to parental "flipping out" about drugs or promiscuous lovemaking.

The strain between the disadvantaged child and his parents represents another casualty of a world that denies opportunity for gratification economically, politically, culturally, or personally. As C. Wright Mills points out, the family (with the church and education) has lost importance as the military, government, and industry have gained.[37] Many of the suggestions for the school and for the street would by themselves help the family. In addition, the following may help both children and parents: (1) Parents should not be required to be adjuncts to either teachers or policemen; (2) Opportunities should be provided for parents to function in paid capacities in school and community activities. Parents should be trained so that they can provide effective performance; (3) Supportive services should be offered round-the-clock to families. These services should range from daycare (and night) facilities to drop-in clinics.

CONCLUSION

There is an enormous variation among the poor, and no simple presentation of personality types can do them adequate justice. They exhibit every characteristic that is found among the more favored, but the distribution is different. The blacks had to deal with the consequences of slavery that led to distinguishing adjustment patterns of language and a style in dealing with the oppressor. The Chicano whose language was outlawed in the wake of military misadventures was pushed along yet another path. The native Americans who were isolated in reservations had yet another row to hoe. The poor whites with no emerging positive social image to provide identification may have been forced into the most lonely of adjustment patterns.

Social adjustment or personality profiles may be viewed as either a cause or consequence of poverty or prejudice. In this chapter the arguments for considering poverty as a function of personal inadequacy were rejected in favor of a position that attributed poverty to a lack of options. The distinctive quality associated with the lifestyles of the poor were explained as efforts to derive a sense of belonging, competence, and usefulness in a world that offered very few opportunities for such gratification.

The personality of the poor is seen as a problem for society and not only the poor — a challenge that may be lost in the shuffle of benign neglect.

---

37. C. Wright Mills, *The Sociological Imagination* (New York: Oxford University Press, 1959).

8

Teaching Achievement Motivation[1]

Alfred S. Alschuler, Diane Tabor, James McIntyre
University of Massachusetts, Amherst

The primary purpose of this chapter is to teach you how to increase students' need to achieve — that is, their desire to strive for their own kind of excellence. The "need to achieve" involves (1) a special way of planning to attain excellence; (2) a set of strong feelings about doing well; and (3) specific action strategies. These three parts of n-Ach (pronounced as two syllables: en atch) have been studied for over 20 years. The use of recently developed educational methods achievement motivation now can be taught directly to students. Later in this chapter we will describe ways you can restructure your everyday classroom teaching to encourage and reward students' achievement motivation. According to research findings courses which increase achievement motivation have stimulated students to initiate more planning to make more constructive use of play time, while school classes restructured for n-Ach often produce dramatic learning gains.

No approach can guarantee that all of your students will become highly achievement motivated. The complexities of contemporary schooling, the hourly problems of coordinating 20 to 30 or more unique minds without becoming a tyrant, and the sheer difficulty of accelerating the pace of personality growth — all guarantee that no magic word solution will turn your classroom into a palace of learning at one stroke. However, application of these new methods is likely to produce a substantial increase in the average level of your students' achievement motivation and may have a strong and significant impact on several of the individual students.

1. From *Teaching Achievement Motivation* by Alfred Alschuler, Diane Tabor, and James McIntyre; Education Ventures, Inc., Middletown, Conn., 1970. Used with permission.

WHAT IS ACHIEVEMENT MOTIVATION?

When desire for achievement becomes a dominant concern for a person, it is expressed in driving energy aimed at attaining excellence, getting ahead, improving past records, doing things better, faster, more efficiently, and finding unique solutions to difficult problems. People with strong achievement motivation generally are self-confident individuals who are at their best taking personal responsibility in situations where they can control what happens to them. They set challenges demanding maximum effort, but goals which are possible to attain; they are not satisfied with automatic success that comes from easy goals nor do they try to do the impossible. Time rushes by them and causes mild anxiety that there won't be enough hours to get things done. As a result they make more accurate long-range plans than people with less achievement motivation. They like to get regular, concrete feedback on how well they are doing so that their plans can be modified accordingly. They take pride in their accomplishments and get pleasure from striving for the challenging goals of excellence they set.

Although one never encounters the "Achieving Man" in bold simplicity, it is possible for psychologists to identify achievement motivation in an individual much as a sensitive musician can listen attentively to the woodwinds while hearing the whole orchestra. In order to study this motive scientifically, Professor David C. McClelland of Harvard University developed methods for measuring its strength. These methods involve counting the frequency of thoughts, actions, and feelings an individual has that are focused on attaining excellence.

With these measuring instruments psychologists have searched for the earliest origins of achievement motivation in individuals and nations. They found, for example, that mothers of young boys with high achievement motivation, comparatively speaking, were more warmly affectionate and used hugging and kissing more often to show approval for independence and mastery. These mothers tended to set higher standards for their children and expected self-reliance at an earlier age than did mothers of children with lower achievement motivation. Researchers found that cultures having many folk tales rich in examples of achievement motivation also stress direct training for achievement in other child-rearing practices. In contrast, cultures having few folk tales containing illustrations of achievement motivation more often stress punishing children for failure to be obedient.

Students need opportunities *and* motivation. The massive U.S.

programs of aid to education, like foreign aid efforts, have concentrated on providing materials rather than developing human resources. It is clear in education, as well, that more up-to-date physical facilities, more sophisticated educational hardware, and even money spent on research will not be sufficient unless students' motivation to use their new opportunities also is increased. Following the successful development of motivation courses for adults, it seemed appropriate to adapt these procedures for students. Since 1965 the Achievement Motivation Development Project at Harvard University Graduate School of Education has adapted n-Ach training for students, explored new methods of increasing motivation, and invented new ways to structure classroom learning to provide experiences in a variety of motives.

Our purpose is *not* simply to stimulate students to make better use of their opportunities in school; but rather to help students attain the goals they set for themselves in or outside school. In fact, research on achievement motivation training for students provides little evidence for increased grades in school, a finding that may disappoint teachers who hope n-Ach courses will raise students' grades in the teacher's favorite academic subject. Instead, n-Ach training most often results in more purposeful planning and action outside of school where students are more clearly "in charge" of their lives. In one way, this finding could not be more optimistic. The ultimate purpose of schooling is to teach students knowledge, skills, values, and feelings that help them live more effective, mature adult lives. This purpose is consistent with the typical and most appropriate applications of n-Ach training to situations requiring personal management in the broadest sense — jobs, athletics, hobbies, administrative activities, and some learning situations; dating, marriage, and raising children.

A LOOK AHEAD

The goal is to provide you with sufficient practical information, experience, confidence, and teaching materials so that you can increase your students' motivation. We believe that n-Ach training is appropriate for those children who need and want increased achievement motivation so that they can respond more fully, effectively, joyfully, and judiciously in entrepreneurial situations. Surprisingly, this could include nearly all of us; according to research findings most people have fairly low achievement motivation. Providing the opportunity for such training is a legitimate responsibility of public schooling.

In the sections that follow, we shall discuss (a) motivation in classrooms; (b) achievement action strategies; (c) learning structures as motivational games; and (d) achievement motivation training.

MOTIVATION IN CLASSROOMS

To increase students' motivation in the classroom it is more important to change the *way* they learn than *what* they learn. The way students think, act, and feel in learning is determined in large part by the rules of the implicit learning game and the teacher's leadership style. Both the rules and leadership style can be readily modified, although generally these methods of motivating students are not consciously used. Teachers can ignore but cannot avoid the direct, pervasive and continuous influence of rules and style on students' motivation. Some teachers, without realizing it, even work against their own declared purposes by having students learn in ways that are inconsistent with the content of their courses. For instance, in many social studies classes designed to teach citizenship, the teacher is, in fact, the benevolent king of a vassal state. In achievement motivation training as well, the rules and leadership style must be consistent with the training courses; more important, however, there must be opportunities outside of the course for students to see their increased achievement motivation — their independent restless striving for excellence — and then deliberately send them into classrooms where achievement motivation is dysfunctional. In order to help you avoid this problem and instead create learning environments that support the motives you want to instill, this chapter describes relevant ways to modify the rules of learning and leadership style in the classroom.

Many teachers say and believe they are most interested in fostering independent achievement motivation but inadvertently encourage submission. There were times for all of us as students when we worked hard for goals that later seemed silly. A high school incident recalled by one of the authors in discussing this chapter neatly illustrated this point. When he got back a math test on which he was to graph a quadratic equation much to his dismay there was a large red "C-" on the top. On closer inspection, it became clear the graph solution was correct. The only errors of omission were the arrow tips at the ends of the ordinate and abcissa. He became angrily determined to submit a perfect paper, an absolute model of detailed accuracy and completeness, no matter how much effort and time it took. With the teacher's standards clear, he decided to meet them through sheer persistence.

At first we thought it interesting that this anecdote was so rich with achievement motivation. We began to realize, however, that the achievement motivation the author possessed had, in fact, been transformed into an energetic desire to comply with the standards set by the teacher, even though these standards were not personally relevant. In retrospèct, working hard for this goal seemed silly. The classroom factors which encourage achievement motivation, compliance, curiosity, or any other motive often are equally subtle, and not adaptable to neat formulas for changing the learning environment.

At another level, achievement motivation and the student's belief in his ability to control his own fate often are clearly discouraged rather than nurtured by schooling. With the increasing demands for higher education to qualify for prestigious and well-paying jobs, there has been a corresponding increase in the importance of academic success. The greatest rewards go to those who demonstrate academic excellence. Sometimes academic success is the self-chosen goal of adolescents. Often it is not. Frequently, achievement motivation is reflected in striving for other less prestigious but no less valuable goals that cannot be pursued in schools. Students with high achievement motivation in fact do not always excel academically and sometimes don't even like school. Their feelings may be due to several structural aspects of schooling. Most school curricula do not encourage individual students to take personal responsibility for setting their own moderate-risk goals. For the lower half of every class, getting an "A" is a very high-risk goal. Yet, striving for a moderate-risk "C" does not yield the payoff so important to later success. It is not surprising that some students with high achievement motivation find school to be at odds with their motivation. Their initiative, independence, and self-reliance either are not seen by the teachers because they are demonstrated outside school or they are noticed by teachers but are viewed as being rebellious, antisocial activity. Categorized as problem students, slow learners, or potential dropouts, these students, not surprisingly, may develop negative self-images and a distaste for school. Their attitudes can result in increased rebelliousness and a sense that they have little power to control their environments and their lives. Their achievement motivation fades or remains latent within schools. The motive most useful to them in economic survival as an adult often is a liability in schooling supposedly designed to help them succeed.

The process as well as the content of formal education should be designed to prepare students to live mature, effective adult lives. The way students learn, the rules and leadership they experience, should be basically similar to the basic rules and leadership styles they will encounter as adults. If survival in the social system (unhappily) required obedience and compliance more than independence, then decreased achievement motivation would be a valuable outcome of schooling. Teaching useful responses to power-oriented situations would be highly appropriate. Whatever motives are taught in school should be consistent with cultural values and societal demands. Often, "loyalty, obedience and sensitivity to those in authority" are valued tactics of our "brightest" students who believe we have the answers necessary to doing well on tests. They slavishly adhere to our requests in order that we will patronize them with good grades and good recommendations. Action instigated by students towards goals that are not consistent with those we hold might conceivably damage their chances for the classroom status rewards. Such a policy does not maximally develop the strengths and potentialities of the individual student but it does make the school, teacher and student aware of what is really happening in the school and world outside.

Teachers' leadership styles, also powerfully shape individuals' motives. This shaping is illustrated by the provocative research of Kurt Lewin. When Lewin left Germany in the 1930's he had an established reputation as a "field theorist." Like other field theorists, Lewin believed that behavior is almost exclusively determined by stimuli in the environment. To substantiate this belief, and simultaneously to help explain German compliance to Hitler's regime, Lewin, Lippitt and White (1939) created three boys' clubs, each with a different type of leader. The "autocratic" (power-oriented) leader was stiff, formal and aloof, gave directions, made rules and did not participate in the boys' activities. The *"laissez-faire"* (affiliation-oriented) leader was informal and friendly; he gave no directions, made no rules and, in general, shared in whatever the boys wanted to do. The "democratic" (achievement-oriented) leader was work oriented, though he helped the boys vote on what they wanted to do. He did not direct actions like the autocratic leader, nor did he let happy chaos reign as did the *laissez-faire* leader. He was a friendly co-participant in the projects chosen by the boys and was concerned with their doing things well independently.

Over time, the three groups developed distinctly different social structures and behavior patterns. There were many more aggressive acts and incidents of scapegoating in the autocratic group. The boys were task involved and compliant but only as long as the leader was present. When he left, anarchy quickly emerged. In contrast, when the democratic leader left his group, the boys continued their purposeful activities while group morale and cooperation remained high. In the *laissez faire* group, the absence of the leader meant even more fun, and even less task involvement. Friendliness and "we-feeling" remained high. After the three social structures were in operation for some time, the leaders switched groups. In this way it was possible to assess how much the boys' behavior was due to the leader and how much was due to the personalities of the boys. Lippitt and White (1958) concluded that in nearly all cases the leadership style, rather than the personalities of the boys, was the principal determinant of behavior. When leaders changed, the behavior changed.

There are several implications for the teacher that emerge from this study. These are, in brief: be democratic, but give directions and involve children in decision-making. Such direction and participation cultivates motivation and independence.

As a social system in miniature, classrooms should reflect cultural values and teach the most constructive and socially useful motives. It is possible to increase students' motivation by changing the classroom learning structure and leadership style. In our experience, it is easier for teachers to modify their leadership style after they have restructured the way their students learn. In fact, when the learning rules are changed, a different teaching-leadership style nearly always is required. In the next section we describe ways to restructure learning opportunities to be consistent with desired motivation. Appropriate changes in leadership style are discussed in this context.

ACHIEVEMENT ACTION STRATEGIES

The following four action strategies, although presented separately, are not completely independent elements of achievement motivation. They combine dynamically to comprise an energetic, restless, innovative individual who is highly concerned with improvement, doing things faster, better, more efficiently, more economically. Together they represent an interrelated pattern that is reflected in getting things done and knowing how to do them effectively. There are four strategies: risk taking, use of feedback, personal responsibility and researching environment.

Risk Taking

In a new situation where a person must rely on his own skill, the high achiever takes carefully calculated moderate risks. He sets goals that are challenging, and not goals that are unreasonably difficult or goals that are too simple and undemanding. Extremely difficult goals make success unlikely. Easy goals make success unsatisfying. The person with high achievement motivation wants a middle position where his skill and dexterity will be challenged, but where he has a reasonable chance of making it, giving his best effort.

Typically, people with high achievement motivation set goals in which their chances for success are roughly 50-50, according to their own estimates of their skills and resources. In these situations the outcome is most uncertain. People with low n-Ach are much more inclined to set extremely high or low goals, usually because there is practically no risk, no uncertainty, and no real challenge for them to produce their best efforts. If they fail to make the high goal they can always attribute their result to the impossibility of the task. A very easy goal is no challenge and does not give the person a sense of accomplishment — in life situations such easy goals usually do not yield very much. In setting challenging goals with moderate risks, people with high n-Ach try hard and end up with more to show for it, because easy goals have little payoff and very difficult goals are seldom attained.

Here are several questions that help focus on individual risk-taking styles and goal setting. What were you thinking and feeling as you selected your goal? Did you have a definite goal in mind? What were you trying to do? Did you think of yourself as competing? In what way?

How meaningful were the goals to you? How did that affect your performance?

Would you consider your behavior in this situation typical of you in competitive situations? Why or why not? Do you do the same thing in other areas of your life? e.g. What kind of risks do you usually take? What kinds of competition generally stimulate you? Or do you avoid competition? What kinds of goal setting and risk taking are involved in your work or hobbies?

What does your behavior in this situation suggest about your attitude towards yourself?

Use of Immediate Concrete Feedback to Modify Goals

Because the person with high n-Ach chooses challenging goals with uncertain outcomes and is highly involved, he likes to know how well he is doing. Thus, he seeks situations that offer regular concrete feedback about his progress or lack of it, and uses the feedback to modify his goals or his behavior. In games this feedback comes from the scores in each round. On the basis of his successive scores, the player with high n-Ach modifies his strategy and behavior to increase his chances for success. For a high achiever, flexibility and experimentation are more typical reactions than stubbornness to feedback. And he needs to be flexible, since he often initially overestimates how well he can do in a new situation. In school feedback comes from the teacher materials and other students. Seeking feedback and using it are important ways of using information to gain increased success.

For the person with high n-Ach, consecutive successes are taken as an indication that an even stiffer challenge is in order. Rather than resting on his laurels, he creates a new situation where the probability of success and the value of success once again demand an energetic effort from him. If feedback shows he is not doing well, or in fact that he is failing, that too is received as information rather than a permanent personal label. He acts to reverse the trend, to make the negative feedback positive by changing the risk, by acting differently, by reassessing the situation, by analyzing the obstacles more closely, and perhaps by seeking help. This procedure doesn't suggest a fatalistic shrinking of aspiration, but more a process of intermediate goal setting that will insure some success experiences along the way as he reaches towards a challenging limit. It also suggests a recognition and appreciation of the realities of work. The process is to work up to success, rather than to give up from failure. In contrast, people with low achievement motivation make more feedback errors. Often, after several successes in striving for a goal of a given difficulty they still aim for the same goal, thus making a "chicken error." They tend not to set more challenging goals. Or, paradoxically, people with low n-Ach sometimes make "dare errors" by setting more difficult goals after repeated failures striving for easier goals.

Among the questions dealing with feedback and how teachers and students use it are:

What feedback is available to tell a teacher how successful he is? What can he look for?

What kinds of feedback are available to students in your classroom? How would you describe the feedback?

What situations do actually offer immediate concrete feedback as a measure of progress toward an achievement goal?

At a more general level, people in the group should consider whether they need concrete, rapid, definable feedback, or if more general and elusive indicators of success satisfy them.

Personal Responsibility

People with high n-Ach like to put themselves "on the line," to test how much they can do. They like situations where they can take personal responsibility for successes and failures. Typically, they initiate activities in which they can assume personal responsibility. Situations where the outcome depends on luck or chance at least as much as skill are not as attractive to them. Thus in darts (skill) or dice games (chance), where the player has a choice between throwing the darts and throwing the dice, the high n-Ach player prefers darts because he has more personal control over the outcome. This is usually the case, even when the person with high n-Ach is a poor darts player, because the sense of personal accomplishment is more important than making points. In contrast, if the task or situation could be described as routine, ritualized, closely defined, or dependent on chance, it is not as attractive to a person with high need for achievement because there is little room for personal decision making. This difference between being "in charge" versus merely responding to the demands of the situation is what has been called the "origin-pawn" dimension. The person with high n-Ach sees himself more as an origin — who causes things to happen — rather than a pawn — who waits for things to happen to him.

However, the need for a sense of personal achievement and the acceptance of personal responsibility does not mean that these people necessarily work alone. A person with high achievement motivation will work just as energetically and enthusiastically for a group project or goal as he will for some private enterprise. The important factor is that the activity must allow for some individual decision-making or contribution on his part, and be concerned with attaining some kind of excellence. Moreover, he does not need public recognition for his contribution or accomplishment so much as some measure of success that tells him he is doing well in terms of objective standards.

Many of the questions suggested to focus on moderate risk taking will also bring up the concept of personal responsibility. Here are some questions that help teachers and students examine their strategy:

What is your usual attitude about games of chance and games of skill? Would you ever call yourself a gambler?

How important is it to you to have control over a situation?

How can personal responsibility be increased and facilitated in the classroom?

Does the role of teacher in the school system allow for true personal responsibility?

Researching the Environment

Persons with high n-Ach approach new situations with a style that is alert, curious, active, and intentional. They might be described as "sizing up" the situation, checking out the limits and possibilities — with the end in mind of accomplishing a goal or moving toward it. They *act* in or on the environment rather than waiting passively for something to happen. Again there is the qualification that the occasion must offer a possible challenge and at least some risk, so that the eventual achievement comes through personal effort. This description does not suggest an exact equation between the high achiever and the person who is thought of as hard working, efficient, aggressive. In fact, it is possible that the high achiever might be careless about details and a little disorganized, although that is not always the case either. Instead, he is ambitious, energetic, and innovative in a more visionary sense. He wants to make something special or do something unique. He will not work conscientiously or indiscriminately at projects solely for the sake of getting the task done. Routine completion of routine tasks is not the arena for his style of initiative or his need to achieve.

This style can exhibit itself even in simple games and school tasks. The person with high n-Ach makes sure he understands what is going on. He wants to know all the rules and what options are open to him. He explores, investigates, plans to try alternatives. He will try to test the materials before performing. For example, in a game of darts, he might try to find out if one way of throwing the darts seems to work better than another, or to pick up hints by watching others.

To help students and teachers focus on their own initiative and degree of exploring the environment, you might ask them some of these questions:

Do you insist on practice?

Do you watch what others are doing, to pick up hints for making their own methods more effective?

Do you test limits? Do you test your own limits?

Do you encourage environment probing in your students? How? Do you ever discourage it, consciously or unconsciously?

The strongest evidence that these strategies work is the success pattern of persons with high n-Ach. The strongest evidence that these strategies have been learned will be found in the students' ability to pick a meaningful goal-setting project and carry it through.

Alfred S. Alschuler, Diane Tabor, James McIntyre   233

LEARNING STRUCTURES AS MOTIVATIONAL GAMES

The "structure" of a situation, whether it is a culture or a classroom, usually means the rules for what you can and can't do, the incentive for doing well, and the penalties for doing poorly. It is as if these rules, incentives, and penalties defined an implicit game with players, a point system, playing fields, and coaches. Using this analogy, we can try to make explicit what kinds of games arouse achievement, fears and other motivations. This explicit analogy will allow you to diagnose and restructure your classroom learning "game" in ways that suit you and your students.

Four characteristics distinguish a *game* from other forms of activity: (1) the rules which govern the activity are agreed upon in advance by the players, (2) the rules describe classes of behavior rather than specific actions, (3) there are obstacles to be overcome, and (4) a scoring system is specified. In general, games are more organized than "play" or "pastimes," but less organized than "rituals." In "play" and other activities which merely "pass time," there are no rules, no necessary obstacles to be overcome, and no scoring. In "rituals" (greeting formalities, graduations, funerals, etc.) the specific actions rather than classes of acceptable and unacceptable behavior are defined. Also there is no scoring present. In general, games are more flexible than "rituals" and less open-ended than "play" and "pastimes."

By this definition, most normal classroom teaching is not a game. Usually the rules are not well specified in advance. When rules are extremely vague, classroom activity often becomes a pastime, literally a way to pass time between more meaningful activities. This forces students to "test limits" in order to discover the unstated rules and boundaries. Limit testing is necessary for would-be game players, but from the teacher's point of view it is a discipline problem and a waste of valuable learning time. Nor is classroom teaching a game when teachers over-specify the minute activities to be performed. This ritualized learning is clearest in older "learning by rote" orientations, but is present today in slightly altered forms, e.g. making specific problem assignments in mathematics and learning through programmed texts.

To arouse students' motivation more effectively in the classroom, learning should have the formal properties of a game, i.e. rules that are clearly specified in advance and that define classes of behavior, obstacles to be overcome, and a well-specified scoring system. It is then possible to vary these properties to arouse the desired motives. The first task is to decide whether to stimulate concerns about excellence, friendship, having influence, or some combination of these motives. The desired motives can be stimulated by creating rules which change the nature of the scoring system, the types of obstacles to success, and the person who is to make the decisions.

Scoring Systems

There are three main types of scoring systems in games: Zero-Sum, Non-Zero-Sum and Shared-Sum. Zero-Sum scoring systems have a fixed number of points. When one player makes points, another player automatically loses points, the sum total number of points thus remaining a constant zero. Arm wrestling, betting games, chess, grading on the curve — all have Zero-Sum scoring systems. In Non-Zero-Sum games the number of points is not constant. Each player is free to earn as many points as he can, independently of how many points the other player makes, e.g. archery contests, pre-set academic grading standards, Boy Scout merit badge progression. In Shared-Sum scoring systems, a score by one player is a score for all players on his team. Almost all team sports have Shared-Sum scoring systems.

Zero-Sum scoring systems set up power goals, since points are awarded only when one side forces the other side to yield or when one side demonstrates superior power, influence, or control. Inevitably in Zero-Sum grading systems, students are in direct competition with each other. Grading on the curve or by ordering students in terms of their academic rankings are Zero-Sum scoring systems, since judgments about a student's performance are determined only by comparison to others. One highly effective strategy for doing well in Zero-Sum games is to sabotage other players. Weakening your opponent, e.g. destroying other students' notebooks, is just as effective as strengthening yourself.

Non-Zero-Sum scoring sets up achievement goals, since it gives greatest value to independent, self-reliant accomplishment. Contrary to Zero-Sum games, Non-Zero-Sum games can be played alone, without direct competition with others. In such games, sabotage is not a useful strategy for earning points.

In Shared-Sum games, affiliation with others is made salient, since making points is a key method of establishing, maintaining, or restoring friendly relationships among team members. Academic situations are rarely Shared-Sum games, thus missing the potential facilitating effect of high affiliation motivation.

Obstacles to Success

In all games points are made when obstacles are overcome. The motivational goals of every game depend on the nature of the obstacles to making points. In boxing, for example, the obstacle is the opponent's strength and skill; in that sport, motives to affiliate with others, and seeking cooperation and harmony are handicaps rather than strengths. N-Ach is a valuable motive when the obstacles are *within the player* himself. To succeed the person must overcome his inadequate personal resources and skills (e.g. ability, habits, shyness, etc.). The question for the teacher is whether she is setting up classroom situations where the obstacles to the goals lie within the student, in interfering with student affiliations, or in demonstrating her own powers. When students respond to their natural affiliation needs in the classroom, more often than not, they are obstructing the teachers' goals. There is a curious logic in such student response: When a teacher creates a classroom based on her need for power, the obstacle to success is in the teacher, her standards, her assignments, her disciplinary and rewarding power. As we have seen, sabotage is an appropriate strategy in power situations. What more effective way is there for students to demonstrate potency than to gang up on the teacher, to sabotage jointly the teacher's efforts? There is greater strength in friendly team effort, and often it is more fun.

Locus of Decision Making

Motivation is a process of decision making. The goals which define different motives define how decisions are made. Obviously, the object of the power motive (n-Pow, to have control over others) is to make decisions for others, *the object of the achievement motive (n-Ach) to make decisions for oneself,* the object of the affiliation motive (n-Aff, to become associated with others) to make decisions agreeable to the majority of members. Similarly, the motivational character of games can be inferred from the decision-making process built into them. In football, the quarterback is encouraged by his position to demonstrate both achievement and power motivation. For the rest of the football players, compliance is required for the sake of affiliation and team power. In the classroom, carrying out the assignments often is less palatable since it serves neither power nor affiliative goals agreed upon in advance. Often students' compliance serves only the *teachers'* achievement goals and the students' interest in avoiding punishment.

Table 3 summarizes the scheme for analyzing the motivational structure of games. The teacher can use it to develop the motives most pertinent to her students and classroom.

Table 3

Motivational Structure of Games

		Motives		
		n-Achievement	n-Power	n-Affiliation
Dimensions of Games	Scoring System	Non-Zero-Sum	Zero-Sum	Shared-Sum
	Obstacles to Success	Personal and Environmental	Opponent	Lack of cooperation: e.g. friction, conflict, distance, tension.
	Locus of Decision Making	Individual Player	Captain or Leader	Team

ACHIEVEMENT MOTIVATION TRAINING

Only a small number of events in a person's lifetime radically change his way of living — the death of parents, getting married or divorced, having a child, involvement in a serious accident, a deeply religious experience. These dramatic, singular events transform a person's outlook, relations to others, and view of himself. By comparison, daily learning experiences in school are undramatic, regularized, and designed to promote steady, small increments in external knowledge rather than abrupt, large changes in life styles, motives, values and relationships. Most of formal education does not change the way students live.

Obviously, we do not want to build curricula around dramatic events and episodes that drastically change students' personal lives. Yet new, more effective teaching strategies are needed to help students develop stronger motivation, clarify their values, and improve their relationship with others and views of themselves. As far-fetched as it may sound at first, it is possible to derive practical ideas about promoting personal growth in normal school courses from these rare life-changing events. These ideas can be transformed into teaching strategies that promote milder, but still significant, changes. The problem is to figure out how to *promote personal growth without traumatizing students.* What is it about these dramatic experiences that triggers the process of personal change? How can acceptable triggering experiences be introduced in the classroom more often? Answers to these questions can guide us in developing gentler versions of the profound life experiences that increase students' independence in setting and reaching their own goals, to help them expand their curiosity, stimulate them to explore their talents more boldly and to develop the confidence and self acceptance that contribute to greater tolerance and loving relationships.

The pattern of significant personal change can be conceptualized in terms of a six step sequence for arousing and internalizing a motive. While such changes are happening the student may feel some confusion and puzzlement because the habitual patterns of his life are changing, his goals and values are likely to be different and he cannot make sense out of what has happened to him. The six step sequence can help the teacher understand the process as it occurs and makes it possible for her to be more confident about promoting relevant school learning experiences. Such learning experiences cause relatively little disorientation yet they are far more intense than the typical school experiences of acquiring impersonal, external knowledge. This is the six step sequence:

1. Focus attention on what is happening here and now.
2. Provide an intense, integrated experience of new thoughts, actions and feelings. (The motive.)
3. Help the person make sense out of his experience by attempting to conceptualize what has happened.
4. Relate the experience to the personal values, goals, behavior, and relationship with others.
5. Stabilize the new thought, action and feelings through practice.
6. Internalize the changes.

Let us examine these steps in greater detail and illustrate them with specific teaching activities we have created to increase students' achievement motivation. (Many more examples and exercises are presented in our book "Teaching Achievement Motivation" and other books listed in the bibliography.)

I. Get Attention

Getting attendance and attention is largely a problem of creating moderate novelty that is slightly different from what is expected. The same old routines are dull and boring. On the other hand, extremely unusual experiences are shocking, disorganizing, confusing. Sometimes an extreme experience can lead to important personal growth, but this traumatic extreme is not necessary or appropriate for managed, maximally effective training. The first way we try to establish moderate novelty is to indicate to the teachers and students all the *prestigious groups* and classes that have been involved in achievement motivation courses. (This may not be appropriate for young children who may be more interested in the overt, active features of the activity.) We also indicate the typical results students can expect if their n-Ach is increased — increased self-confidence, more intiative, greater ability to make long range plans, better risk taking.

We also try to find a moderately novel setting so that n-Ach training won't become just another course meeting once a day in a classroom. Short periods generally work against continuity, impact and sustained attention, although what is short will obviously depend upon the age of the students. For high school groups we have tried to use a large block of time (1 1/2 hours per day). With younger groups we recommend periods of much shorter length. We have also tried to get some article of clothing, for example, a T-shirt that had an insignia which reinforced the students' association with this special program. We also made our own signs and equipment — posters, collages, dart boards, mobiles, goal setting charts. In these ways we tried to achieve some of the novel, attention-getting advantages of a special program or unusual setting; separateness, continuity, warm interpersonal relationships.

Teachers' attitudes are crucial in establishing a productive, relaxed, moderately novel climate for learning. As the old saying goes, "Expect trouble and you'll get it." The teachers' positive or negative expectations create a frame of mind about how students will behave and their ability to change. Once, during a course, when some of the faculty were mulling over what to do if students came late — or if they weren't interested — one teacher advised, "We have so much else to plan, let's handle those situations when they happen, if they happen at all." The teachers created a frame of mind that assumed that the students were interested and would change — that they would participate, would be considerate of each other and would think well of themselves. When such an attitude is sincere, and when the teachers, as participants, live up to it themselves the attitude is communicated to the students. Similarly, if the teachers doubt that the students can ever "guide and direct" their own behavior and doubt they will ever want to change, these doubts will be subtly communicated to the students even if they are never voiced. Teachers' expectations tend to become self-fulfilling. The teacher's own attention, involvement and hopes can be contagious.

A final factor that helps get and keep attention is the sequence of methods used to increase n-Ach. Not only should these methods be moderately different from those in regular classrooms but there should also be variation and contrast in the sequence of methods in order to maintain novelty, attention and interest. Many methods can be gained through reading our book and other books discussing procedures of applied motivation: games, projects, role plays, group presentation. Most schools have equipment to use visual media — movie projectors, overhead projectors, slide and tape machines and occasionally a videotape apparatus. These alternatives, plus any more that you can invent to keep the teaching pace quick, varied, and moderately novel will help sustain students' attention.

Getting and sustaining attention is the first problem to be solved in teaching achievement motivation. Without this attention no learning of any kind can take place.

II. Provide an Intense Integrated Experience of the Motive

The only way to know achievement motivation is by experiencing it. Descriptions of n-Ach fall far short in conveying the nature of this motive, in the same way that colored slides cannot give to others the special joys and lasting effect of your most recent vacation. To increase a person's achievement motivation, it is necessary to have him experience n-Ach vividly, intensely, in all its complexity — the goal setting, planning, risk taking, hopes, fears, anxiousness, and satisfaction. Then it is possible to label the experience meaningfully, talk about it in relation to one's life situation, values and ideal self. After the experience is understood in these ways, the person can make a knowledgeable choice about whether or not to practice and strengthen his achievement motivation. An intense, integrated experience of the motive is the keystone of the course.

One way we have provided such an experience is through simulation games like ring toss or darts. For most players, involvement in the games means working for achievement goals, such as improving personal performances or coming out ahead of other players. Because the games cue so strongly for achievement motivation, the players learn, by experience, what n-Ach is like.

The most obvious criterion to keep in mind is that the game or situation should encourage individual goal-setting in a context that encourages achievement goals. In addition, the participant should be free to determine his own goals measured objectively against the performance of other players, or a stated criterion, or his own performance from round to round. There should be provisions for regular, specific feedback on one's performance. The scoring system should encourage moderate, carefully calculated risk taking. The situation should be complex enough to include the thoughts, actions, and feelings associated with the motive, and be challenging enough to make players really care about winning or losing. Yet the content of the game should be sufficiently different from everyday activities to allow non-threatening experimentation with one's behavior. It is more important at this state in the course for students to enjoy the n-Ach experience and want more, than for them to take away an immediate, lasting personal insight. An intense, integrated experience of achievement motivation cannot be fully digested quickly any more than peak growth experiences or traumatic life-changing events are understood immediately and applied to one's life. Understanding, applying, and internalizing increased achievement motivation goes beyond the course into school and the child's personal life.

III. Conceptualize the Motive

Once students have intensely, thoroughly experienced the motive, it is appropriate then to help them make sense out of what happened. Labeling the planning, feelings, and action strategies makes it easier to discuss what happened in the game. A very natural labeling process can occur in the discussion after the games as people compare what their goals were and describe the strategies they used and the feelings they had. Learning the achievement vocabulary makes the course experience easier to remember and to use in everyday life situations and also promotes learning.

Since most people experience some, but not all aspects of the motive syndrome, teaching the vocabulary has the effect of helping the students find the gaps and holes that exist in their n-Ach. Discovering these gaps helps a person to understand his achievement-oriented behavior in and outside the courses. Such a vocabulary has meaning and use to the students if it is related and employed with activities in which they engage, e.g. building wooden airplanes, playing kickball. For instance, a pattern of low risk taking is more understandable when the person discovers he seldom has hopes of success and success feelings. The person who always dreams of success but never gets anywhere can pinpoint the problem accurately when he realizes he never thinks about personal and world obstacles, and the activities necessary to surmount them. The consistently high risk taker who never makes it big can see more clearly the self-defeating aspects of his risk-taking style.

We try to keep attention by alternating n-Ach experiences with efforts to build conceptual understanding. For example, often we start out with games and then examine what has occurred. This sequence gives students (over 5 or 6) a chance to apply and practice what they've learned and at the same time provides a better experience base for teaching how to plan their activities. With a little labeling and a minimum of description, nearly everyone has a clear idea of action strategies such as moderate-risk goal setting, use of feedback, and taking personal responsibility rather than relying on chance.

IV. Relate the Motive to Important Aspects of the Person's Life

Increased achievement motivation is appropriate for a person to the degree that it helps him get along in his world, enhances his view of himself, and is consistent with his basic values. When the person knows what n-Ach is and has the words to talk about the experience, it is easier for him to assess the desirability of developing this motive.

New personality traits can't be gulped in like candy. They have to be taken in like solid food, chewed and digested until the nutritious value is extracted. Since it is important that the course participant be convinced, for himself, of the value of this personal change, a good part of the course should present materials and opportunities to help the student evaluate how the change will affect his actions and growth. The student should consider whether there is a practical value in acquiring the motive. Would demonstrating achievement behavior be consistent with the demands of reality. Secondly, even if n-Ach is practical, will it enhance the student's self-image? Thirdly, is n-Ach behavior compatible with his basic values or will it conflict with other goals and values he has learned and accepts?

A way to help students consider how realistic n-Ach is for them is to distinguish between situations where achievement behavior is valuable and situations where it is a hindrance, or less appropriate than another motive. A good teaching technique is simply to discuss the variety of areas that reward achievement goal setting: career, sports, some aspects of education, play time. For many students, the most convincing point often is that an individual who cannot determine for himself what he wants to do and how he wants to do it, generally winds up doing what other people want, or not doing at all. An ability to choose and to accomplish is inherent in self-confidence and self-esteem.

Although these points can be introduced fairly casually, there are important follow-through activities that can demonstrate their validity. Students (over 6) can interview people they admire and consider successful, and then discuss goals and strategies revealed in the interviews. Speakers can be invited to class. Through it all it is especially important to recognize what the reality looks like from the student's point of view. While some students have long term goals, most students have much more immediate and short term projects. Some live in a reality where it is easier to have no goals at all, because all aspirations seem thwarted from the outset. Part of the role of teachers in the course is to make time for students to talk about their own lives and concerns, and then help them establish appropriate connections between the motive and the situations they describe.

Turning to the question of real and ideal self-images and whether n-Ach will enhance such images we find a more complicated picture. Do children know "who they are"? Can they talk about self-image? If they can, will they talk in front of a group, even a small one? Although professional opinion is divided, we found it most effective to use less direct, and less verbal, methods of examining the ideals they have for themselves. All of the techniques should help the student to think about what he is like now, and what he would like to be ideally, then to think about ways of drawing the two images together.

For example, in several of our courses each student filled out an "admiration ladder." He was asked to indicate the name of someone he admired on the top rung. On the bottom rung he named a person he did not want to be like at all. Somewhere in between he wrote his own name, indicating how he felt about himself in comparison to these two people. Afterward, we discussed what qualities the students value in the people they most admire. If they wanted to be more like those people, what would they have to do? When it was relevant, we talked about how achievement motivation could be helpful in reaching that kind of personal goal.

Potentially this area is one of the richest, most creative parts of the course — especially if teachers are willing to experiment with art, drama, and other techniques. Students can present themselves in an artistic collage, using photographs or newspaper fragments. If teachers are interested in improvisational drama or have had theater experience, they might like to try skits, improvisation, pantomimes, or role plays. These activities can range from personal closeups, in which the students play themselves and each other, to situations in which students play historical or public features that come closest to their secret or real selves. The important criteria for any of these activities is, first of all, expressed acceptance and support for the way people present themselves, and secondly, the attempt to understand more clearly the nature of the gap between a person's real and ideal self. For many students this can be a first occasion to see themselves as potentially high achievers.

Even after a student acknowledges that n-Ach is of practical value in his world, and is a desirable aspect of his self-image, he may still experience conflict about the motive unless it is consistent with the values of the groups to which he belongs. One can easily speculate about family structures that squelch a young person's positive self-image and his opportunities for independence and personal decision making: general discord in combination with authoritarianism or over-protection by parents. Another area of potential value conflict is school itself. If a classroom is structured to preclude decision-making and goal-setting by students, if there are few provisions for feedback and initiative and a rigid, limited system for being successful, then students cannot be expected spontaneously to show achievement motivation. A third area of value conflict occurs when a student belongs to a group that sees achievement concerns as part of what's wrong with America. In many people's minds there are links between an ethic that espouses individual achievement and current societal ills, such as power monopolies in big business, a materialistic money orientation, and callousness to the plight of small individuals. The argument may strike one as simplistic, accurate, a confusion between greed and achievement, or just as inevitable. The course could bring cultural values and students' perception of them into the open as a topic for discussion, not to change the students' values, but to clarify what those values are, and to explore the ways they are consistent and inconsistent with the n-Ach values of self-reliance, independence, and concern with excellence.

Often it is difficult to sustain a meaningful conversation about cultural values with young students. We have found several approaches that work successfully. One is to use current media. For example, newspapers and magazines continously focus on youth and school issues. These writings can provide lively discussion about values held by the students, or confronted by them. Popular songs, popular heroes, and popular causes are useful in evoking a clearer notion of cultural values. Another procedure we have found effective is to discuss student responses to such questions as: "It is more important to do well than to be popular; I'd rather have fun in the present than worry all the time about what I'm going to do in the future." A more elaborate version is to ask students to read a series of prepared profiles about young people approximately their own age and to choose which three of 10 they would choose to represent the best of American youth. The profiles you create should represent different value orientations, from high priority on gregariousness and popularity, to concern with developing skilled hobbies, concern with money, race, etc.

The most challenging part of the course is the effort to help students relate the motive to their own life situation, ideal, self-images, and values. It is hard to get such conversations going, and even more difficult to keep students on the track without being wooden and constantly saying, "Now what does this have to do with n-Ach?" Teachers should aim for obvious interest and involvement on the part of the students and a growing tendency to speak personally and specifically — to say "I," to refer to one's own family and group of friends. If the films and readings are remote to the students, that will be fairly obvious in short order. The general rule for teachers is this: If interest begins to fade, stop and do something else. Just because there is a great deal of material does not mean that it all must be thoroughly taught and learned. Help students maintain the initiative by creating a learning environment in the course that supports achievement concerns, enhances students' self-images, values their independence, and responds to their initiative.

V. Practice the Motive

An integral part of any n-Ach course is to have students actually practice using the motive by carrying out a goal-setting project. Without this application of what has been learned, the motive is cognitively understood but not used and useful. As with any new skill, the first attempts to engage consciously in n-Ach planning, feelings, and actions usually are halting and difficult. Teachers must be especially patient and inventive in keeping the course lively and fun. Once students choose an appropriate n-Ach goal they want to pursue, the details of n-Ach planning and action can be evoked to increase the likelihood that their practice will be satisfying and successful.

Experience has led us to anticipate certain obstacles in this practice phase. If the teachers aren't careful the project can come across as "just another assignment" so that students will set up some vague goal as their project just to fulfill their obligation and then put in little or no effort to achieve it. It's important that staff get the idea across that the project is not homework, and instead that it is an opportunity to experiment in the goal setting technique with a goal important to the student himself. In fact, while the students should be encouraged to do a project they should not be forced. Some students who are reluctant at the beginning may try projects later, particularly if they have seen others enjoy success by so doing.

Once a student has settled on a goal that is an achievement goal his next step is to be specific about it and devise concrete methods of feedback and measuring progress. The teacher can help in various ways: assist by showing students how to plan in detail; subdividing larger projects into smaller parts with separate deadlines; getting away from the idea that spending more time indicates more knowledge or greater progress. The point is to imagine and devise a specific, concrete goal with intermediate goals and built in check-points (action strategies). Another reason for student vagueness about planning can simply be lack of interest in the goal. Ability to be detailed and specific about something shows involvement. Thus, another approach to the vagueness malaise is to encourage the student to think about a goal that is more important to him.

Above all, stay flexible, not every student can or wants to declare a precise goal, completely analyze all the obstacles, and know ahead of time exactly how the hurdles will be surmounted. This style may be appropriate in getting the Apollo spacemen to the moon but not always for every other goal. Some students feel that this degree of analysis beats a fond notion to death, leaving little room for spon-taneity. True enough. Not everyone should set and implement goals in the same way. Those students with particularly low self-confidence may need a lot of ego propping, praise, and group encouragement before starting seriously for a goal. There are as many styles as in-dividuals, and the teaching task outlined in this section should not bar a student's unique brand of initiative.

VI. Internalize the Motive

Paradoxically, the most important thing for a teacher to do in helping a student to internalize n-Ach is to stop doing anything. Support for continued strong achievement motivation must be gradually transferred from external sources to the person's own inner resources. The trick is to leave on time — not too soon because guidance is needed in the early phases, and not too late because that retards essential self-reliance.

After those wise words to you we should admit that we have no guaranteed cues for you to use in staging perfectly timed exits. As a general rule, however, we do believe that teacher support and/or students' peer-group support should continue for some time after the instruction is over. This phased withdrawal can begin during the goal-setting projects. The follow-up reports encourage record keeping and show continued interest in the students' progress.

Internalization is the process of taking a skill, idea, value, or motive from an outside source and voluntarily incorporating it into one's own repertoire to such an extent that the behavior in time becomes the person's own. In our research studies of achievement motivation training we have collected systematic follow-up data on how much internalization takes place as the result of different types of teaching procedures. Here are four guidelines we use to find out how much internalization has taken place.

Wait a year: Internalization takes a while. After a year, if the person does not show various new energetic strivings for excellence, then whatever short-term motivation developed during the course probably was not deeply meaningful.

Look for voluntary concerns with excellence: Almost everyone has within his repertoire of responses sufficient achievement motivation to deal with those situations which demand competition, planning and energetic pursuit of excellence. What distinguishes the person with high achievement motivation is his spontaneous, voluntary concern with excellence even when it is not necessarily demanded by the situation. Thus, we look at how a person uses his leisure time and the personal goals he sets.

Look for displays of the motive in several areas: If achievement motivation is meaningful, useful and valued, it will be evident in several areas. With students we find that leisure time, sports, hobbies, work, and — to a lesser extent — school are the most likely places to find evidence of increased n-Ach.

Look for evidence that the person values and enjoys his increased effectiveness: Internalization will not occur if the motive syndrome is dysfunctional in the person's life. The best way to find out is to ask the person. Our lengthy follow-up interviews reveal large differences in the degree to which the person values and enjoys achievement concerns.

A BEGINNING

To "close" this chapter with a summary would contradict the forward-looking attitude we hold and advocate. It is appropriate to ask where you go from here. The theories presented in this chapter, the suggested sequence in training, the use of curriculum materials, even achievement motivation itself are convenient tools for you to use in giving your first course in psychological education. It is our hope and expectation that this will be only a beginning.

Like hundreds of other teachers who began with experience in an achievement motivation course you too can transform this stimulus into your own unique contribution to teaching and learning. We cannot predict where and how you will progress but we can tell you that many teachers have modified and adapted the six step sequence, altered our free wheeling style of teaching and content of our course with successful results. Read further, get materials, attend workshops, set up your own intermediate specific goals and concrete procedures.

And now, where will you go from here?

9
Selected Techniques in Affective Education to Promote Involvement and Motivation

Robin D. Montz
University of California, Santa Barbara

We in the United States have gained wealth beyond our wildest early dreams and world influence far above the speculations of the founding fathers. We can, for the first time in history, manipulate and control much of our environment — the chemistry of the human body, the climate of a city, and even the basic power of the universe itself, the atom. Much of our success in these achievements is due to our democratic system and that system's insistence on the education of all its citizens. We have developed a second industrial revolution in recent years, the computer revolution, that has placed mankind in the position of being able to retrieve data and control machines more quickly and efficiently than ever before. We have almost reached the point in technological progress that whatever the mind of man can conceive, the hand of man or his machines can create. Although we take justifiable pride in our accomplishments, some observers are beginning to point to some dangers inherent in our dependence upon technological power. These social observers and critics say that the primary ethic of our country is fast becoming that whatever is technologically possible ought to be done and that we are confusing the possible with the desirable. With this "technological determinism" comes an exaltation of the mechanical and dehumanization in life and a depreciation of human values.

Whether or not one agrees with these critics, one must agree that the public education system has been at least partially responsible for the development of our technological power and ability. That system has fulfilled its function in this endeavor by focusing its attention on the development of those students' cognitive-intellectual functions deemed necessary for material progress. Cognitive development — the development of the thinking function — has long been considered important in planning school curriculum. Since the early 1960's cognitive development has become established as perhaps the single most important pursuit of schools.

As a result of our concern for the development of cognitive skills, we have often ignored the affective-emotional experiences of the individual — his concerns, his feelings, his perception of himself and his environment, and his motivations. By ignoring these affective experiences schools not only have inhibited the development of feelings and motivations in individual children, but also carried often the implicit message that the individual's concerns and feelings are not worthwhile and therefore are to be denied and cut off, or at least buried beneath the surface. We often see the child only as a student — as a learner — who needs to be "filled up" with information and skills rather than as a whole human being who also stands in need of self-actualization, self-discovery, development of awareness, and emotional maturity.

This condition has not been universal. In many schools there have always been good teachers who are concerned about the whole child, who work with children as individuals in their classes, and who do not ignore the affective experiences of children, but rather use those experiences to enrich the learning environment. Surely all of us can remember at least one such teacher in our own experience, and for the most part, what we remember about that teacher is not how much cognitive material we learned but rather how that person affected our real lives — how she helped us to overcome our fears, shared her excitement about life, communicated to us that we were worthwhile and that we could do what we set out to do, and insisted that we take responsibility for ourselves. These teachers were not only able to enrich our life and help us to grow, but they also made the subjects they taught more exciting and meaningful.

In my thirteen years as a student, I can only remember two of my teachers with those particular qualities; some people can point to fewer than that. Much more often my teachers were characterized by almost total concern for intellectual attainment, data memorization, and other completely cognitive skills; their concern for me as a human being, if any, was hidden and poorly communicated. Their very lack of concern for me and depersonalized approach to teaching made it difficult for me to get any more involved and enthusiastic than they themselves were. If my experience is typical, and from my reading and discussion with others I have reason to believe that it is, then there is little wonder that there is a growing gap between what happens in school and what happens outside school. This very gap has been a major contributor to the disenchantment and escapism of a large segment of today's youth.

Teachers are beginning to sense that the attitudes of the children they teach have changed considerably in the past few years. It is much more difficult to teach cognitive subject matter to many of today's children than it was to their counterparts of just ten years ago. It is harder because it is more difficult to find ways to motivate today's children to want to learn. Children expect subject matter to be relevant and meaningful to their lives and are less likely to respond to learning for the sake of traditional extrinsic rewards as their counterparts did in the past. The traditional subject matters of schools have many valuable things to offer children, but unless today's children can see personal meaning and relevance in school material, they "turn it off " and fail to pay attention and ignore much of what we offer them. Instead of learning or outwardly rebelling they turn aside and ignore our curricula. Although these attitudes and concerns are not present in every child in every classroom, they are appearing with increasing frequency and regularity. The schools appear to have increasingly less influence upon the very individuals for whom they were established because classroom approaches and topics do not seem willing to relate to the real concerns of children. Judged in terms of impact upon the lives of students the schools appear to be an institution of declining power and significance.

In the middle stands the teacher. Parents seem to want the same kind of education for their children that they had, even though they may not have been entirely satisfied with their own educational experience. Children are often turning off to the traditional subject matters that schools have provided. Administrators, government officials, schools of education, other teachers, and nearly everyone, it seems, are crying for changes and innovations in the "educational establishment." The teacher is caught in the middle — responsible for actually implementing any changes that might take place but not given much help or guidance in discovering new directions to take and methods to use to get there.

It is my conviction that most teachers are of good will — they want their children to mature and to learn the skills and attitudes that will enable them to live satisfying and fulfilling future lives. I do not believe that educators have conspired to do harm to children by dealing seriously only with their minds and ignoring everything else. I am convinced that teachers are not aware of the effects of a total emphasis upon cognitive skills. If they realized the consequences of this one-sided approach, they would want to modify their approach in the classroom and deal with children as whole persons rather than as mere learners of data. I am convinced that many teachers want to do more in this direction but fail to do so because of a lack of knowledge concerning specific steps to take and uncertainty of the consequences of this approach to teaching.

Part of the problem lies in the fact that until recently few alternatives were available for teachers. The few teachers that dealt directly with affect in the classroom did so in spite of the methods they had been taught in teacher-training institutions. Especially since 1957 (when the United States suffered a massive attack of wounded pride and lack of confidence in itself and its institutions as a result of Russian space triumphs), the official attitude of government and education has not encouraged life-centered and child-centered curricular approaches. The social and political situation is changing now, and new alternatives are becoming more readily available. One function of this book and this chapter is to provide teachers in early childhood education with some alternative methods in the direction of a more humanized educational approach.

By way of introduction to the sections dealing with specific teaching techniques the paragraphs that follow describe general strategies to follow in deciding upon the content and structure of daily lessons. In this way the reader can examine techniques in the context of overall strategies and thereby gain greater insight and perspective than could be achieved by merely looking at the techniques in isolation.

Although there are many ways to combine and interrelate affective and cognitive learning, a good strategy at the outset is to pick some conventionally taught lesson — any lesson — and see if there is any part of that lesson that could be experienced more directly by the children through some kind of simulated situations. For example, a social studies lesson about the function of police in the community could be supplemented not only by a visit to the police station and conversation with policemen, but also by the delegation of certain police powers in the classroom. The delegation of powers could include shifting from individual to individual the responsibility for carrying out rules made by the class or by the teacher and for enforcing those rules either in the room or on the playground. Students could then be asked not only to reflect upon what policemen do, but also, and this is crucial, upon how they felt when they had that kind of power. What did the power do for them? What did that power do for the class?

The teacher should determine, if possible, what emotional responses are inherent in the material itself and then plan to capitalize on these emotional responses should they be forthcoming to further the educational function of the lesson. For example, if the lesson on police functions is taught in a ghetto school, children even as young as pre-schoolers will probably experience some negative feelings toward the role of the police and toward the individual policeman in the community. The school can perform an important function for the child by helping him work through feelings that form a very real part of his world and by teaching him about the role of the police at the same time. (As will be discussed later, there are ways of working with negative feelings so that constructive outcomes result.) To extend our example, feeling responses related to power are inherent in the lesson on policemen — how we feel about having power over another, how we feel when someone tells us what to do, whether we prefer controlling or being controlled, and other such important considerations. Sublessons that deal directly with these important parts of real life could be incorporated into the lesson on policemen and thereby make the total lesson much more effective and meaningful. Examples of such subplans will be discussed later.

While she is teaching any lesson the teacher should be aware of what kinds of emotional responses arise in the classroom. Obviously children do not come to school as "blank tablets" on which we can write anything we choose. Each day they come to school changed in some way by what has just happened to them in the immediate or recent past. For example, a child whose parents had a fight at breakfast cannot function in the same way at school as a child whose morning was happy, peaceful, and full of love. To take another example, children who fought with each other at recess cannot usually come into the room and work together effectively on a group project unless their anger is released or dissipated through an intervening process. As has been mentioned, and as will be discussed further, there are methods by which teachers can guide children toward constructive use and resolution of such negative emotions as anger or frustration and thereby help them to move on and solve other problems or learn school material.

Finally, the teacher should keep in mind that some goals of education fall almost totally within the affective domain and that part of the time devoted to learning within the classroom should be spent dealing exclusively with these goals. These purely affective goals include: developing awareness, both of self and of the environment; developing communication; developing responsibility and control; and developing attention, motivation, interests, creativity, cooperation, and many other social and personal goals of education. All of these goals and associated capacities are important — not only because their development helps the child to be a more effective learner but also because their development assists the child to formulate skills with which he can create for himself a life-style that is varied, satisfying, and creative, and with which he can cope with many of the demands of a rapidly changing, technological society.

It is impossible in the space we have here to deal with all of the affective learnings that are of importance to children in early childhood. It is also not possible to list all of the techniques that have been developed for teaching these concepts, skills, and behaviors. The reader should view the approaches that follow as only being illustrative of the much wider range of teaching and learning behaviors from which they are drawn. Most of these techniques were developed by teachers for specific groups of students learning specific things. Most have been so very successful and versatile that it is possible to use them with children of other ages and backgrounds for purposes other than the ones for which they were originally intended. Some of the exercises are useful for more than one purpose. For example, some that were originally intended to develop awareness are also equally valuable in developing communication or creativity.

Teachers who intend to use these techniques should be aware, however, that the outcome of these lessons will be influenced by the attitudes, emotions, moods, and temperament of the person using them. It is best for teacher and students if the teacher employs those techniques with which she is comfortable rather than the ones she feels she *should* use. By comfort we mean a sense of competence and control of the situation. If that feeling of comfort is absent, the associated insecurity will surely be communicated to the children and perhaps will cancel much of the benefit of the exercise. Therefore there is no reason to try all of the techniques in this chapter. Indeed, there is every reason not to try any of them until you feel comfort and competence in doing so and are willing to take responsibility for what occurs.

With these comments as background, it would be wise for the teacher to bear in mind several important "ground rules" for working with affective learning. First, and perhaps foremost, no child should be coerced into doing anything he does not want to do. Coercion of any kind is harmful to the general spirit of affective learning, especially to its emphasis upon individual responsibility and the freedom within which such responsiblity is exercised. The teacher who plans on trying some of the teaching strategies in this book should keep this ground rule in mind; perhaps the teacher should provide some alternative activities for children who choose not to participate in affective learning experiences.

Secondly, teachers must be aware of the kind of satisfactions they are receiving from this form of teaching. One of the very real dangers of work in the affective domain is that individuals sometimes see themselves as "instant group leaders" or as agents of salvation for the children in their classrooms. Those people who have done significant work in this field know that any growth that is taking place in the individual comes about as a result of that person's own work, rather than through the work of the teacher, facilitator, or therapist. It is legitimate and understandable when a teacher feels satisfaction that a child takes responsibility for himself after a particular classroom exercise. A teacher who thinks "I'm certainly happy that I was able to get Johnny to take responsibility for himself. See how much I've done for him?" is manifesting a rather unhealthy view of her role in the learning process. Learning is done by the student. The teacher's function is that of guide and environment-provider. There is no place in any kind of meaningful education, including affective education, for people who are on "ego trips" of their power and influence.

Thirdly, teachers and children should respect each other's individualities. This ground rule implies that there would be no "gossiping" about the personal things that might emerge during work in the affective domain. Children and teachers alike should feel free to discuss what was done in class, what kinds of activities went on, what things they did, and how they themselves felt about it. Personal communication should remain personal and, thus, privileged. Teachers and children should understand this tradition and agree to adhere to it from the first day of school until the last, and even after the year is over.

Finally, the teacher should realize that using "techniques" without any other reason than to "try them" tends to make those techniques into "gimmicks." The use of affective exercises and techniques should be a natural part of a larger framework of learning — each technique should be utilized for a sound reason and as a part of the total learning experience of the children. Otherwise the attitude of gimmickry is communicated to parents and children who are likely to resent, and perhaps fear, the fact that the teacher is experimenting without clear goals and responsibility. Teachers should be able to justify the use of these teaching strategies in terms of somewhat conventional learning goals. They must be able to demonstrate, for example, that children are being taught to be more aware, not only in the senses of seeing more, hearing more, or feeling more with their fingers (although those are very important by-products) but also in terms of maintaining greater contact with the real world (taking responsibility for their actions in that real world and understanding what they are doing).

If the teacher can accept and implement these four ground rules, there is every reason to expect very positive results from integrating affective learning into her curriculum and teaching style. Of course, the teacher should not expect overnight miracles. She should look at each child as a person in the process of development, realizing that development of real and meaningful changes takes a great deal of time. The teacher using affective techniques can look forward to seeing some very positive growth take place eventually in most of her children. She can anticipate that she will see smiles where there were frowns, contact where there was avoidance, children beginning to take responsibility where they previously shirked, people relating to and trusting each other where they had previously been isolated, and youngsters gaining an awareness and respect for their feelings and ideas that they previously ignored and denied.

TECHNIQUES FOR DEVELOPING AWARENESS

Much of the content of school curriculum as we know it emphasizes the past and the future. Even in working with preschool or primary children, teachers often ask their pupils to learn about things that happened in the past and to plan for what might happen in the future. In other words, we ask children to conceptualize the past and visualize the future. Although there is nothing wrong with this orientation per se, it is often associated with ignoring the time dimension of "Now" that is the most important of all to young children. By ignoring this dimension of the present we teach children that their present experiences are not as important as what is outside them — in books, in films, and in the mind of the teacher. The present moment is the only contact we have with the real world. What is past is gone, and our minds may have distorted much of what took place. What is future has not yet occurred, and we have no way of knowing what will occur. Only in the present, the Now, do we have the possibility of contact with reality. Everything else is fantasy. By emphasizing the past and the future to the exclusion of the present, we also teach our children that fantasizing is more important than contact with what is real. One of the most important sources of information in classroooms and one that is almost completely ignored in most cases is the child himself. That source of information is useful only if its senses can be made available in the immediacy of the learning situation. If the child can be taught more fully to be aware, really to see, taste, smell, feel, and hear, to experience the world around him and the world inside him, and to take responsibility for his own experiences, then we will have helped him move toward a life that is based on reality rather than on fantasy, on contact rather than on escape, and on the knowledge that he is worthwhile because his experiences are valid and meaningful.

Exercises in Awareness of the Physical Self

1. *"Now" games*: Have the class sit in a circle. (If the whole class is too large, do this exercise with part of the group while the remainder is busy with some other activity.) The teacher begins by saying, "For a few

minutes I am going to talk about what I know about me right now. I am sitting in this chair. I feel my feet on the floor. I see you looking at me . . ." (Continue with statements that are true of that moment. Examples: I can hear my voice; it sounds soft and warm. I see Billy moving his hand. I hear voices on the playground.) After you have given enough examples for the children to know what is expected, ask, "Who would like to do it now?" The teacher listens carefully and helps the children only if they wander from the present tense. A variation of the game is to have the children describe what they can see in the room right now. Another is to say, "Today we will look at ourselves. What parts of yourself can you see here and now?" Games like these give children practice in concentrating on what is really going on at the present moment and are important introductory awareness exercises.

2. *Finding your space*: This preparatory exercise for other physical awareness exercises involves having the children lie on the floor and asking them to close their eyes. Closing eyes is often difficult for children to do. It is important to allow them to open and close their eyes at will until they feel comfortable in closing their eyes for an extended period of time. With very young children you might even need to assure them that you have your eyes open and you will see that nothing harms them while they have their eyes closed. Have them find their space by discovering and repeating the patterns that do not bring them into contact with anyone else. Ask them to imagine how big their space is, then say, "Can you tell where the person next to you is? Without opening your eyes, imagine where that person is." After a few minutes have the children open their eyes to check the size of their space. After the first time or two, the teacher can ask the group to lie down and find their space without any reference to where the other children are. This also can be done in a standing position (with eyes closed) so that the children can move their arms without touching anyone else.

3. *Body concentration*: Employ the eye closing procedures described in the preceding paragraphs and have the children lie on their backs. Then say, "Now feel the floor where you are touching it. When I ask you to think about some things in a moment, just quietly think of the answers. Don't talk to someone else or say your answers out loud. You will be able to tell us about what you were thinking later." Then ask the children to concentrate on the various parts of their bodies that are touching the floor (e.g., Is your head touching the floor? How does it feel? How do your shoulders feel?) In a variation of this exercise, the children could sit in chairs and close their eyes, concentrating on the relationship of their bodies to the chair instead of to the floor.

4. *Breathing exercises:* Have the children lie down on the floor in their own space and request that they close their eyes. This time ask the children to concentrate on their breathing, simply to pay attention to their breathing without making any effort to change it. Ask them to feel the air going in and out, and suggest to them the further possibilities of placing their hands near the nose or mouth to feel the air as it moves. Then ask them to place their hands on their stomachs and see what happens as they breathe. After about one minute have them place their hands at their sides on the floor and be aware of how they feel. Then ask them to allow their eyes to come open slowly, "as if the sun were just coming up in the morning," and to see what they can see, "as if you've never seen it before." This exercise is especially appropriate after coming in from energetic playground activities or at the end of a long session of work or study.

5. *Touch conversation*: Divide the class into dyads (partners, groups of two) and have them stand facing each other with their eyes closed. Have them join both hands and ask them to "get acquainted, using just your hands." After a short time say, "Now we're going to do some things using just our hands. Don't move your feet. Just imagine that we do everything with our hands and with our eyes closed. First, using just your hands, go for a walk together . . . now have your hands run together . . . and if they can jump . . . just with your hands, now, see if you can dance together . . . tell each other a secret using just your hands . . . now just be together with your partner's hands . . . now have your hands say goodbye to each other very slowly . . . now let your partner go, and see how you feel by yourself . . . now open your eyes and talk to each other about what you did and how you feel about it."

6. *Mirror games*: Divide the class into dyads. One of the partners is a person looking into a mirror. The other partner is the mirror, reflecting what it sees. The mirror cannot talk. The person using the mirror should move slowly so that the mirror can copy him without too much effort. After a while reverse the roles. More advanced versions of this game involve concentrating on facial expressions and on tuning in to the real feelings of the person, with the mirror actually trying as closely as possible to be the other person. At the end of the exercise, ask the children to deal with such questions as, "What did you learn about your partner by being a mirror?" "What did you learn about yourself by looking into this mirror?" and "Which did you prefer, being a mirror or being the one looking into the mirror?"

Exercises in Awareness of the Environment

1. *Experiencing objects*: Ask the children to sit in a circle and to

close their eyes. Have ready a number of common objects (pencil, eraser, cup, stone) and say, "I am going to pass something around the circle. Take an object and feel it with your hands and see if you can guess what it is. Don't say what it is, just think it. Just sit now and wait until the person next to you passes the object to you." Then begin passing the objects around the circle. Each time you repeat this exercise, the objects you use should be less and less familiar. After a while change the emphasis from guessing what the object is to such activities as seeing how the object feels, seeing how the object makes you feel, or concentrating on how heavy or light, soft or hard, smooth or rough the object is. At times after completing the exercise, the teacher might allow the children to see the objects and to comment on the difference (or similarity) between how the objects look and how they feel.

2. *Experiencing space:* Have the children stand. Move all furniture out of the way (or use a large room without furniture). First, let the children move around the room in any way they want. Then ask them to imagine that the floor is made of soft rubber and that they are bouncing on it. Then have them imagine that each of them has a large rock that has to be pushed up a hill and that is very heavy (teacher should demonstrate). Next, ask the children to imagine that the room is filled all the way to the top with jello and that they have to move through the jello. (The teacher might vary this part by stating the flavor of the jello — lemon, lime, strawberry — or alternately stating that the jello is their least favorite flavor, and then later by saying that it is their favorite flavor.) There are many different ways of experiencing space. You could ask the children to experience the space as birds, as snails, as rabbits, or as other animals. They could see what difference it makes if everyone moves in the same direction or if they move in different directions. They could experience the space standing still. They could experience the space with their eyes closed. The variations are as many as the teacher's imagination will allow.

3. *Exercises with moving:* Teachers can develop many new and different kinds of movement exercises, or they can use the traditional ones to which they are accustomed. Most early childhood teachers use some kinds of movement or dance exercises to develop physical dexterity and rhythm. The critical addition that works the feelings into the lesson requires that the teachers ask the children to deal with their feelings associated with the particular movements. One typical sequence could be "Now imagine what it would be like to be an elephant. See if you can stand like an elephant. Now try to move like an elephant. See if you can really be an elephant who is moving. Now,

when I play this music, see if you can be an elephant dancing (etc.)"
Then, after a while say, "All right, how did you feel when you were an
elephant? Did you like the way elephants move and dance? What do
you like about it? What do you dislike about it?"

4. *Blind work:* In ordinary life most of us depend so much on the use
of our eyes that we often lose or overlook much of the information that
our other senses give us. In order to reawaken the senses of touch,
hearing, smell, and taste, those who work with children in affective
learning often temporarily block the sense of sight to heighten attention
upon other senses. (Closing the eyes, described earlier, is involved in a
number of the exercises described in this chapter.) The basic situation
involves asking the children to close their eyes and to experience
something without seeing it. Often young children are afraid to close
their eyes, and sometimes the use of blindfolds is helpful. It is always
important that children feel free to open their eyes or to remove their
blindfolds whenever they wish so that they feel they have control of the
situation. Darkness is often frightening, and children doing these
exercises need to feel free not to participate whenever feelings of fear or
distrust upset them. However, children who are constantly opening
their eyes to identify things or to satisfy curiosity should be encouraged
to keep their eyes closed and experience the exercise without vision.
Blind work can enable the teacher to achieve two goals: (1) increasing
awareness by development of the nonvisual senses and (2) increasing
trust by following others with pleasurable and safe consequences.

The blind exercise with the greatest potential is the Blind Walk, also
known as a Trust Trip. In the Blind Walk, children are asked to choose
a partner. One of the partners closes his eyes (or uses a blindfold), and
the other partner leads him around and introduces him to all kinds of
sensory experiences involving touching various textures, smelling
different kinds of things, and even tasting, if something edible is handy.
This exercise is best performed outdoors, when it becomes a wonderful
way to experience nature. As a variation, it can be done inside the
classroom or cafeteria. After about five or ten minutes (or longer with
older children), the roles are reversed; the leader becomes the blind
follower and the follower becomes the leader. After both partners have
experienced being the blind follower and being a leader, they are asked
to evaluate their experiences, including the questions, "How much did
you trust your partner?" and "Which did you enjoy more, leading or
being led?"

5. *Experiencing nature:* In addition to the Blind Walk, there are
many exercises that can help children experience nature more fully and
thus appreciate it and understand it better. For example, children can

be taken outdoors on a nice day (or even better taken to a park or wooded area, if possible) and asked to sit with their eyes closed and pay attention to the sounds. They might each be assigned to one square yard of grass and then be asked to explore that territory in detail, seeing what kinds of creatures live in their territory. Another exercise involves giving each child a rock after he has closed his eyes and having him experience the rock through the senses of touch and smell. The same activity could be done with a pine cone, a leaf, or another natural object. The teacher could ask the children to become animals and to simulate their behavior (e.g., become baby salmon hatching out of the egg; become salmon going to sea; become salmon returning up river to spawn; become a bear trying to catch the salmon). What is important in these exercises is that the child experience nature directly, in its own forms and processes, that he express his feelings about what he experiences, and that he experience nature in a way that is not usual (with touch instead of sight, for example). In this way children can begin to use much more of themselves in the process of discovery of all things and will have more of themselves available for other kinds of tasks. The more of themselves they can experience, the more they are able to experience other events and processes.

TECHNIQUES FOR DEVELOPING COMMUNICATION

An area of traditional concern in public schools is that of teaching children to communicate more effectively with one another. Teachers have always dealt with speaking, writing, listening, and other social and literary skills involving communication. It is unfortunate, however, that with all of the emphasis on interpersonal communication, the schools have stressed verbal and written communication virtually to the exclusion of any other form. They have largely neglected the rather obvious fact that everything we say bears with it other kinds of signals — body posture, tone of voice, twinklings of the eye, gestures, previous relationships — that condition what we say and give it meaning. We invest our words with emotional energy, and often the words we use are the least true thing we are saying. How frequently a person will say something like, "Oh my dear, that is such a lovely dress," yet by other signals indicate that she really does not think the dress is lovely at all. To decipher the message we have learned (usually by hard experience and not in school) to look for other clues. Many people, however, never learn very well how to detect double messages, and they are continually being duped, disillusioned, cheated, or made to appear foolish in their gullibility because they were never taught to communicate with more than the face value of their words. Thus they are often used by their more aware and sophisticated acquaintances.

Teaching children to communicate more fully should begin in their very earliest years. More total communication will be available to children if they can be taught to listen, not only to what words someone says (although that is important) but also to the other nonverbal cues that the person is giving; if they can be taught to talk to each other openly and honestly, without fear of being punished for telling the truth; if they can feel free to communicate in more diverse ways than with just words; and if they can learn how to "jump into the other's place" and experience a situation as the other person must feel.

A teacher can employ many methods to help children learn how to listen more completely. Many of the exercises discussed under developing awareness are also appropriate in developing better listening techniques. When children tune in to themselves, they are in a very real sense listening to themselves, to their inner voices, to messages given off by their bodies. When they really see someone else, they are at the same time more able to hear him. Teachers can help children develop their sense of hearing by isolating that sense (having children close their eyes and concentrate on what they hear) and asking them to attend to increasingly subtle sounds. As has been observed before, listening is more than better hearing. A few examples of techniques for verbal and nonverbal listening should suffice here. What is important is that teachers constantly help students become aware that there may be double messages and that what they hear with their ears may not be the real message being conveyed by the other person.

Exercises in Listening

1. *Listening to the movement:* Form a circle (ten to twelve children per group is ideal). Play some particularly evocative or rhythmic music on the phonograph. Begin by having all the children move to the music in any way they want. After some time (perhaps the second or third time this exercise is done) encourage individual students to make some kind of personal statement of themselves ("do *your* dance"), of another ("dance how you feel about someone else"), of the season ("dance how you feel about summer"), or of whatever through movement or dance. The rest of the group should concentrate on "listening to the movement." This might be difficult with very young children, but if appropriate wording were used in the instructions, they might be able to listen and communicate in this way.

2. *Listening to physical cues:* During classroom discussions, there are many times when a student will say something and his facial expression

will say something different. (E.g., a child smiles while he is saying, "I'm mad at you" or a child on the verge of tears says "There is nothing bothering me.") If children are made aware of these double messages as they are occurring, eventually they will begin to pick them up on their own. If possible, this awareness should come about as a result of questions asked by the teacher, rather than as direct statements by her. Teachers should be alert to the presence of double messages and point them out to students when they occur.

In addition to facial expression, body posture provides another set of cues. If someone is sitting with legs and arms crossed and says, "I would like to get to know you," the listener can be fairly certain that the words are false since the speaker is physically all closed up. If he said the same words with legs and arms uncrossed and leaning forward with a smile and a sincere ring to the voice, the listener could be more certain that the speaker was telling the truth. If children can be made aware of physical cues and listen to the facial expression and body posture of those speaking to them, they will be much better listeners.

3. *Listening to avoidance:* This is an exercise for teachers more than for young children. Older children might be able to handle this, but primarily this is an exercise for adults. When children (or other adults) are talking, one can often gain insight into the real message (or other very important "side messages") by listening to what the speaker leaves out. This is especially true when the person is speaking about personal experience. Often in sharing time or in incidental conversations with the teacher, children will talk about their family, their feelings, their hopes, and their desires. It is often just as important for the teacher to be aware of what the child fears to talk about and what he avoids as it is to listen to what he actually says. By learning how to listen to the avoidances skillfully (and not overinterpreting) the teacher can gain a set of insights about children that are not available if they only listen to what is actually said.

Exercises in Communicating

1. *Revolving discussion sequence:* This is an exercise in verbal communication. Begin by dividing the group into dyads (groups of two). One of the partners makes a statement (the subject matter is up to the teacher — it could be something personal or could involve a problem in the curriculum or whatever). After the first speaker finishes his statement, the other person states his maximum *agreement* with what the first one has said. Then he may state his disagreements or anything else he wishes to say on the subject. The other person then responds in the same way. Using this with very young children might be difficult

but not impossible. It may be more effective if the teacher, instead of talking about agreement and disagreement, said, "Now tell your partner what you liked about what he said . . . Now tell him what you didn't like . . . Now tell him whatever else you think about the subject." If young children are doing this exercise, prior demonstration by teacher examples could serve as an effective method of specifying what is *appropriate* and required.

2. *Ticket to talk:* Begin by getting about four volunteers. Place them around a small table in the center or in the front of the room. Give each of them ten cards or pieces of paper. These are tickets to talk. Only one person may talk at a time, and they must put their ticket in the middle of the table in order to talk. The person who puts his ticket into the center of the table first gets to talk. Everyone else must listen to him. The object is to get rid of all ten tickets first. What usually happens is that few people in the "discussion" know what the discussion is about since they are concentrating on getting their tickets into the center of the table and not on listening. Evaluate by discussing what other things we do in conversations to avoid listening to what is going on — stare out the window, tap our feet, or think about something else, for example. This is an example of a contrived learning experience where the children discover the moral by discussing the events that have occurred in the group. Such learning experiences generally benefit from further discussion and games to clarify the underlying point. (Exercise three is an example of such a follow-up.)

3. *Gibberish games:* Often our communication is not as effective as it could be because we do not put enough of ourselves into it. We may appear to the world as rather shallow, surface-level people because we feel that the words themselves carry enough feeling. One method for helping children put more of themselves into their communication is to take away from them for a time the use of meaningful words. This can be achieved through the use of gibberish — meaningless words and syllables. The teacher should begin by presenting various illustrations of what gibberish means. One effective method is to go to a child and, using a gesture, indicate the command to stand up. Use a sound to accompany the gesture — "Gasomona!" If the child is slow to respond, repeat the sound and strengthen the gesture. Using gibberish, then, ask other students to do other kinds of things — sit down, take out a pencil, open a book, open the window. Then divide the class into dyads and have them play with gibberish for a while. After they are more or less familiar with the use of the nonsense (no-symbol) speech, say, "Now tell each other something funny that happened to you, using gibberish . . .

Now tell each other a secret with gibberish ... Tell each other something sad ... something happy ..." and so on. What normally happens when the children use gibberish is that they depend much more on gestures, voice inflections, facial expression, movement, and other dimensions of communication usually neglected in regular speech.

4. *Becoming the other:* The best and most complete understanding of someone else would occur if we could really step into someone else's skin for a moment and experience life through his senses. Of course this is not possible (unless we accept the testimony of psychics and mediums). It is possible, however, to approximate such a transfer through fantasy. If, for example, two children in the class are angry at each other or have quarreled, the teacher could ask them to close their eyes and in their imaginations relive the entire episode as they originally experienced it. After they have accomplished this objective ask them, with a bounce of the imagination, to jump into the other person's place and to see the whole incident again but from inside the other person. Often just this experience will resolve the difficulty. At least it will facilitate communication between the two antagonists if they really allow themselves to do the exercise. Another way of handling this same issue is to have the two children role play the parts of the other child in a dispute. Such exchanges give the child an opportunity to become the other party in a dispute and learn how to communicate with more than one perspective.

5. *Classroom climate:* The classroom climate is probably the single most important influence in developing genuine and resourceful communication in children. A teacher can try all the techniques in the world and still fail to develop much genuine communication if the children perceive that the teacher really does not want them to be real and honest and open. If children experience the teacher as being real, they usually will respond by being real. Children usually respond in kind to a teacher who is open, unafraid, and honest in her dealings with individual children and the group. The key to teacher-student communication lies in seeing other people, no matter what their age, as being genuine individuals with personal integrity deserving of respect and honesty. If children feel that their teacher is really interested in them as individual people and is also honest, open, and real with them, they in turn will begin to develop more fully the resources of communication that are available to them and will become increasingly able to listen and communicate with each other and with the wider world around them.

TECHNIQUES FOR DEVELOPING
RESPONSIBILITY AND CONTROL

One of the most important characteristics of the mature person is that he takes responsibility for himself and his actions. He does not blame others or his past or the environment for his actions and mistakes, but he accepts full responsibility for them himself. A person who is mature, therefore, obviously is aware of what he is doing and that he is the agent and source of his actions. He also has control over himself, and his actions are the result of a choice among alternatives. The responsible person is a free person who is aware and has control over himself.

Responsibility cannot exist without freedom. If I am compelled to do something, I am not responsible for what happens. If I choose to do something, then I am responsible, no matter what factors or fears were involved in the decision. In the final analysis, all men are free in one very important respect — they are free to say "No!" even though, in some cases, saying that might mean their deaths. We are all responsible for what we do, and it is a mark of a mature person that he accepts responsibility for what he is and what he does.

Although we cannot expect little children in early childhood to take full responsibility for themselves, there are some very significant ways that teachers, by their actions and expectations, can introduce those children to behavior patterns and habits that will affect their ability and willingness to take responsibility in later life. Children at that age normally do what they are taught to do, and taking responsibility for oneself is something that can be learned and increasingly developed during the early years of school.

Before anyone can take responsibility for himself, there are at least three preconditions that must be met. These are that the person must be (1) free to choose between alternatives; (2) aware of what he is doing; and (3) aware of what behavior is appropriate to the environment. Turning to the first of these, responsibility follows only if there is freedom to choose among alternatives. As has been observed above, responsibility cannot exist without freedom. Although the quality and extent of freedom will vary with the age and maturity of the children in a particular class, a teacher cannot expect to teach children to take responsibility for themselves unless she gives those children some genuine measure of freedom of choice. Freedom with the possibility of ultimate veto by higher authority (the teacher in this instance) is essential before the children can feel personally liable for their decisions. If we are to teach responsibility, we must create islands of freedom within which children experience total freedom of choice and must accept the responsibility of the result. I am not advocating anarchy in the classroom. On the contrary, I am suggesting that children need to be given increasing amounts of freedom, increasing areas over which they have total control, so that they can also experience the responsibility that accompanies that control. For example, very young children can be given a choice of activity A, B, or C and made aware of their responsibility for making that decision. Later, when they can comfortably handle three alternatives, the number of choices can be increased. As another example, a teacher may decide that by the end of the first grade children can handle responsibility for the neatness of a part of the classroom, and she might choose to give her class the responsibility for determining some of the specifics of such tasks. Of course, they would also be free *not* to clean up that area, in which case they would have to bear the consequences. If the area is left uncleaned and unstraightened and if the teacher then steps in and cleans up that section of the room herself, she has violated the students' territory, and their sense of responsibility suffers. It would be legitimate, however, for her to comment on how the room looks, how the messiness makes her feel, and what actions she feels are required to make for effective work and play space. The cardinal rule in providing opportunities for exercising responsibility is this: Do not do for someone else what he can do for himself. If I continually do things for the children in my class that they could do for themselves, I rob them of experiencing the feelings of strength and ability that come with performing those tasks on their own. In those instances, I have robbed them of the possibility of growth.

The second precondition for developing responsibility is awareness by the child of what he is doing. A child cannot actively take responsibility for something unless he knows what he is doing or not doing. Even though the child is actually responsible in an objective sense, he does not *feel* responsible because he does not know what he has done. In order to develop responsibility in the children in her classroom, a teacher must help them first become aware of what they are doing.

The third precondition is only slightly less important than the first two: The person must be aware of the environment; he must know *where* he is doing what he is doing. The concept of responsibility, to a considerable extent, lies in knowing in what context certain kinds of behavior are appropriate. Awareness of self, awareness of environment, and communication are not only important prerequisites for responsible behavior, but are also necessary elements in teaching children the feeling of responsibility. However, although an individual should always strive to be honest in his relationships with others, there are many situational factors that may lead to different interpretations of what is also appropriate. One would not always do at a large gathering of people what one does in the privacy of his own home; someone who did might be labeled irresponsible (among other things) in some situations. Teachers can help their children develop the ability to discriminate among contexts for behavior by helping them develop an awareness of their environment and by assisting them in broadening their repertoire of techniques of communication. One very effective technique for dealing with responsibility in the classroom is really quite simple and yet has enormous potential. First, the teacher must assist the child to focus on what he is actually doing and how he is doing it. Then the child must "own up" to the fact that it is he that is doing that. In other words, the child must know what he is doing and accept responsibility for doing it. (See exercise 1 of this section for examples of this technique.) If the child can take responsibility for what he is doing, his feeling of responsibility is strengthened, his sense of control is strengthened, and he stops playing the "blaming game." In this way, children are encouraged to begin to grow up emotionally as well as physically and intellectually, and we help them to develop responsible relations with the environment in which they live.

Exercises in Controlling and Taking Responsibility

1. *Two examples of the fundamental responsibility-training technique follow.* These examples illustrate how the teacher can bring the child to an initial focus on his role and participation in a social or individual activity. From this initial step the teacher can follow up with exercises 2 and 3.

"Billy, what are you doing?"
"Johnny stole my crayons!"
"What are you doing?"
"Johnny took them, and he won't give them back!"
"Billy, what are you doing?"
"Hitting him."
"Who is hitting Johnny?"
"I am."
"Now can you put that all together in a sentence beginning with 'I'?"
"I am hitting Johnny."

●●●

"What are you doing, Sally?"
"Drawing a picture."
"Who is drawing a picture?"
"I am drawing a picture."

"How are you drawing your picture?"
"Quietly, all by myself."
"Who is working quietly, all by herself?"
"I am working quietly, all by myself."
"When you finish, would you like to put your picture on the board?"
"Yes, I would."
"That's fine."

The important elements in this technique, as can be seen above, are that the teacher focus the attention on what the child is doing, who is doing it, and how he is doing it. The question that should be avoided in this situation is "Why?" To ask a person why they are doing something forces them out of awareness of what is actually happening and into their brain to invent some reason or rationalization for their behavior. If we look at the behavior and ask how or what, we can get much better cues to what is happening to the child than if we ask why and force him out of contact with reality. Besides, there are so many answers to the same why question. If you ask a child why he is hitting another child, the answers could vary from "He hit me" (which avoids responsibility) to "My mother beat me this morning" (which avoids responsibility also) to "I'm tired of sitting" (which takes responsibility for the feeling of tiredness but avoids the responsibility of hitting.) There are probably at least fifty different answers to the same "why" question. There is only one answer to the what question, "What are you doing?" — "I am hitting Johnny." There is only one answer to the how question, "How are you drawing your picture?" — "I am working quietly, all by myself." Both of these questions deal with taking responsibility for present behavior.

2. *I am in control of myself:* Seat the children in a group. Ask, "Who makes you do things?" Accept all of their answers. After they have answered ask, "How do these people make you do things?" Again accept all of their answers. Then, through discussion using the examples the children have given, ask them to take one specific thing and to describe what they do in detail. Begin each sentence in this sequence with the word *I.* For example: "When my mother makes me practice the piano, I go to the piano; I take out my lesson book; I take out my music; I sit down; I do my scales; I play the pieces I know; I try the new pieces I am learning; I make my fingers run along the keyboard; I get up when I am done and go out to play." Perhaps through this kind of concentration on just what is really taking place the child will be able to accept responsibility for what he does.

3. *I am a robot:* Have the children pretend they are all robots. They

can do nothing unless they are told to do it. Begin with the teacher giving very specific instructions. After a while let a student control the rest of the group. Just help the class do exactly what the leader says to do. In the evaluation of the exercise, have the children deal with how it feels to be controlled and how it feels to be in control.

Other games similar to these can be developed by teachers who are in touch with what is taking place in the classroom. When the teacher perceives that someone is markedly controlling someone else's behavior, she can make that control explicit by asking the children involved to describe how they control others, how they allow themselves to be controlled, and how controlling or being controlled feels. Any time a child does something that is new for him or that he thought impossible the teacher can make that explicit by helping the child take responsibility for his achievement and by helping him "own up" to being able to control himself. This is one of the key elements in a classroom environment that is conducive to growth and maturation and should be one of the central concerns in a teacher's mind at all times. Through such intervention strategies the teacher can develop the concept of personal autonomy and its place and value in personal development.

TECHNIQUES FOR DEVELOPING COOPERATION

For many years education has had as one of its goals the development of cooperation, effective group membership, ability to work together effectively, or whatever any local school district might call it. The following exercises are included as somewhat novel approaches to this very important educational goal and might offer teachers another strategy in developing such competences in her children.

Exercises in Cooperation

1. *Who Started the Motion?:* Form groups of ten. Seat the children in circles and send one child from each group out of the room. While the child is out of the room each group chooses a leader, and the leader begins some kind of motion that the whole group copies. The one sent out now comes back in and stands in the center of his group. The leader slowly changes the motion, and the group copies him. The one in the center tries to guess who the leader is. If the selection is too easy, suggest to the group that they need to move more slowly so they can move at the same time and make it harder to guess who started the motion. This exercise helps in increasing awareness as well as providing experience in group cooperation.

2. *Group acting projects:* Divide the group of ten into half-groups of about five. Give the group an imaginary rope and ask them to have an imaginary game of tug-of-war, five against five. Be sure all the children in the group are hanging on to the rope, side-coaching them that the rope cannot stretch and that combatants cannot move in opposite directions at the same time. Also, no one can let go of the rope until the game is over. Other similar activities involve having all ten children arrange chairs so that they seem to be in a large rowboat. Have them row together, increasing the speed of the boat after a time. Using the same arrangement of chairs, suggest that they become a bus or trolley car that goes over bumps and whose "parts" all bounce together in the same rhythm. The teacher might also ask the children to imagine that they have to move an enormous boulder. It will only move about one inch at a time; so, they will have to work very hard and work together. In the evaluation of these lessons, ask the children such questions as, "How did working together feel? What did it feel like when you couldn't get together?"

3. *Slow motion follow-the-leader:* Have one child be the leader. Standing in one place, he begins some movements with his hands, arms, and body in extremely slow motion. The class, also standing, copies him and tries to make the motions at one time as a group. This exercise is very similar to the Chinese process of meditation through movement called T'ai-Chi Ch'uan, and the exercise can perhaps take on additional meaning if, after it is over, children express how they felt while moving, what new things about themselves they became aware of, what new things in the environment they could see, and other questions focusing on the personal experience.

4. *Task-oriented exercises:* Many methods for fostering cooperation are task-oriented. For example, giving a group a task to accomplish, perhaps setting some time limit, and thereby assuring that some kind of group process takes place, will probably further cooperation in the group. One such exercise (that probably should only be done by teachers who have a great deal of self-confidence) involves telling the children that they have been stranded on an island without hope of being rescued and that they will have to provide for themselves. The teacher may first act as a group member but then sits down and says no more, even when asked. The children must grope toward a solution of the situation by developing some kind of rudimentary government and solving such basic life problems as food growing or hunting and resource distribution. Occasional prompting may be necessary, with the teacher saying such things as, "You've been two days now without food or water. If you don't get busy, you'll die of thirst or starve to death."

This game involves a great deal of chaos and uncertainty and usually lasts more than one or two days, but almost always it is successful in getting children to take responsibility and to learn cooperation in a simulated island environment. As has been observed, such an exercise is not for the faint hearted or for the teacher who has difficulty coping with unstructured situations or who has problems with the teacher in the room next door. A lesser variation of this exercise may be used in social science teaching dealing with such social issues as police, rules, and sanitation.

5. *Cooperative-classroom climate:* Teachers can also assist in the development of cooperation if the climate of the classroom is not highly competitive. If teachers place great value on students working together instead of against each other, cooperation will be encouraged and rewarded, and children will learn to help each other and to work together. This can be done with children teaching other children or working together on class projects.

TECHNIQUES FOR WORKING WITH NEGATIVE FEELINGS

Often in our work with children we tend to ignore some negative feelings — fear, anxiety, and frustration — of the youngsters in our classes while repressing others — anger and aggression. The general avoidance of negative feelings stems from a variety of reasons — negative feelings might frighten or alarm us; we might feel incompetent in dealing with them; we might feel that expressing such feelings would have more destructive than constructive consequences. Yet we all know that if a child is frustrated, angry, frightened, confused, or aggressive, those feelings get in the way of his learning process, influence his actions, affect his perceptions, and intrude upon his memory and motivation.

The two negative feelings that most often interfere with learning are the feelings of anger and frustration. Anger, or hostility, is usually expressed in some form of overt aggression or by directly or indirectly "acting out" an impulse. Frustration, an often subtler feeling, can be expressed in a number of ways — the child might quit trying or he might become so frustrated that the frustration becomes anger or he might escape the reality of his frustrations by daydreaming and losing contact with reality. Whatever their manifestation, negative feelings have to be handled constructively if children are to be able to learn how to cope with them and use them rather than being controlled by them.

One of the most effective set of methods for dealing with children's anger is described in a small book by Janet Lederman, *Anger and the Rocking Chair* (McGraw-Hill, 1969). Lederman uses with exceptional success Gestalt awareness techniques for dealing with the hostilities, frustrations, and other negative feelings in her children. The book describes her techniques and processes in a poetic and pictorial essay of great beauty. Her methods place strong emphasis upon helping the child discover what he is doing in the immediate situation and upon expressing his hostile feelings in fantasy. She assists the child to deal with his anger and aggression by expressing that anger in ways that are neither harmful to the child nor seriously threatening. The child who takes responsibility for his own anger, instead of blaming someone else, can begin to "own" all of his feelings and thus gain greater control over them.

Other teachers have used other methods and approaches in the constructive use of anger and frustration. Several of these different approaches will be described to provide examples from which the teacher can draw and elaborate.

Exercises in Working with Anger and Frustration

1. *Pushing:* When children are angry at each other, it is often helpful to allow them to "work through" their anger by pushing against each other. This physical contact is safe — no one can be harmed — and it allows the children to experience their own strength and the strength of the other child; in addition, the hostile feelings are usually worked out in the struggle. Sometimes the teacher can ask the children to push with their hands above shoulder level, sometimes they can push shoulder to shoulder, and sometimes they can push back to back. All of these positions require a large investment of energy, and the children soon become tired and work through their anger quickly.

2. *Resent, demand, appreciate:* When a child expresses anger or resentment toward someone who is not present, ask him to imagine that the person is sitting in an empty chair situated directly in front of him. Then ask the child to talk directly to the person and tell him what makes him angry. Be sure he makes the resentments explicit. Have the child begin each sentence with the word *I.* Examples: "I don't like you to push me around. I hate your dumb smile. I resent it when you tell me to brush my teeth." Follow these statements of resentment by asking the child again to go over that which makes him angry by firmly telling the other person what he should do to satisfy him. Examples: "Stop pushing me! Quit smiling that way! Don't nag me! Leave me alone!" Follow this by asking the child to tell that fantasied person what they like about them or appreciate about them. Examples: "I like the way

you play baseball. I like you to show me how to draw pictures. I like your cooking." When a person (child or adult) works through this sequence of resentments, demands, and appreciations, he often finishes up an unfinished situation in his mind and then is able to use his energies for more constructive purposes.

SOME CONCLUDING COMMENTS

This chapter has concentrated on selected examples of affective teaching procedures for developing involvement, cooperation, and creativity and for dealing with negative feelings that interfere with learning. Affective learning also should be of importance to teachers in teaching concepts and topics that involve cognitive learning. Many things that are taught in schools have little or no effect on children because they cannot really experience what is being taught. If teachers will look carefully at their subject matter, they will see some concepts, ideas, and processes can be experienced by the children in ways that are much more direct than reading or hearing. For example, in a science lesson on the growth of the bean seed, if the children not only plant bean seeds and watch them grow but also become bean seeds in fantasy, they might gain additional information on how plants grow, flourish, or wither. In another example, in teaching about the services of community government (fire, police, hospitals) a teacher could ask the children to reflect on who takes care of them in emergencies, how they feel when they are taken care of, if they have ever taken care of someone else, how that felt, and other similar considerations. One strategy for developing lessons that deal with both the cognitive and affective dimensions of learning was described in the example of the police station presented in the introduction to this chapter.

If you are interested in pursuing affective education further, there are many places to go for more information and experience. Workshops are given regularly through institutes in various parts of the country and under the auspices of many University Extension services. In these workshops teachers can experience directly the kinds of activities they might be employing in their classrooms and thus gain valuable expertise. Other kinds of information and further sources of techniques can be obtained from the books listed in the bibliography to this chapter and others in this book. Even more important, as you begin to use affective techniques in the classroom and begin to see, after a time, that children are growing and maturing and gaining control over themselves in new ways, you will be able to visualize other possibilities, other strategies and techniques for further development of the affective part of your children's personalities. You will also realize what it means to teach the whole child — to be able to develop teaching techniques that speak to the complete, unified person. Then you will discover that every day is really different because every child is different every day, and each new learning situation is a new opportunity for growth and development and maturity.

REFERENCES

Brown, George I. *Human Teaching for Human Learning.* New York: Viking Press, January, 1971.

Castillo, Gloria. *Left-Handed Teaching: Affective Teaching Procedures.* Unpublished manuscript, available from the author at University of California, Santa Barbara.

DeMille, Richard, *Put Your Mother on the Ceiling: Children's Imagination Games.* New York: Walker and Co., 1967.

Gordon, W.J.J. *Synectics Making It Strange,* New York: Harper and Row, Publishers, 1968.

Lederman, Janet. *Anger and the Rocking Chair.* New York: McGraw-Hill, Inc., 1969.

Schutz, William C. *Joy: Expanding Human Awareness.* New York: Grove Press, 1967.

Spolin, Viola. *Improvisation for the Theater.* Evanston, Illinois: Northwestern University Press, 1963.

10
In Support of Creativity

Joyce Hagen Sonntag
California State University at Northridge

A wide variety of procedures have been proposed to develop and increase creativity (e.g., Torrance 1962; Taylor 1964). My own experiences have lead me to favor an approach that seeks to develop and extend creativity by fostering social relationships that permit greater awareness and expression. This approach is based on the assumption that the child's greatest resources for creative expression are already present within him and that the environment can best facilitate creative expression by helping him recognize and trust his ideas and feelings. There are certainly other approaches to fostering creativity that deal with strategies (e.g., Synectics 1968) and specific procedures (e.g., Torrance 1962), and I do not argue their significance or effectiveness. What I do say at the outset is that such procedures are likely to be of limited effectiveness unless the teacher is able to create an atmosphere of trust and acceptance. Without such an atmosphere the child is unlikely to feel free to explore, recognize and express the unusual, original, and different thoughts that are uniquely his. In this chapter I shall discuss some of the major ways in which teachers can develop such an atmosphere.

Let me begin with a summary of the major ideas to be presented in this chapter. I define and conceptualize creativity as a style of openness to, respect for, and integration of inner and outer experiences. I assume that classroom development of this style rests upon (1) the creation of relationships among the learners and their teachers that support and stimulate this individual process and upon (2) the satisfaction of the personal needs for safety and feelings of belonging that might otherwise drain off the attention and energies of the individual and thereby reduce creative expression. I propose a model for developing creativity that begins with (a) a focus on self-awareness, and moves to (b) an interaction between awareness of self and awareness of others, and goes from there to (c) the involvement of the group in supportive and responsive relationships with one another. In the course of presenting this model I will present examples of curriculum that support the development of individual creativity. In spite of my own personal convictions, I should share with you the knowledge that there is no hard evidence that these procedures (or any others) necessarily result in more creative adults. Teachers concerned with this issue should look instead for positive and negative evidence in the way in which their students relate to their work and to one another. Some perspective on that point may be useful in evaluating the goals and outcomes of programs intended to increase creativity.

A PERSPECTIVE ON EVALUATING RESULTS

During the last few years, we have seen a great deal of research devoted to clarifying the sources of creativity and developing methods for increasing its occurrence. Although that research has been helpful to educators interested in increasing creativity in the classroom (Gowan, Demos, and Torrance 1967), the effectiveness of these procedures is far from certain. We have no longitudinal studies that show that specific educational interventions at any point in a child's development are associated with higher levels of creativity in his later relationships with people and things in the real world. The literature on creativity does not offer evidence that children who achieve high scores on tests of fluency, originality, and divergent thinking grow up to be highly creative adults. Essentially, the research on improving creativity[1] relates certain kinds of procedures with improved scores on tests that enjoy some face validity as measures of creativity. In this sense the study of increasing creativity is much the same as studies of increasing intelligence or academic performance, all of which depend on certain test scores as indices of ability or attainment. Studies of creative adults by Barron, MacKinnon, and Maslow have found creative adults to be characterized by certain personality traits, and clinical data by Rogers indicates that these traits can be developed within "helping" relationships. The program recommended in this article derives from these personality and clinical studies and is designed to support creative behavior in children by meeting un-

---

1. Reviewed in *The Journal of Creative Behavior*, a new journal that describes and analyzes studies on creativity.

derlying needs and by providing a network of those relationships that have been found to induce personality changes toward greater creativity in adults. I have found this program to be effective — if effectiveness is to be judged by statements from children who have participated in such a program and from their parents who have reported that changes in self-awareness and self-trust have occurred. Since I have not made any formal assessment of this approach and do not have test scores to report, I do not want to give the (misleading) impression that I have a guaranteed, reliable method for increasing creativity. What is presented are a set of well thought-out and tried-out ideas and procedures that I have found to be useful and effective in working with teachers and students in California. Hopefully, either I or someone else will do a more comprehensive study of their effectiveness in the future.

At the same time, I should point out that the available evidence on the process of creativity and personality traits of creative people is consistent with the model and teaching procedures I propose. There is, at this point, no agreement among investigators of creativity as to how such abilities are to be recognized and measured. If anything, the most accepted position among investigators in this area is that what is judged to be creative differs from culture to culture, from time to time, and from one social group to another. Judging creativity in terms of test scores is certainly one way of removing a portion of the social and humanistic connotations of that word, but such an act does not necessarily make those scores more useful or meaningful to the teacher. I am more concerned with humanizing the classroom and helping children utilize their powers than I am with developing tests of creative expression.

In defining creativity it is important to indicate what is *not* central to the creative process and put some popular impressions to rest. Creativity is not identical to intelligence, and there are many instances where very creative people have only normal intelligence and where very intelligent people are not creative (Getzels and Jackson 1962; MacKinnon 1962). Creativity is not necessarily associated with being unconventional and different. Although many creative people are indeed unconventional, their unconventionality is an expression of their personality and not a cause of their creative works. People who act unconventionally are not thereby more creative — they are merely different. To find out whether that difference is original, effective, and an integrated part of their personality requires closer examination. Two other common misconceptions are that creativity is revealed by lack of inhibitions and by intellectual sharpness and speed. Although it is true that many creative people do express their impulses freely and are quick-witted, it would be erroneous to confuse the outward manifestations of a style with its underlying processes. Expressing anger, smearing paints, and expressing thinking skills may be reflections of creativity, but they can also be surface or fringe expressions of less original personalities.

Studies of the personality characteristics of creative people have revealed several common traits. Among these traits are a willingness to take risks; high levels of flexibility; open and independent styles of thinking, perceiving, and interpreting; a playful attitude toward work that allows the person to see new possibilities in the familiar; "primary process" thinking that is free of traditional logic, reason, and time and marked by fluidity and contradictions; self-trust and confidence in one's own abilities, impulses, and perceptions; and a respect and appreciation for the unusual and asymmetrical in the person himself and the outside world (Barron 1955; Cropley 1967; Getzels and Jackson 1962; Roe 1963). Combining the evidence on personality traits of creative people and theories of the creative process leads me to a working definition of creativity.

Creativity is defined in terms of a personal style that includes flexibility, openness, awareness, self-trust, and intensity. This definition does not focus on scores of particular tests of creativity or on the creation of a particular tangible product. The definition emphasizes the general and long-term personality traits of the individual rather than the short-term characteristics that can be produced or manipulated in the classroom. The approach I describe is intended to increase a child's general powers to create rather than to produce short-term improvements in creative expression. The approach is consistent with the parental training that has been repeatedly found in the background of creative individuals (Cropley 1967; Getzels and Jackson 1962; MacKinnon 1962). These parents appeared to have a high degree of respect for the opinion of their children, they were confident that their children could and would perform well and appropriately, and they allowed them to make decisions for themselves. They expected their children to behave in a reasonable and responsible fashion and gave them the independence and privacy to act in that way. These parents were themselves expressive, they respected differences, and they did not impose their own values and views on their children. They tended to be authoritative but were not dominating or authoritarian. In general, they treated their children with acceptance and respect and were tolerant of playful actions and inconsistencies. They gave the child space for exploration and were not always concerned and vigilant that he perform and succeed.

The Back of the Teacher's Mind

There is abundant evidence that a teacher's expectations and beliefs are as powerful an influence on children as is her behavior (Rosenthal and Jacobson, 1968). It follows therefore that an inclusive approach to teaching for the development of creativity would begin with a collection of ideas that the teacher should consider having in the back of her mind. In the procedure to be suggested here, thinking and doing are inextricably twined and grow out of one another. Unless the children's sensitive interpretation of nonverbal cues leads them to believe that the teacher really thinks some of the following thoughts, the corresponding behaviors will not be effective. Before you embark on a consideration of strategies, consider the following ideas:

- every child is potentially creative, especially everyone in this class. If some of us have lost touch with the creative part of ourselves, that is a serious matter and needs our attention.
- each person in this room is very important.
- we each experience everything in our own way and that is a little different from other people's ways.
- everyone here has the unquestionable right to be who he is, to think what he thinks, and to see things his own way. (How to deal with differences between people has to be considered but does not mean that the individual's rights are to be limited at the outset. Feldman in chapter 3 and Coopersmith in chapter 4 discuss this issue in this volume.)
- ideas are interesting, and it is exciting to find out how people come to think as they do.
- our mistakes are valuable and a useful source of information.
- spontaneity is valuable. People being and expressing themselves spontaneously are delightful. Acting spontaneously in this class is a good and desirable way of behaving.
- what comes to us from within ourselves is uniquely valuable and has a place in this classroom if we feel like sharing.
- this classroom is a place where it is safe to share a glimmering of an idea, an improbability, a frustration, a fear, a fantasy, a fact.

If these are comfortable thoughts, try reading them again, adding "and that includes me" or some form thereof, after each one. When you have found that these ideas are comfortable and make sense, you will begin to feel your own ways of translating these beliefs into action.

In general, I find it helpful to remember that creativity begins with a feeling or an impulse within a person and that the development of creativity depends first upon bringing these feelings and impulses to awareness.

Getting Started

It may be difficult to direct the child's attention to himself. After a couple of years of school, many children believe that when the teacher says, "How do you feel about that?" or "What do you think?" she really means, "Guess how I think you should feel about that," or "What do *I* think?" Many children have to be reminded that they are producers of ideas and feelings before they can learn to value and trust their own productions.

An easy way to help the child experience himself as a producer of ideas is through the use of classroom games designed by Torrance (1962) and others to improve children's performance on measures of creativity. Ask a question like "What could we do with a piece of string?" or "How many ways could we use a safety pin?" and collect answers. Repeat (in a kind of savoring way) the suggestions called out by the children; as the ideas begin to come more slowly, wait expectantly so that the children understand that more answers are possible if they choose to keep looking.

After the children have played such games a few times, it will not be necessary for the teacher to repeat each idea. Her acceptance and valuing will be assumed, and if she continues (beyond the point of initial need) to funnel all communications through herself, communication and exchange of ideas between the students will be retarded. When children are not used to having their ideas valued, they are quite unable to value — or even to listen to — the ideas expressed by one another. After the teacher has set a model for the acceptance of a wide variety of answers to a question, she can withdraw from the central position and encourage students to direct their communications to one another. This strategy will probably be more successful if the students are seated in a circle so that each child can see every other child.

More appreciation is available from the total membership of a group than from the teacher alone, and this group resource should be available to the members. The experience of *giving* appreciation is as important to a growing individual as the experience of receiving it; children cannot participate in both of these experiences unless the teacher removes herself from the center.

Sharing ideas is less risky than sharing feelings; when it has been established that unusual and far-out ideas are interesting and enjoyable, children may be ready to risk themselves on an even more personal level.

A low risk beginning for the sharing of feelings is included in a curriculum for the development of musical creativity written by Martha Wampler. She asks the children to notice how it feels to be in their classroom and to remember how it feels to be in a room in their own home. "Is the feeling different?" she asks . . . and, "How is it different?" Leaving one child alone in the room while everyone else steps outside gives him the chance to see how that feels and to compare it with the feeling of when everyone returns. Someone can leave the room to notice how it feels to leave — and how it feels to return. She suggests making the room as dark as possible and talking about how it feels to be in the dark: it might feel different when there is absolute silence from when everyone is talking at once. Does the feeling change when the teacher lights a candle? Discussion of these and similar questions heightens the child's awareness of himself and validates the importance of his changing feelings.

Again, the teacher serves as a model for hearing and accepting the feelings of others and for being interested in how feelings differ. As soon as the children begin to incorporate her actions and attitudes into their own behavior, she should step out of the center and allow the children to alternate their experience of sharing themselves with the experience of receiving from one another.

We remember that children cannot learn to give attention, appreciation, or love without having received them; we sometimes forget that having received, they need the opportunity to be giving and to feel that their own giving is received. Personal wholeness and feelings of integrity come from a balanced alternation between affecting the environment and being affected by it. Rollo May emphasizes this alternation in *Love and Will*, saying, "If you cannot receive, in your giving you will dominate your partner. Conversely, if you cannot give, your receiving will leave you empty." Teachers must remember to receive from children and to teach them to receive from one another; children benefit from the feeling of giving as well as receiving from the teacher and other children. A classroom where the teacher only gives and the children only receive supports dependency, not emotional growth and personal development.

Theoretical Foundations

It may seem to be an unreasonable escalation of the level of discourse to jump from children listening to and accepting ideas and feelings for one another to a discussion of wholeness and integrity in personal relationships, but there is a logical connection. A way of conceptualizing the progress from one to the other is presented in the statement by Krathwohl and a committee of distinguished educators (1956) on the development of the affective domain. In their model, growth proceeds from attending, or awareness, to receiving, from receiving to responding, and from responding to valuing.

It is useful to think of each of these levels as having three aspects. For example, on the awareness level the child must first feel the attention of a significant other person; from this experience he becomes aware of and learns to pay attention to himself. Subsequently he needs and benefits from the opportunity to develop his awareness of others. Likewise, from (1) the experience of being received by others, he can develop (2) receptivity to what comes from within himself and (3) grow from there to the capacity for receiving others. In this application, the term "response" denotes a uniquely personal consequence of prior receiving. The receiver has been touched in some way by what has just come into him from another person, and he replies from the place that was touched. Again, the child needs the experience of being responded to — not in a sentence uttered by someone who was waiting for a turn to speak but in words that express ideas and feelings that did not exist before the child's message was received. He needs a place in his life where he has the opportunity to feel the response of others and to respond to them in return. As he is responded to, he can learn to respond to himself.

Each of these levels is developed through alternately experiencing the self and the other, as the child progresses from awareness to valuing. When the teacher involves her class in the activities suggested here as a means of focusing the child's attention on himself, it is important that she keep the total model firmly in mind. She can then watch for the opportunity to shift the focus to the feelings of others so that the children may alternate the giving and receiving of attention, appreciation, value, and love. She can employ procedures that give the child an opportunity to play different roles, experience positive and negative feelings, and learn to expand and generalize his feelings. (See Montz, chapter 9.)

Although creativity rests upon the development of many noncognitive aspects of personality, what we know about the development of cognition suggests that there is considerable *similarity between* supporting conditions for the development of cognitive capacities and the development of creative characteristics. From the work of Piaget we have a picture of the human infant building his conceptual structures by acting, observing the result, repeating actions, establishing norms, predicting from norms, checking predictions, observing discrepancies, modifying actions and predictions, observing the results, and so on in an unending and increasingly complex pursuit of meaning.

Creative persons behave in much the same way. Their abilities may include the capacity to view the world from the point of view of other people and to profit from the experience of others, but that part of their work that is unique and original proceeds through individual action and the development of personal meaning. (See discussion in this article on p. 280, getting started (p. 282), connections (p. 288); other articles dealing with this point are in chapters 4, 5, 6 and 9.) In infants, the process seems to be stimulated by a sense of self that arises in the relationship with a mothering person; in children and adults the process derives from our earlier experiences and present networks of meaningful personal relationships. Teachers interested in stimulating creativity need to consider ways of involving students in the kind of relationships that support them in their personal creation of meaning.

According to Maslow's studies of people who developed and utilized their potentialities fully, creativity can be blocked by unmet needs for safety, a feeling of belonging, esteem, and competence. The development of creativity in the classroom will require provision for the satisfaction of needs in these areas. Unless these basic needs are met, the children are unlikely to feel free to recognize, accept, and express their original but more abstract ideas and feelings.

The teacher alone cannot give the child the feelings of safety and belonging that enable him to advance to higher levels of motivation. Regardless of his relationship with the teacher, a child who is frightened of the other children will be so involved in the problems of psychological survival that he will have little energy to invest in the development of his creative powers. Rogers has found that a teacher who is authentic, empathic, and loving in a nonpossessive way establishes growth-promoting relationships with students (1961). To secure an area for the development of creativity, the teacher will also have to teach the children how to form growth-promoting relationships with one another so that each child can find his safety and belongingness and the stimulation to his creative growth in a network of such relationships. The peer group must support the value system that the teacher has been conveying if the classroom is to be a place in which children feel like risking individual originality.

BUILDING COMMUNICATION AND SUPPORTIVENESS

In a curriculum that was published by the California State Department of Education, I have described some procedures that were useful in developing a network of communication and supportiveness in groups of gifted children with whom I worked in experimental summer workshops.[2] Since that publication was not made widely available, I would like to repeat some of the same ideas here, along with related suggestions. There are many ways of working with children to stimulate creativity in a classroom setting, but the major focus of this presentation is on stimulating growth through group processes. The topics I will consider here are (a) reducing anxiety, (b) forming connections, and (c) building a responsive group.

Reducing Anxiety

An early process in group development is pairing: each person finds someone to look at when he speaks. Once an individual has established such a connection, he is more comfortable about speaking in the group and more likely to express himself. To facilitate this process, I create several opportunities during the first meeting of a class for children to pair off for the purpose of getting to know each other in different ways. However, choosing partners is a fairly high risk activity because it involves the possibility of rejection; so, it should be preceded by some involvement that lowers anxiety to the place where it is possible for children to begin choosing partners in relative freedom from excessive anxiety.

Sometimes I divide the children into groups of five and ask them to find out the names of the other people in their group and then to talk about what they hope will happen in this class. In this situation, each child has two jobs: to find out what each other person wants out of the class and to tell them what he wants. If some groups are being dominated by one or two members, I interrupt and remind everyone that they have *two* jobs. I remind them that they have the job of receiving as well as giving to others. (In the process, the children go through the processes of receiving, discovering themselves, and interacting with one another.) After about five minutes I ask if the groups need more time. When they are ready, a volunteer from each group introduces the other members, and another tells us what the people in their group are hoping will happen in our class. I note the goals on the board as they are reported. By the end of the first twenty minutes of the first morning, the following things have been accomplished by every child:

---

2. The workshop is titled "Developing the Creativity of Gifted Children" and is directed by Professor John Gowan of California State University at Northridge. The curriculum guide that grew out of my work there is *Action Centered Explorations of Communication and Relatedness,* 1972.

He knows some other children's names and is known by name to them.

He has said something to some other children, been listened to, heard his idea repeated, and seen the teacher write it on the board.

He has listened to some other children with the intention of remembering what they said.

He has heard his name spoken in the room.

He has involved himself with the future of the total group by proposing a goal.

This is a simple sequence of events with a low level of involvement, but the feeling in the room will have changed rather dramatically; so, allow space for the children to become aware of the change. Ask them to go back in their imaginations to when they entered the room, looked around, found a chair — to remember their feelings at that time and how they expressed them or held them back. Then ask, "Notice how you feel now. Is it any different from the way you felt then? Would anyone like to say how it is different for them?" These questions further the objectives discussed above of focusing the child's attention on his own experience and on the meaning an individual moment has for him. By giving importance to each individual's experience of the group, the teacher can help the children to incorporate the idea of varying individual perceptions into their concept of their own group and to see these differences as a source of richness by which their own ideas of the possible ways of seeing things can be enlarged. By defining the group in this way the children can gain a group feeling that supports, rather than restricts, individual creativity. If the children come to understand that the "Johnness" of their group includes their perceptions of John, *and* John's experience of them, their group can be inclusive and participative, rather than rejecting and tyrannical — as peer groups can sometimes be.

In discussing the question "What happened in here that made it different for you?" each child is helped to analyze his own experience and to hear the aspects of the common experience that were meaningful to other members of the group. The teacher should participate in this discussion; she should put words on the changes in her own feelings and try to identify what happened that made *her* feelings change.

Some of the anxiety in the group will have been dissolved in the trust that has begun to develop, but there may be another kind of anxiety present. Children often feel uneasy about allotting school time for the purpose of becoming acquainted, and they wonder whether they should not be "getting to work." It comforts them to hear the teacher say that getting to know another person is very hard and that learning to know and understand one another takes all of the concentration and skill we have. Industry-oriented elementary school children are interested in the information that out in the world people are more likely to lose their jobs because they could not work with other people there than because they could not do the work. The idea that relating to other people is important work is generally new to them. I suggest that the children talk it over with the grown-ups in their life to see how important working with other people is for adults. At the same time I suggest that they try learning to know some of the people in the class and to see whether it is easy or hard. It is important for many children to be assured that this kind of work in the classroom has value in the outside world and connects with the struggles experienced by adults in the "real" world.

Forming Connections

After anxieties regarding knowing others have been reduced the teacher can create or utilize other experiences for children to work in pairs. Such pair experiences generate further growth in forming creative interpersonal relationships. I like to create occasions where the work of the pair is to be aware of one another and of the communication between them. Several such experiences build a net of connectivity within the group, wherein each child is known by and knows several other children in a special way.

I ask the children what they have learned about the other people in class so far and follow with "What did you see (hear) that made you think that?" This question helps them to consider what they mean when they say they "know" something, the kinds of evidence that enter into their experience of "knowing." Then each child chooses a partner — someone he does not know very well yet — and they try to get to know one another better by conversing while sitting back to back on the floor. I acknowledge that it will not be easy and ask them to notice how it feels to try to learn to know someone when all you can use are your ears and your voice. After about ten minutes, they discuss the experience as a group. (How was that for you? What did you like? What didn't you like? What did you learn about your partner? How did you learn that? Is there anything else you want to know about your partner? Can you think of any way you could learn that? Ask him if you like — he won't answer unless he wants to. Did it get harder or easier as you went along?)

The next assignment can be to try to get to know another person while spending thirty minutes with him and not talking. The partners can go anywhere on the school grounds (or whatever limits seem appropriate) as long as they do not disturb anyone else. They are to try to see if they can tell what their partner wants to do, as well as to see if they can let their partner know what they want to do and what they enjoy — all without words. (George Brown (1971) has pointed out that children need permission to be embarrassed, and this is one of the times that I find it helpful to say, "It's OK to be a little embarrassed — most people are when they are trying something new.") I add that the first five minutes of not talking are the hardest and that if they can make it to the sixth minute, it will probably get easier. If they forget and begin speaking, they can stop talking as soon as they remember and try to finish the time in silence, in order to know what it is like. When they come back together, they can share their experiences. (How was it to be together without talking? When was it hard, and when was it easy? Do you know anything about your partner that you didn't know when you chose each other? What happened that let you learn that? Did your partner understand what you wanted to do? Did one person do all of the deciding or did you take turns? How did you know when your partner wanted a turn to decide? How did you let your partner know when you wanted a turn? How do you feel about your partner? Is there anything different about the way you know this partner from the way you know the partner you talked to when you couldn't look at each other? What's the difference?)

Another partnership experience that provides valuable opportunities to analyze the feelings of knowing and wondering and trusting and mistrusting is the "blind walk." For adults, the newness of this experience may lie chiefly in the feeling of complete dependence on the partner who leads them while their eyes are closed and guides their sightless exploration of the environment. Adults and children share the wonder of the heightened experiences of their senses of touch, taste, and smell. The most unfamiliar part of the experience for children may lie in the feeling of being responsible for another person. Some preparation for this is necessary, such as, "When your partner's eyes are closed and you are leading him, you will be taking care of him in a very important way. You will be thinking about how to make the walk interesting for him by finding different things for him to touch and explore; you will be thinking about being sure that he is very safe." To help the children put their experience into words and to clarify it for themselves and for one another, I ask questions like, "Did you trust your partner? Was it easy to trust him sometimes and harder other times? What made the difference? What did you like (didn't you like) about your blind walk? How did it feel to lead your partner? Did your partner trust you? How could you tell? How did it feel to be trusted? . . . not trusted? Did you find out anything about when you trust people and when you don't? Did you find out anything about when people trust you and when they don't? Did you see anything when you opened your eyes that you hadn't noticed before? What did you look at first when you opened your eyes?"

These discussions relate to the support of creativity because it is characteristic of creative people to be in close touch with their own inner world — with what they like and do not like, want and do not want — *and* to have heightened awareness of the beauty and wonder and ugliness and horror of the world around them. Awareness of what is outside depends on awareness of what is inside since beauty, wonder, ugliness, and horror are feelings internal to the individual. Discussions such as the ones I am recommending here help children to experience the unity and wholeness of this inner/outer awareness.

Building a Responsive Group

The children's increasing awareness of themselves and of others can be called upon and nurtured in group situations. Theater games developed by Viola Spolin (1963) are very useful in building group responsiveness. Although *Improvisation for the Theater* was not intended for teachers, it contains many ideas that are directly applicable to the classroom. One game that I have found to be successful is called "What am I doing?" The teacher says, "I'm going to start doing something. As soon as you figure out what I'm doing, figure out a way that you can help, and start helping. If someone is already helping, figure out what they are doing, and find a way to fit into what is happening, and to help it along." Then the teacher starts (in pantomime) washing dishes or painting the wall or mopping the floor, and the children join in as they think of a way to help. If it starts to get hectic, Spolin suggests that the teacher call out "SLOW MOTION" and adjust her movements accordingly. The game stops when everyone who wanted to get involved has become involved and the players have a chance to tell each other what they were doing, if there were some ambiguous actions. They can suggest ways in which the communication could have been improved. The students will have ideas that they want to try and will need some turns at being the leader. I remember one situation as being remarkably vivid: a boy pantomimed noticing with horror that the wall was falling inward toward the classroom. He caught it with his shoulder and pushed against it. We all joined him, and after slow and heavy pushing, we got the wall back where it belonged. It was a very satisfying experience.

In a physical way, the group supports the spontaneous creation of an individual, and each member adds his own invention in support of the rest of the group. The game requires each player to attend to and interpret the movements of each other player, as well as to move in a way that communicates his intentions to the rest of the group. It provides an opportunity for originality in response to the problem and also provides the opportunity to take a low level risk and join in, in a conforming way. (The pattern of responses follows the giving and receiving described earlier in this chapter.)

"Mirroring" is another Spolin game that takes these skills of receiving and giving one step further. It requires that the players attend to their own movements and to those of their partners at the same time: The children take turns being the "person" and the "mirror." After each partner has had his turn and the partners have polished their performance and established a physical sensitivity to each other, a group mirroring game can be played to music. Then after each child has had time to find his own way of responding to the rhythm of the music, the children can take turns being the leader. While they are leaders they can demonstrate their rhythm to the rest of the group who will mirror the movements as they get the feel of them.

The children also can get the feeling of being part of a group from the experience of responding to one another in a game where one member of the group leaves the room while the rest pick a leader. All follow the leader's movements, and the point is to follow them so closely that the child returning to the room cannot tell who is the leader.

Experiments in group conformity suggest that those children who are secure in their feelings of membership are more inclined to exercise independent judgment when it differs from the judgment expressed by the group; those who do not feel connected to the group are more inclined to behave in conforming ways. These findings support Maslow's assumption that individuals must have satisfied their need to feel that they "belong" before their energies can be released for independence and self-actualization. An approach that enhances feelings of belongingness is to form groups that are required to cooperate if successful completion is to be attained. For example, to ask two children to perform a skit, run a relay, or prepare a project permits closer activities and communication. Children learn to work with others and have to gain as well as give feelings of respect and support before they utilize and enjoy other persons.

SOME OTHER CURRICULUM FOR CREATIVITY

Creativity depends on translating one's unique inner life into the common arena — the interaction with the people and things in the environment. By centering learning activities on the learners, the teacher helps a child to respect his own thinking processes; the child who respects his own mind as a source of ideas and a creator of knowledge, is ready to learn anything he needs to know in a personal way — in a way that connects to what he already knows and adds meaning to his previous experience. Curriculum that emerges around the learner, offering him opportunities for the growth of personal knowledge, supports the learner in developing his own unique ways of organizing and integrating experience. This type of curriculm also translates the learner's unique approaches, ideas, feelings, and meanings into the broader world of people and work.

John Holt says that when we find ourselves tempted to tell children what to do, it is always better to ask, "How many ways can you think of to do it?" "How many ways can you hold a pencil and still write with it?" "How many ways can you think of to make a capital A — that will still be recognized as an A by the other people here?" "How many different numbers can you combine to make 5? . . . How can you be sure you have found all there are?" These questions from his book *What Do I Do On Monday?* (1970) transport fluency-promoting behaviors from the area of games into the heart of the curriculum. Holt describes an incredible richness of activity springing from the children's study of their differences in height, weight, speed (walking, running, hopping, carrying someone piggyback), endurance, ability to estimate time and distance, and rates of improvement among the children on these activities are examined for possible relationship to such factors as height/weight ratios, length of leg, differences in age or sex. Holt writes, "Children are naturally and healthily competitive. They are interested in knowing who does things best, and they are all deeply interested in doing whatever they do today a little better than they did it yesterday." (p.23) His book includes a wide variety of suggestions for using the child's interest in himself to involve him in researching an infinity of questions.

Martha Wampler (1971) uses the names of members of the group to encourage children to play with sound and to discover its properties. "Whose name is just one sound? Which are two sounds? Try grouping several names, and see which sound interesting together." Her pupils organize and chant the names of their friends in patterns of increasing complexity, developing the forms of musical composition. They form connections from the sounds they speak and see what patterns they can invent — either with or without music.

In a curriculum for the study of microbiology by gifted elementary school children, Raquel Muir proposes that the child begin by growing the microorganisms from his own fingerprints in a culture. He can touch parts of the culture medium with "clean" fingers, "dirty" fingers, and leave part of it untouched. The students will need to establish commonly accepted criteria for "clean" and "dirty," to find ways to identify the parts of their culture, and to record and compare their results. She describes a flow of learning experiences that lead the student into controlled experimentation and observation, that extend from himself, his body, and his own interests into what Holt calls the *continuum of experience* — the integrated wholeness of the world.

The areas of knowledge a student explores in this way become truly his — his to speculate about, to take liberties with, to improvise upon. It becomes the raw material of creativity. Knowledge that belongs to someone else can be memorized and stored away, but it is not available for taking apart and putting together — for use in creative thinking.

These examples of curriculum support the development of individual creativity; similar examples can be found in curriculum guides for all subjects. A teacher who skims existing material with an eye for activities that center around the learner will find all she needs in the way of places to start and directions that the explorations might take. The actual directions will be different for each group of students and will evolve out of the interactions among the teacher, the children, and the material.

THE BACK AND FRONT OF THE MIND

Before summarizing we return to the important part the teacher's beliefs and assumptions play in fostering creativity in her students. As I have emphasized in this chapter, creative people are in close touch with their own inner world and have great awareness of the world around them. Awareness of what is outside depends on awareness of what is inside because both are based on the person's feelings of what he experiences. In order to increase the child's ability to recognize and respect *his* ideas and feelings it is essential that the teacher accept and value the different ways in which children perceive and respond. Teachers who wish to foster awareness and differences in responses have to give up the idea that there is only one "right" way to do things. In the back of their minds these teachers must affirm the right of each child to ask questions, seek answers, define and redefine problems, and inquire, or they cannot expect their students to be flexible and open to solutions. These teachers must communicate their approval and acceptance of the child's explorations and express their pleasure at his individuality. They must be willing to allow and encourage their students to look beyond traditional, conventional, and "right" answers and accept different ways of expression. They must give up the traditional role of the teacher as the source of "correct" methods and solutions and as helping the students employ the right technique to get answers. These teachers learn to emphasize the process of discovery and appreciate that there are many ways of solving a particular problem. The teacher who wishes to encourage creativity recognizes that children can learn and gain support from other children and that she is not the center and source of teaching. These teachers play down the importance of being right. They value questions and do not readily drop important issues because of time and schedule. They encourage their students to seek answers that make sense and work for them, and they recognize that play is the work of the child and a serious matter to him. These teachers value imagination, humor, and exploration and regard playfulness as an asset rather than a liability. They are more impressed and interested in the open spirit of inquiry than in being right. Creativity increases when the teacher is interested in and aware of creativity, when she is flexible, and when she is motivated to increase such states in others (Torrance 1963).

IN SUMMARY

Creativity is conceptualized as a style of openness to, respect for, and integration of inner and outer experiences. Classroom procedures that provide social support and feelings of belongingness apparently help the individual to recognize, respect, and express his own unique ideas and feelings. A three-part model for developing creativity is proposed on the basis of my teaching experiences and appraisal of studies in creativity. The model begins with a focus on self-awareness, moves to an interaction between awareness of self and others, and then moves to an acceptance and involvement of individuals into mutually supportive social relationships. Examples of procedures and curricula supporting this model are presented. The values, beliefs, and importance of the teacher are examined and it is suggested that creativity-motivated teachers are themselves flexible, tolerant of differences, open to alternatives, and adventuresome in their own thinking and approach to teaching.

SUGGESTED READINGS

The readings are divided into two sections. The first *"For Understanding"* is for teachers who wish to gain knowledge about the processes involved in creativity, awareness, and personal growth. The second *"For Doing"* is for teachers who want to implement these ideas and practice them in their classrooms.

For Understanding

Bower, Eli, and Hollister, William. *Behavioral Science Frontiers in Education.* New York: John Wiley & Sons, Inc., 1967. (particularly the chapters by Bower, Biber, Suchman, and Thelen)

Gowan, John; Demos, George; and Torrance, Paul. *Creativity: Its Educational Implications.* New York: John Wiley & Sons, Inc., 1967.

Jourard, Sidney. *The Transparent Self.* New York: Van Nostrand Reinhold Co., 1964.

Kagan, Jerome. *Creativity and Learning.* Boston: Beacon Press, 1967.

Keen, Sam. *To a Dancing God.* New York: Harper & Row, Publishers, 1970. (particularly the chapter on "Education for Serendipity")

Koestler, Arthur. *The Act of Creation.* New York: The Macmillan Co., 1964.

Krathwohl, David; Bloom, Benjamin; and Masia, Bertram. *Taxonomy of Educational Objectives: Handbook II, Affective Domain.* New York: David McKay Co., Inc., 1956.

Lederman, Janet. *Anger and the Rocking Chair.* New York: McGraw-Hill, Inc., 1969.

Leonard, George. *Education and Ecstasy.* New York: Delacorte Press, 1968.

Maslow, Abraham. *The Goals of Humanistic Education.* Esalen Monograph. Big Sur, Calif.: Esalen Institute.

―――. *Toward a Psychology of Being.* New York: Van Nostrand Reinhold Co., 1966.

Perls, Frederick. *Gestalt Therapy Verbatim.* Lafayette, Calif.: Real People Press, 1969.

Perls, Frederick; Hefferline, Ralph, F.; and Goodman, Paul. *Gestalt Therapy: Excitement and Growth in the Human Personality.* New York: Julian Press, 1951.

Polyani, Michael. *The Tacit Dimension.* Garden City, N.Y.: Doubleday & Co., Inc., 1966.

Reps, Paul. *Square Sun Square Moon.* Rutland, Vt.: Charles E. Tuttle Co., Inc., 1967.

Rogers, Carl. *On Becoming a Person.* Boston: Houghton Mifflin Co., 1961.

Rogers, Carl, and Stevens, Barry. *Person to Person: The Problem of Being Human.* Lafayette, Calif.: Real People Press, 1967.

Rosenthal, Robert, and Jacobsen, L. *Pygmalion in the Classroom.* New York: Holt, Rinehart & Winston, Inc., 1968.

Stevens, Barry. *Don't Push the River,* Lafayette, Calif.: Real People Press, 1971.

For Doing

Barron, F. "The Disposition towards Originality." *Journal of Abnormal Social Psychology.* 51(1955):478-85.

Borton, Terry. *Reach, Touch and Teach: Student Concerns and Process Education.* New York: McGraw-Hill, Inc., 1970. (includes annotated bibliography)

Brown, George Isaac. *Human Teaching for Human Learning: An Introduction to Confluent Education.* New York: The Viking Press, Inc., 1971. (useful bibliography included)

Cropley, P.J. *Creativity.* London: Longmans, Green, 1967.

DeMille, Richard. *Put Your Mother on the Ceiling.* New York: Walker & Co., 1967.

Getzels, J.W., and Jackson, P.W. *Creativity and Intelligence.* New York: John Wiley & Sons, 1962.

Gunther, Bernard. *Sense Relaxation.* New York: Collier, 1968.

———. *What to Do until the Messiah Comes.* New York: Collier, 1971.

Holt, John. *What Do I Do Monday?* New York: E.P. Dutton & Co., Inc., 1970.

Kohl, Herbert. *The Open Classroom.* New York: Random House, Inc., 1969.

Lyon, Harold C., Jr. *Learning to Feel Feeling to Learn.* Columbus, Ohio: Charles E. Merrill Publishing Co., 1971.

MacKinnon, D.W. "The Nature and Nurture of Creative Talent." *American Psychologist* 17(1962):484-95.

Maupin, Edward. *On Meditation.* Esalen Monograph. Big Sur, Calif.: Esalen Institute.

Otto, Herbert, and Mann, John. *Ways of Growth.* New York: Grossman Publishers, 1968.

Roe, A. "Psychological Approaches to Creativity in Science." In *Essays on Creativity in the Sciences,* edited by M.A. Coler. New York: New York University Press, 1963.

Schutz, William. *Joy: Expanding Human Awareness.* New York: Grove Press, Inc., 1967.

Shaftel, Fannie, and Shaftel, George. *Words and Actions: Role-Playing Photo-Problems for Young Children.* New York: Holt, Rinehart & Winston, Inc., 1967.

Sonntag, Joyce Hagen. *Developing Self-Knowledge and Community among Gifted Children: An Affective Curriculum.* Sacramento, Calif.: California State Department of Education, 1972.

———. "Sensitivity Training for Gifted Children." *Gifted Child Quarterly,* Spring, 1969.

Spolin, Viola. *Improvisation for the Theater.* Evanston, Ill.: Northwestern University Press, 1963.

Synectics, Inc., *Making It Strange.* New York: Harper & Row, Publishers, 1968.

Taylor, C.W., ed. *Creativity: Progress and Potential.* New York: Wiley, 1964.

Torrance, E.P. *Education and the Creative Potential.* Minneapolis, Minn.: University of Minnesota Press, 1963.

————. "Developing Creative Thinking through School Experiences." In *A Sourcebook for Creative Thinking*, edited by S.S. Parnes and H.F. Harding. New York: Charles Scribner's Sons, 1962.

Wampler, Martha. *Orff-schulwerk: Design for Creativity.* Sacramento, Calif.: California State Department of Education, forthcoming.